ARCHAEOLOGY
AND THE OLD TESTAMENT

BY JAMES B. PRITCHARD

PRINCETON UNIVERSITY PRESS · 1958

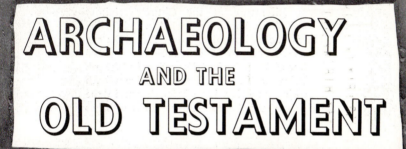

ARCHAEOLOGY
AND THE
OLD TESTAMENT

PREFACE

ARCHAEOLOGY is a science in which progress can be measured by the advances made backward into the past. The last one hundred years of archaeology have added a score of centuries to the story of the growth of our cultural and religious heritage, as the ancient world has been recovered from the sands and caves of the modern Near East—Egypt, Jordan, Israel, Syria, Lebanon, Turkey, and Iraq. Measured by the number of centuries which have been annexed to man's history in a relatively few years, progress has been truly phenomenal. This book deals with the recent advance and with those pioneers to the past who made it possible.

Interest in biblical history has played an important part in this recovery. Names such as Babylon, Nineveh, Jericho, Jerusalem, and others prominent on the pages of the Bible, have gripped the popular imagination and worked like magic to gain support for excavations. This book is written from the widely-shared conviction that the discovery of the ancient Near East has shed significant light on the Bible. Indeed, the newly-discovered ancient world has effected a revolution in the understanding of the Bible, its peoples, and their history.

My purpose is to assess, in non-technical language which the layman can understand, the kind of change in viewing the biblical past which archaeology has brought about in the last century. Since the text of the Bible has remained constant over this period, it is obvious that any new light on its meaning must provide a better perspective for seeing the events which it describes. In short, I am concerned with the question, How has history as written in the Bible been changed, enlarged, or substantiated by the past century of archaeological work?

v

One might suppose that the story of archaeology in Palestine, the land of the Bible, would provide the answer to the question. But it has supplied only a part of the relevant data. One of the surprises of modern archaeological discovery has been that the peripheral lands of Mesopotamia, Egypt, Syria, and Anatolia have added to biblical knowledge. From each of these neighboring areas have come written documents and monuments of great importance for an understanding of the life, literature, and history of the peoples of Palestine, and any fair appraisal of archaeology's contribution to an understanding of the Bible must take into account these widely scattered remains.

Whenever possible, I have tried to let the evidence speak for itself. In presenting the picture of new material made available by archaeologists, I have sought to place before the reader a translation of a relevant document or a photograph of a significant archaeological object. These translations and pictures, for the most part, are taken from two large collections which I have edited for the use of scholars and advanced students in the field of Old Testament studies. *Ancient Near Eastern Texts Relating to the Old Testament*, Princeton University Press, 2nd edition, 1955 (abbreviated *ANET*), contains translations of texts made by thirteen specialists. For their collaboration in this undertaking I wish again to express appreciation to: W. F. Albright, H. L. Ginsberg, Albrecht Goetze, A. Jamme, S. N. Kramer, Theophile J. Meek, A. Leo Oppenheim, Robert H. Pfeiffer, Franz Rosenthal, A. Sachs, E. A. Speiser, Ferris J. Stephens, and John A. Wilson. *The Ancient Near East in Pictures Relating to the Old Testament*, Princeton University Press, 1954 (abbreviated *ANEP*), reproduces relevant artifacts and monuments which have come from the lands of the Bible and gives a documentation for each. It is hoped that the present volume will provide the interested non-specialist with an introduction which will enable him to make use of these larger and more complete collections.

The men who have made the discoveries and deciphered the texts are an important part of the story. I have tried to satisfy in a measure, by some specific details, the general curiosity as to who the archaeologists were, how they chanced to take up their occupation, who supported them, how they lived and worked in the field, and what were the costs of exploration and excavation.

The passages from the Old Testament have been quoted from *The Holy Scriptures According to the Masoretic Text*, Philadelphia, 1942, with the generous permission of the publisher, The Jewish Publication Society of America. In the quotations from *ANET* there have been eliminated editorial conventions which are customarily used by scholars to indicate relatively certain reconstructions of a broken text and the addition of words required by English idiom for a better understanding of the original. These important devices of technical scholarship, along with explanatory footnotes, may be found in the original publication of the translations in *ANET*.

A glance at the arrangement of the chapters in the table of contents will show that I have proceeded from the geographical center to the periphery. Chapters 1 and 2 provide illustrations of methods and results from the excavations and explorations which have been carried on in Palestine (modern Israel and Jordan). Chapter 3 is concerned largely with work done in Syria (modern Lebanon and Syria) and with an important discovery in the area of ancient Moab (now in Jordan). Chapters 4 and 5 provide materials which have come from the area of Mesopotamia (modern Iraq), where the ancient empires of Assyria and Babylonia flourished. The final chapter, Chapter 6, draws from the results of excavations in Mesopotamia, Egypt, and Anatolia (modern Turkey).

PREFACE

As the field of Near Eastern archaeology is immense, it can be readily understood that this volume is intended to serve only as an introduction to a study of those results of the past century which relate to the Bible. Obviously, one who is at home in this field of research will miss much which may be of importance to him. In general, I have tried to choose those examples which can be understood by the layman who has had no occasion to study the languages of the ancient Near East, and who has not concerned himself with the more minute problems of philology and history.

J. B. P.

Berkeley, California
January 1958

CONTENTS

PREFACE   v

LIST OF ILLUSTRATIONS   xi

1. THE SCIENCE OF PALESTINIAN
   ARCHAEOLOGY   1

   The Essential Alphabet of Archaeology   1
   A Supplement to Jeremiah   10
   Sennacherib before Lachish   18
   War and Commerce at Megiddo   24
   Jerusalem Underground   35
   Scrolls from Caves Overlooking the Dead Sea   42

2. THE MAKING OF A MAP   53

   Pilgrims and Soldiers   53
   The Founder of Palestinology: Robinson   57
   Surveying Western Palestine   62
   New Sources for an Ancient Map   65
   Surface Exploration for Pottery   82
   Excavating for a Map   85

3. BAAL AND THE RELIGION OF
   CANAAN   91

   The French in Phoenicia   91
   Monument of Mesha, King of Moab   103
   The Canaanite Bible from Ugarit   106
   Sex, Fertility, and Religion   124

4. ASSYRIA, ISRAEL'S ENEMY   127

   Learning to Read Cuneiform   127

ix

CONTENTS

The Palace of Sargon 134
The Black Obelisk 139
Tiglath-pileser's Conquests in Palestine 148
Sennacherib at Jerusalem 156

5. MYTH IN THE ANCIENT NEAR EAST 160

All Mankind Returned to Clay 160
Gilgamesh, Most Splendid among Heroes 170
Conflict and Creation 183
Adapa's Lost Chance for Immortality 193
Flood and Creation in Sumer 201

6. LAW AND WISDOM 206

Hammurabi, the King of Justice 206
Five Codes of Cuneiform Law 215
All the Wisdom of Egypt 228
Babylon's Wise Men 239

POSTSCRIPT 246

GLOSSARY 251

SOURCES FOR ILLUSTRATIONS 255

INDEX 257

INDEX OF BIBLICAL REFERENCES 263

ILLUSTRATIONS

1. Map of the ancient and modern Near East   xiv-xv
2. W. M. Flinders Petrie   xvi
3. Archaeological sites in southern Palestine   3
4. Strata of occupation at Tell el-Hesi   5
5. Types of pottery found in Palestine   7
6. Letter IV from Lachish   16
7. Sennacherib receiving booty from Lachish   19
8. The attack upon Lachish by Sennacherib   20
9. The tower of Lachish under siege   21
10. Walls of Lachish as traced by excavation   23
11. Crest of an Assyrian's helmet from Lachish   25
12. Egyptian attack upon a Canaanite fortress   28
13. Stables of the Solomonic level at Megiddo   32
14. A royal victory, on ivory from Megiddo   34
15. Siloam tunnel at Jerusalem and inscription   38
16. Plan of the Siloam tunnel   41
17. Scroll fragments from the Dead Sea caves   46
18. Khirbet Qumran under excavation   48
19. Copy desk from scriptorium at Qumran   50
20. Sites excavated in Palestine   51
21. World map with Jerusalem at its center   55
22. Edward Robinson   58
23. Sites north of Jerusalem identified by Robinson   61
24. Egyptian execration figurine   67
25. Places listed in annals of Thut-mose III   69
26. List of Asiatic conquests of Thut-mose III   70
27. Gold bowl of General Thoth   72
28. Shackled Syrian prisoners of Ramses II   73
29. Ramses II's conquest of Ashkelon   74
30. The town of Yanoam under attack by Seti I   78
31. Handle of wine jar inscribed with "Gibeon"   88
32. The rock-cut pool discovered at Gibeon   89
33. Sites in the northern part of Canaan   93
34. Ernest Renan   94
35. Sarcophagus of Eshmunazar, king of Sidon   96
36. Air view of Byblos under excavation   98
37. The sarcophagus of King Ahiram of Byblos   99
38. Inscription of Mesha, king of Moab   104

ILLUSTRATIONS

39. The alphabet of ancient Ugarit 108
40. Canaanite god receiving an offering 114
41. Baal of the lightning, from Ugarit 115
42. A seven-headed fiery dragon 121
43a. Fertility figurine of molded clay 123
43b. A Canaanite god covered with gold 123
44. Ivory carving of a woman at the window 126
45. Assyrian cities on the upper Tigris 128
46. Inscription of Darius at Behistun 130
47. A drawing of Sargon's palace at Khorsabad 134
48. Sargon and an officer before a god 135
49. Portrait of King Sargon of Assyria 137
50. Shalmaneser receives tribute from Jehu 141
51. Portrait of Shalmaneser III 146
52. Shalmaneser III takes tribute from Tyre 147
53. Tiglath-pileser III, king of Assyria 148
54. Assyrian soldiers capture the town of Astartu 150
55. Siege of Gazru, on a relief from Nimrud 151
56. Plan of excavations at Nineveh 155
57. Assyrians attack a city with siege-engine 158
58. Clay tablet with account of the Flood 163
59. Assyrian hero clutching a lion 172
60. Contest scenes on a Babylonian seal 176
61. Hammurabi before the sun-god Shamash 177
62. The goddess Ishtar riding on a lion 178
63. The god Marduk of Babylon 186
64. A winged deity drives out a monster 187
65. Enemies of King Eannatum caught in a net 188
66. Contest with the great serpent-dragon 189
67. Akh-en-Aton and Nefert-iti with offerings 195
68. Statue of Dudu, a Sumerian scribe 202
69. Air view of Susa, biblical Shushan 207
70. Stela of Hammurabi inscribed with laws 208
71. A cuneiform document with clay envelope 212
72. Cities of lower Mesopotamia 216
73. Scenes from the stela of Ur-Nammu 220
74. Hittites, as depicted by the Egyptians 223
75. An Egyptian scribe from Sakkarah 229
76. An Egyptian nobleman and his wife 231
77. Silver model of a boat from a tomb at Ur 247
List of Sources for Illustrations 255

xii

ARCHAEOLOGY
AND THE OLD TESTAMENT

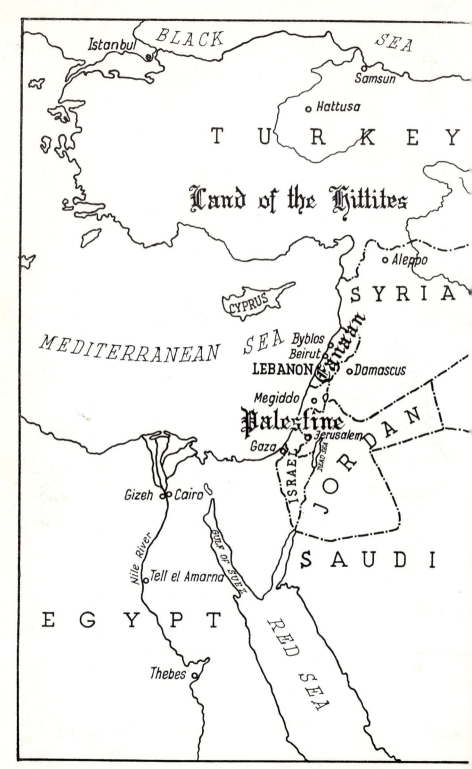

Fig. 1. Map of ancient and modern Near East.

FIG. 2. The Nestor of Palestinian archaeologists, Sir W. M. Flinders Petrie, 1853-1942, who set the pattern for over a half-century of excavations.

CHAPTER 1

THE SCIENCE OF
PALESTINIAN ARCHAEOLOGY

THE ESSENTIAL ALPHABET OF ARCHAEOLOGY

THE science of Palestinian archaeology was born in the
spring of 1890, when a rare genius, W. M. Flinders Petrie,
found an ancient mound of buried cities worthy of his
ability to observe and interpret. In a scant six weeks of digging, this pioneer set the pattern for over half a century of
excavations. Others, to be sure, had dug in Palestine before, but none had hit upon a sure means for dating the
ancient ruins which he had uncovered. It remained for
Petrie to discover the secret of method.

Petrie was an Egyptologist who had been asked by the
Palestine Exploration Fund of England to direct its excavation in southern Judah. Although he was only thirty-
seven years old at the time, he had a decade of experience
to his credit in Egypt; and through the publication of ten
archaeological volumes he had made a considerable reputation for himself. A sum of £1,110 had been raised, mostly
from hundreds of small gifts in response to a special appeal
by the Fund, for which Sir Walter Besant, a popular
English novelist of the time, had served as secretary and
financial genius. Years of patient effort had finally resulted
in permission to carry on excavations granted by the
Turks, who at the time ruled Palestine.

This first archaeologist to excavate scientifically in Palestine began his serious study of the ancient past even before he went to Egypt. As an amateur numismatist at the
age of eight he launched what proved to be an eighty-year

1

career in archaeology. With this early start he was able, just ten years before he died, to write his autobiography under the startling but accurate title of *Seventy Years in Archaeology*. In the number of excavations made and of books written—he was responsible in whole or in part for ninety-eight volumes, not to mention a great number of scientific and popular articles—he has as yet had no rival.

Petrie's first archaeological expedition was in 1880, when he went out from England to Egypt to attempt to measure accurately the Great Pyramid of Gizeh. He had been led into this venture some fourteen years earlier by the purchase of a curious book written by Piazzi Smyth, *Our Inheritance in the Great Pyramid*, a work of fantastic theories based on an amazing correlation—so Smyth alleged—between the measurements of the Great Pyramid and the history of the world as it is written in the Bible. Petrie's father, who was a friend of Piazzi Smyth, encouraged the young Flinders to enter this enticing field of seeming coincidence. Alas, the facts established through the painstaking labor of this first season at Gizeh did not support Smyth's theory, but in the demonstration of its fallacy Petrie had found his career.

Many years later, as he looked back at the day he purchased Smyth's book, Sir Flinders reflected: "I little thought, how, fifteen years later, I should reach 'the ugly little fact which killed the beautiful theory.' "[1] The "ugly little fact" was the discovery that the measurement of the base of the pyramid was not 9,140, as supposed by the theorists, but 9,069 inches. A difference of 71 inches may not seem like much, but when an inch was supposed to represent a year it was enough to convince Petrie that there were no chronological secrets in the measurements of the pyramid.

In his final report on the work of measurement Petrie was optimistic enough to believe that many of the theo-

---

[1] Flinders Petrie, *Seventy Years in Archaeology*, London, n.d., p. 13.

rists would agree with an American who had been a believer in the theory when he came to spend a couple of days in Egypt with Petrie, but who, after seeing the sure results produced by the young Englishman, said in a saddened tone: "Well sir! I feel as if I had been to a funeral."[2] But Petrie's optimism was unfounded; many people continued to accept the theory in spite of the facts.

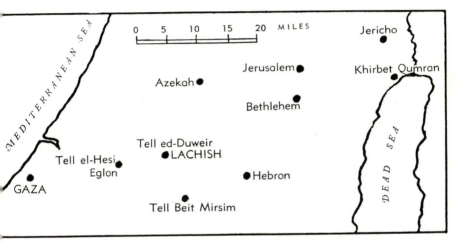

FIG. 3. Sites in southern Palestine.

So well did the twenty-seven-year-old archaeologist do his work of surveying, which was published with scrupulous regard for detail in 1883, that it remained the standard work on the subject until 1925, when another surveyor, with more modern instruments, was able to refine further the measurements.

In March of 1890, Flinders Petrie arrived in Palestine, waited in Jerusalem for several weeks for the arrival of the necessary permission from the Turkish government, and finally, as a one-man archaeological expedition, made his way to the supposed site of ancient Eglon. Arriving at a camping place, he pitched his tent and fell asleep.

2 W.M.F. Petrie, *Pyramids and Temples of Gizeh*, London, 1883, p. xvi.

"During the night I was awoke," he wrote in his report to the sponsoring Palestine Exploration Fund, "by a dog getting in, and again by a slight noise, and looking up, saw a gap in the tent—in it, a man's head and shoulders, and heard the intruder fumbling over the tool-bag, too heavy to carry off, and awkward to open. I challenged, he ran, and four bullets went over his head to improve his pace."[3] Such incidents were not unusual in the early days of excavations in Turkish Palestine.

The next day Petrie was off to see the site to which the Fund had sent him. Alas, there was only a little broken pottery lying about, and what there was belonged to the Roman period. This, he concluded, surely could not be the ancient Eglon, the prominent biblical city. He moved to a place which bore the name of Lachish, but after three days of work there he was persuaded that neither was this the site of the ancient Judaean city which bore that name. Six miles from his camp, however, he found a mound, called by the Arabs Tell el-Hesi, where there was an abundance of ancient pottery, a site which he judged was "worth a dozen of all the other places put together." And it was at this site, sixteen miles east of Gaza, that the science of Palestinian archaeology was born. Although Petrie mistakenly thought of it as the ancient Lachish, it now seems likely that it was actually the ancient Eglon, the supposed identification of the place to which Petrie had at first been sent by the Palestine Exploration Fund. Without knowing it, he had in fact carried out his orders.

Tell el-Hesi was a mound of earth measuring about 200 feet on each side at the summit and towering more than 100 feet above the plain. The eastern side had been eaten away by the erosion of the water of the stream Wadi Hesi, turning this side of the mound into a cliff sloping at about a 45-degree angle.

With practiced eye Petrie recognized that the torrents

---

[3] *Quarterly Statement of the Palestine Exploration Fund*, 1890, p. 220.

4

which swept down the wadi each year had already laid bare a thousand years of history. The gash into the hill on the east side, as Petrie wrote in his first report, "gives us at one stroke a series of all the varieties of pottery over a thousand years," adding prophetically that, "in future all the tells and ruins of the country will at once reveal their age by the potsherds which cover them."[4] A more picturesque description of the site of Tell el-Hesi was written by an American visitor who dropped in on Petrie's dig and who, upon his return to Detroit, described it as "a gashed and broken tell lying by the waterbrook like some hurt creature of the geologic ages fallen in its dying agonies."[5]

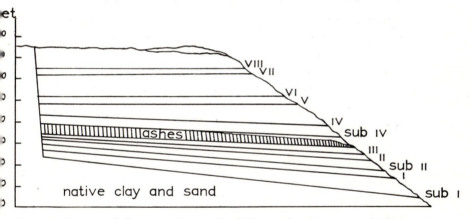

Fig. 4. Section of the mound at Tell el-Hesi, where Petrie and Bliss cut through the remains of eight cities which stood on the site.

For six weeks the excavation was directed by Petrie singlehanded; about thirty men were employed as laborers, each assisted by a woman who carried off the debris in a basket. Then came the harvest season, when his laborers were drawn away to their crops. Petrie left with his notes and plans, not to return to dig again in Palestine for over thirty years.

4 ibid., p. 165.
5 ibid., pp. 166-167.

Unable to persuade Petrie to leave his chosen field of Egypt for another season, the officers of the Palestine Exploration Fund found an American, F. J. Bliss, the son of the president of the Syrian Protestant College (later the American University of Beirut), and engaged him to continue the work. After a short apprenticeship with Petrie at Meidum in Egypt, Bliss went to Tell el-Hesi. By January of 1893 he had cut away about one-third of the ancient tell, down through 65 feet of debris, laying bare the remains of eight cities (Fig. 4).

The labor of almost three years of digging disappointingly produced no artifacts for museum display. The only object of value was a clay tablet, measuring 2 by 2½ inches, with twenty-six lines of cuneiform writing, which Bliss found in what he called city III. The tablet could be dated to the time of the famous Egyptian king Akh-en-Aton, in the fourteenth century B.C., and mentioned the well-known prince of Lachish, Zimreda.[6] This object served to date the layer and the pottery in it. Everything below this must be older than the fourteenth century; the cities above it were, of course, later.

But the importance of this early excavation in Palestine cannot be measured in terms of museum pieces. The great discovery was the demonstration by Petrie and Bliss that the history of ancient Palestine was written in the forms and shapes of broken fragments of pottery.

In the early days of archaeology excavators had searched only for treasure, often plundering the past for museums, which, as Petrie once remarked, are "ghastly charnel-houses of murdered evidence."[7] Careful observation of the circumstances and context of discoveries had been conspicuously absent, as had been attention to the small but universal things such as potsherds. In such a monumental publication as the thousands of engravings of Egyptian monu-

6 *ANET*, 490.
7 W.M.F. Petrie, *Methods and Aims in Archaeology*, London, 1904, p. 48.

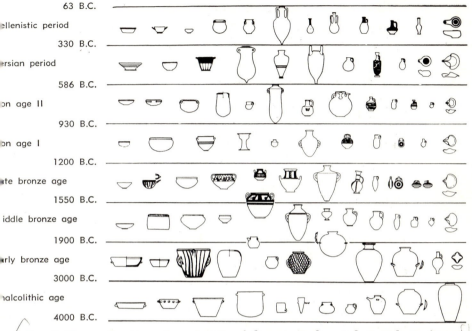

63 B.C.	
ellenistic period	
330 B.C.	
rsian period	
586 B.C.	
on age II	
930 B.C.	
on age I	
1200 B.C.	
te bronze age	
1550 B.C.	
iddle bronze age	
1900 B.C.	
rly bronze age	
3000 B.C.	
alcolithic age	
4000 B.C.	

FIG. 5. Types of pottery characteristic of the principal periods in Palestine's history. Pottery is the essential alphabet of archaeology.

ments in C. R. Lepsius' *Denkmäler aus Ägypten und Äthiopien* (Monuments from Egypt and Ethiopia), published in Germany at the middle of the nineteenth century, there was only one page of illustrations of pottery.

It was Petrie who established the need for scrupulous and accurate recording of every scrap of evidence. His publication of the results of six weeks of reconnaissance at Tell el-Hesi has five large plates of drawings of pottery, each piece carefully marked with the depth at which it was found.

The observation that certain types of pottery belonged to certain layers of occupation and the dating of these strata by the presence of objects whose date was known made possible the skeleton for the chronology of ancient Palestine. This trustworthy standard has been checked,

7

revised, and improved since Petrie first proposed the principle that pottery is "the essential alphabet of archaeology," but the principle remains the same.

Attention was given first of all to form—particularly the shapes of handles, rims, and bases; then to decoration, such as combing on the wet surface, painting, and burnishing of the leather-hard vessel with a pebble before firing; and finally to the texture of the clay and the way in which the pottery had been fired in the kiln. Combinations of these factors made possible many distinctive variations, each of which seemed to hold for a time and then to be superseded by a new type. The fragile nature of pottery accounts for the great number and variety of broken pieces preserved. Once a pot was broken it had to be replaced, and the preference was for a newer style. Thus it was that changes took place rapidly in form, shape, and decoration.

Petrie estimated that during his six weeks at Tell el-Hesi he must have looked over 50,000 or more pieces of pottery, while in Egypt, he said, "about 3,000,000 pieces have been clearly looked at by me."[8] This is the essential business of the archaeologist, who should be known for the shortness of his finger-nails and the toughness of his skin (he should grow his own gloves, Petrie once advised). "Why," he exclaimed in his book on *Methods and Aims,* "one might as well try to play the violin in a pair of gloves as to profess to excavate with clean fingers and a pretty skin."[9]

The enthusiasm of this newcomer into the Palestinian field for the importance of broken pottery did not fail to be challenged by some who had long worked there. C. R. Conder, responsible for much of the great Survey of Western Palestine, objected that deductions from pottery "are apt to mislead." He considered that lettering on texts, character of tombs, masonry and architecture form to-

[8] *Quarterly Statement of the Palestine Exploration Fund*, 1891, p. 68.
[9] W.M.F. Petrie, *Methods and Aims in Archaeology*, p. 7.

gether much safer data. But Petrie could not be dissuaded from his newly-found key to Palestine's history. Said he: "With the brief view of Palestinian pottery gained in a few weeks, on one site at Tell Hesy (Lachish), I found it possible to ride over mounds of ruins and see the age of them without even dismounting."[10] It is this discovery of the value of pottery as an index to chronology, the essential alphabet of archaeology, which more than anything else entitles Petrie to the title given him by William F. Albright, a later master in the field, "the revered Nestor of archaeologists."

Petrie saw a mound of debris as a treasure as rare and valuable as any manuscript. Carelessness was plunder. This respect for the record written in ruins was later written into the law of the land, which prohibited even the owner of land to dig in his own back yard if antiquities were discovered there. The earnestness with which he undertook his task is apparent in what Petrie wrote about the aims of archaeology. The past, he says, has rights, which the careless and ignorant may not abrogate. "To murder a man a week before his time we call a crime," he argues, but "what are we to call the murder of years of his labour?"[11]

Digging has no place for the dilettante. "Let us be quit," he wrote, "in archaeology at least, of the brandy-and-soda young man who manipulates his 'expenses,' of the adventurous speculator, of those who think that a title or a long purse glorifies any vanity or selfishness."[12] Knowledge and training are essential, for excavation without knowledge is like undertaking a surgical operation in ignorance of anatomy. Most of all, an archaeologist must know the history of the many small things such as pottery and beads, for it is "sadly true that he does not find anything that he does not look for."[13]

10 *ibid.*, p. 17.   11 *ibid.*, pp. 176-177.   12 *ibid.*, p. 3.
13 *ibid.*, p. 1.

A SUPPLEMENT TO JEREMIAH

Flinders Petrie gave to Palestinian archaeology its method; it remained for others to apply it. A strict regard for observing and recording layers or strata (stratigraphy) and a careful study and analysis of the pottery (typology) were first demonstrated to be of value by Petrie in 1890 and then bequeathed to his successors.

One who learned his craft directly from Petrie was James Leslie Starkey, a British archaeologist who had the good luck of making a truly great find. On March 13, 1935, there was cabled from Palestine a news report announcing the remarkable discovery by Starkey at Tell ed-Duweir of a dozen letters written in good biblical Hebrew. They were written with iron-carbon ink on potsherds and were dated from the time of the prophet Jeremiah.

This was news for several reasons. First, although there are many references in the Bible to people sending letters from one place to another—for example, the famous dispatch of David to Joab, instructing him to dispose of Uriah, Bathsheba's husband—no such correspondence had ever turned up before in scores of excavations in Palestine. Secondly, with the exception of a Hebrew inscription cut into the wall of the Siloam tunnel and some scattered ostraca, mostly containing proper names, there was in existence no ancient Hebrew outside of the Bible, and the Bible was known only from manuscripts written hundreds of years after the events described. And thirdly, the newly-announced file of correspondence came from an exceedingly important and interesting period in the history of the kingdom of Judah, the conquest of Judah by Nebuchadnezzar, which resulted in the Exile.

For these reasons scholars in America and in Europe anxiously awaited the publication of the unique documents. By November, Professor Harry Torczyner of the Hebrew University in Jerusalem, to whom the letters had been committed for publication, had published photographs of four—the number by this time had increased to eighteen—in a twenty-page article written in modern Hebrew.

With the opportunity to see a sample of this important collection so soon after its discovery, orientalists in various parts of the world took up the study and offered proposals for the reading of this correspondence.

Within three years after it had come from the ground the entire material was made available in a sumptuous publication—including photographs, drawings, commentary, and Torczyner's translation. This publication produced a flood of suggestions as to readings and meanings. A recent bibliography of serious articles on the Lachish letters—not including news reports—lists, for the years from 1938 to 1940, thirty-nine serious works on the subject, written in ten different languages. Rarely have so few words been studied so intently by so many in so short a time.

Starkey was forty years old when he made the discovery. It was his third year as director of the Wellcome Archaeological Research Expedition to the Near East. Like Petrie, he had not had a rigid, formal education. At the age of fifteen he had left school and started to work for an antiquity dealer in London, making use of the reading room of the British Museum in his spare time to follow his natural bent for the study of antiquity.

With the coming of the First World War he went into the Royal Naval Air Service and was fortunate in his assignment to a lighthouse on the English coast, where he was able to spend much of his time reading textbooks which he had sent out to him. Upon demobilization he enrolled for evening classes at University College in London, where he met Petrie and studied Egyptian hieroglyphs.

In 1922 he abandoned a promising business career for

archaeology. He spent two seasons in Egypt in the Qau-Bedari district, where he worked with Petrie and Guy Brunton. Another two seasons he spent in the Fayum as field director for a University of Michigan expedition. At the age of thirty-one he went with Sir Flinders to Palestine and assisted him in three important excavations, learning not only Petrie's methods but the pottery and artifacts of Palestine.

In 1932, accompanied by Mrs. Starkey and their children and a staff of eleven and supported financially by Sir Henry Wellcome and Mr. H. Dunscombe Colt, Starkey began work at the great eighteen-acre mound, Tell ed-Duweir, which he thought to be—as it in fact proved to be—ancient Lachish. The systematic destruction of this mound was a long-term program. Near the southwest corner of the mound a modern camphouse was built of mud, stones, and plaster; and a grove of acacia and almond trees was planted for a garden. To facilitate the work of digging, a steel chute was installed to take the debris quickly down the slope to the dump. Through the generosity of Sir Robert Mond, another patron, light railway equipment, including over 700 yards of track and eleven cars, was purchased (this railway was eventually sold to aid the Allied cause at the time of Rommel's advance toward Egypt). The comforts, as well as the mechanical contrivances, had increased considerably in the forty-two years since Petrie had gone out alone to live in his tent at Tell el-Hesi.

Work continued on this elaborate scale at Tell ed-Duweir until 1938, when the project ceased with the death of its director before much had been done on the mound itself. On January 10th, Starkey left the camp at Tell ed-Duweir to attend the formal opening of the new Palestine Archaeological Museum in Jerusalem. Just outside of Hebron he was killed by armed bandits. A loyal staff has carried on the publication of the results, but no work has been done at the site since 1938.

The first of the Lachish letters was recognized on January 29, 1935, by the writing on a small piece of broken pottery found in a deposit of black debris which underlay a Persian roadway through the gate to the city. Immediately, all the pottery fragments from this debris were taken to Starkey's camphouse and "carefully washed in filtered water, the forefinger being used to remove any dirt that adhered to the surface. No brush or abrasive action was employed." And, wrote Starkey, "on that memorable evening we saw many texts for the first time."[14]

The search was now extended. All soil from the Persian roadway was passed through a sieve; even the dump-head was recovered and screened, with the result that another fragment was added to this precious collection. The total number of inscribed potsherds salvaged that season was eighteen, sixteen of which were among the hundreds of jar fragments found in the debris of a guard room of the bastion of the outer city wall. Many of the sherds in the room had been affected by the intense heat of the fire which had destroyed the building, so there was no way of knowing how much correspondence had been lost.

In 1938 three more letters came to light, adding some new names to the corpus of Hebrew inscriptions. As a result of the digging at ancient Lachish about a hundred lines of more or less readable Hebrew written in the time of Jeremiah the prophet have been made available.

The letters are a file of correspondence received by a certain Yaosh, probably the military commander of Lachish, from a subordinate, Hoshaiah, who was in charge of an outpost to the north. The form of the composition of these Hebrew letters is of interest. In two letters the addressee, Yaosh, is named at the very beginning, "To my lord

14 H. Torczyner, *Lachish I: The Lachish Letters*, London, 1938, p. 12.

Yaosh," while another opens with the statement, "Thy servant Hoshaiah hath sent to inform my lord Yaosh." Frequently, the formal—and to us stilted—third person singular is used; the sender refers to himself usually as "thy servant," and to his correspondent as "my lord."

Under the military emergency which the letters obviously reflect, one might suppose that the niceties of polite address would be neglected. But they are not. Frequently there is the complimentary opening, "May Yahweh cause my lord to hear tidings of peace." The sender of the letter goes a step farther than our nineteenth-century "your obedient servant," and uses on several occasions the phrase, "who is thy servant but a dog," an expression of polite address on the part of a subordinate to a superior in the Bible as well (II Samuel 9:8, for example). Another conventional phrase is the emphatic "as Yahweh thy God liveth," an oath which is also a part of biblical speech.

The more specific content of the letters is difficult to grasp because of the loss of the correspondence which passed in the other direction, from Yaosh to Hoshaiah, as well as of other letters which are mentioned but which were not in the file. When we read "as for the letter of Tobiah, servant of the king," or "and now according to everything that my lord hath written," or "and with respect to what my lord hath written about the matter of . . . ," we can only conjecture as to the contents of letters which were transmitted, but of which no copies were kept or have survived.

Letter III is the longest of the entire correspondence. In it, Hoshaiah seems to be answering charges brought against him that he has been indiscreet in informing himself of—and perhaps disclosing—the contents of important letters which passed through his hands. Letter III indicates that he himself is unable to read, and he asserts that he has not called a scribe to read for him. In addition to the paragraph of objection to this charge, he adds a report of military intelligence and a note about a letter which may have contained some political information. The text of the letter follows:

> Thy servant Hoshaiah hath sent to inform my lord Yaosh: May Yahweh cause my lord to hear tidings of peace! And now thou hast sent a letter, but my lord did not enlighten thy servant concerning the letter which thou didst send to thy servant yesterday evening, though the heart of thy servant hath been sick since thou didst write to thy servant. And as for what my lord said, "Dost thou not understand?—call a scribe!", as Yahweh liveth no one hath ever undertaken to call a scribe for me; and as for any scribe who might have come to me, truly I did not call him nor would I give anything at all for him!
>
> And it hath been reported to thy servant, saying, "The commander of the host, Coniah son of Elnathan, hath come down in order to go into Egypt; and unto Hodaviah son of Ahijah and his men hath he sent to obtain . . . from him."
>
> And as for the letter of Tobiah, servant of the king, which came to Shallum son of Jaddua through the prophet, saying, "Beware!", thy servant hath sent it to my lord.[15]

Important for the geographical information it gives, is letter IV, beginning on one side of a broken piece of pottery and continuing on to the other side (Fig. 6). It describes the breakdown of a system of communication in the area of the outpost held by Hoshaiah, who, with the failure of the signals from the biblical city of Azekah, is entirely dependent for vital information on the signals from Lachish.

[15] *ANET*, 322.

FIG. 6. Reverse of Lachish Letter IV containing, "we are watching for the signals of Lachish."

The letter reads:

May Yahweh cause my lord to hear this very day tidings of good! And now according to everything that my lord hath written, so hath thy servant done; I have written on the door according to all that my lord hath written to me. And with respect to what my lord hath written about the matter of Beth-haraphid, there is no one there.

And as for Semachiah, Shemaiah hath taken him and hath brought him up to the city. And as for thy servant, I am not sending anyone thither today, but I will send tomorrow morning.

And let my lord know that we are watching for the signals of Lachish, according to all the indications which my lord hath given, for we cannot see Azekah.[16]

[16] *ANET*, 322.

16

Another letter, VI, acknowledges the receipt of an important correspondence, a letter of the king himself and letters of the princes. Hoshaiah gives his opinion of the letters of the princes in a phrase which recalls the charge brought against Jeremiah during the final siege of Jerusalem, "he weakeneth the hands of the men of war that remain in this city."[17] Hoshaiah is alarmed and advises his lord Yaosh to reprimand through a letter of protest these seditious words on the part of the princes. Although poorly preserved, the letter has been translated thus:

To my lord Yaosh:

May Yahweh cause my lord to see this season in good health! Who is thy servant but a dog that my lord hath sent the letter of the king and the letters of the princes, saying, "Pray, read them!" And behold the words of the princes are not good, but to weaken our hands and to slacken the hands of the men who are informed about them . . . And now my lord, wilt thou not write to them, saying, "Why do ye thus even in Jerusalem? Behold unto the king and unto his house are ye doing this thing!" And, as Yahweh thy God liveth, truly since thy servant read the letters there hath been no peace for thy servant. . . .[18]

From these few scraps of what must have been a considerable correspondence, it is clear that the commanders of outposts in Judah were concerned with, if not involved in, the web of political intrigue of king, princes, and prophets in the last days of Judah's autonomy. In one short letter Hoshaiah modestly asks the question, "How can thy servant benefit or injure the king?"[19] We may surmise from this defensive question that there had been at least some talk of his political activity against the king.

None of the principals in this correspondence can be identified with persons mentioned in the Bible as the de-

---

[17] Jer. 38:4.   [18] *ANET*, 322.   [19] *ANET*, 322.

fenders of Judah at the crisis that marked the end of the rule of a single dynasty which had lasted more than four hundred years. Yet this dossier of a military commander gives us, for the crisis of 588-587 B.C., an insight which is lacking in the official annalistic history of the period.

The Lachish ostraca have indeed added a new chapter to the books of Kings and Jeremiah. It is a miracle that this revealing, and at the same time tantalizing, literature has been preserved for over twenty-five hundred years in the soil of Palestine. Recently, less than twenty years after the recovery, a scholar who examined these letters in a museum case, where the envelopes of dirt and sand which had preserved them for centuries had been removed, reported that "the ink on the ostraca seems to be slowly fading away."[20] One wonders if the illustrations in the Lachish publication, now scattered in various libraries over the world, will last as long as the ink on the sherds before they were taken from the debris in the sixth-century guard room at Lachish.

SENNACHERIB BEFORE LACHISH

A little more than a century before the conquest by Nebuchadnezzar, Lachish was involved in another time of troubles, when the Assyrian king, Sennacherib, came down upon it "like the wolf on the fold." From the Bible it had long been known that Sennacherib, in 701 B.C., took all the "fenced cities" of Judah, with the exception of Jerusalem, and that this great Assyrian king made his headquarters at Lachish for a while. From here he sent emissaries to negotiate with Hezekiah, the Judaean king in Jerusalem. But there is no record in the Bible as to how Lachish was taken, or what its defenses were.

These bare references to Sennacherib encamped at Lachish have been supplemented and illustrated by two

[20] Olga Tufnell, *Lachish III: The Iron Age*, London, 1953, p. 331.

FIG. 7. Sennacherib seated on his throne receiving the booty taken at Lachish. At the left three Judaeans, citizens of the town, do obeisance to the Assyrian conqueror. The countryside is represented as hilly and covered with grapevines.

FIG. 8. The taking of Lachish by Sennacherib in 701 B.C. The walls of the city are shown in the upper right-hand corner. Assyrian spearmen and archers advance up the steep hill on which the city is located.

Fig. 9. The taking of Lachish by Sennacherib in 701 B.C. A siege-engine is pushed up an earth-ramp; bowmen advance, protected by shields, up other ramps. Prisoners are leaving the tower in the center. At the lower right, Assyrian soldiers are impaling three citizens of Lachish on poles outside the city.

archaeological discoveries, the first over a century ago, and the second during Starkey's work at Lachish in the 1930's. The first was made by the Englishman Austen Henry Layard, not in Palestine itself, but in distant Nineveh. It was of a picture of Sennacherib taking Lachish and was found in the elaborately-decorated palace of Sennacherib. Almost a hundred years later another British archaeologist, by tracing the city walls at Tell ed-Duweir, recovered from the ground the plan of the city defenses; and this plan seems to match in detail the representation of the defenses made by Sennacherib's artists.

The famous campaign of Sennacherib to Syria and Palestine in 701 is described not only in several books of the Bible but in a well-preserved cuneiform inscription written by the king's own scribes. Fortunately, about one-third of the long text deals with the resistance and eventual submission of Hezekiah, king of Judah (see p. 157 for the text). The royal scribe goes into specific detail about the means employed by the Assyrians in taking the "walled forts" of Judah. They built well-stamped earth-ramps for the battering-rams and gained entrance to the city by means of mines, breaches, and sapper work.

Of all the forty-six cities conquered, Lachish seems to have been the prize, the source of Sennacherib's greatest pride upon his return to his palace at Nineveh. Within one of the rooms of the palace which Layard discovered at Nineveh in 1849, were thirteen slabs of stone in bas-relief depicting in minute detail an attack upon a well-fortified city (Figs. 7, 8, 9). Just in front of the king, who was enthroned on a hill before the besieged city, was a short cuneiform inscription stating that Sennacherib sat on his throne as he reviewed the booty taken from Lachish.

Here for the first time appeared an ancient illustration of the taking of a biblical city, showing the clothing worn, the city walls and other defenses, the Assyrian armory, the methods of attack, and numerous details about daily life.

The artists had taken the pains to label the extensive panorama of this important event so that its identity was unmistakable. Layard wrote enthusiastically, "an undoubted representation of a king, a city, and a people, with whose names we are acquainted, and of an event described in Holy Writ."[21]

Even at first glance at the bas-reliefs it is apparent that Lachish was defended by two city walls, one outer wall,

FIG. 10. The city of Lachish protected by a double wall. A model made on the basis of Starkey's excavation.

from whose towers the inhabitants fought, and a second inner wall, farther up toward the summit of the city, which served as a second line of defense. Both city walls are built with recessed panels. In the center of the scene appears a tower or bastion, detached from the walls above. The tower is under heavy attack by a siege-engine with a batteringram, which is being pushed up a roadway constructed for it. The city is set in a hilly countryside covered with trees and vines.

While the technique of attack as depicted on the relief corresponds to the description of well-stamped earthramps, battering-rams, mines, breaches, and sapper work

21 A. H. Layard, *Discoveries among the Ruins of Nineveh and Babylon,* New York, 1856, p. 129.

listed in Sennacherib's annals, the most compelling evidence for the accuracy of the carved scene came as a result of Starkey's six seasons of work at Lachish itself.

In the final report of the excavation of the Iron-Age city at Lachish, the archaeologists describe the remains which they actually found at the site: ". . . during the ninth and eighth centuries B.C. the city was surrounded by two lines of defense, an upper wall of brick following the edge of the escarpment, and a lower wall or revetment of stone half-way down the slope [Fig. 10]. Both walls were planned with recessed panels. . . . [There was a] bastion at the southwest corner, which appears to have been a free-standing block, unattached to the lower revetment in its earliest phase. On and near the roadways leading to the city were the missiles of the attack: iron arrowheads used by the bowmen engaged in the assault, stone slingshots used by the rear ranks of slingers, a spearhead, and part of a bronze crest mount worn by a spearman [Fig. 11]—all embedded in a thick layer of ash which spread out over the road."[22]

Through the collaboration of artists who lived in Nineveh at the beginning of the seventh century B.C., Hebrew scribes who kept records in Jerusalem, Austen Henry Layard, who discovered the palace of Sennacherib at Nineveh, and James Starkey, who unearthed ancient Lachish, the episode of the capture of this strongly fortified Judaean city has become one of the most fully documented events in the history of ancient Palestine.

WAR AND COMMERCE AT MEGIDDO

By all odds Israel's wealthiest king was Solomon, the builder of the temple in Jerusalem. A discovery which has shed light on the period of this magnificent monarch was made at Megiddo, where, through the backing of Mr. John D. Rockefeller, Jr., Palestinian archaeology has had its most ambitious excavation.

[22] Olga Tufnell, *Lachish III: The Iron Age*, p. 55.

Megiddo—later known as Armageddon—was a city which commanded a strategic pass across the range of Mt. Carmel. Over this pass went one of the oldest international roads of the world, a highway which connected the two continents of Africa and Asia.

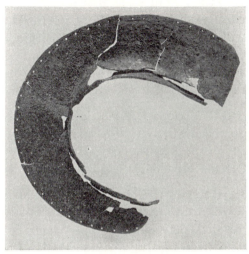

FIG. 11. Part of a bronze crested helmet worn by an Assyrian soldier. This was found in the debris at Lachish, which was taken by the Assyrians in 701 B.C. Compare the helmet worn by the spearman at the lower left of Fig. 8.

On May 7, 1468 B.C., the great Thut-mose III, king of Egypt, encamped with his army on the south side of the Carmel range and held a conference with his military staff on how best to cross the mountain and meet his enemy on the other side. His advisors suggested the advance over one of two alternate routes, since, in their opinion, the direct pass of the Aruna Road by Megiddo was too narrow for the rapid advance of the large army. The account of this staff meeting has been preserved for us on the walls of the temple at Karnak in Egypt:

They said in the presence of his majesty: "What is it like to go on this road which becomes so narrow? It is reported that the foe is there, waiting on the outside, while they are becoming more numerous. Will not horse have to go after horse, and the army and the people similarly? Will the vanguard of us be fighting while the rear guard is waiting here in Aruna, unable to fight? Now two other roads are here. One of the roads—behold, it is to the east of us, so that it comes out at Taanach. The other—behold, it is to the north side of Djefti, and we will come out to the north of Megiddo. Let our victorious lord proceed on the one of them which is satisfactory to his heart, but do not make us go on that difficult road![23]

In reply to this counsel of caution, Thut-mose III decided to proceed daringly against his enemy in the plain beyond through the narrow defile leading to Megiddo. It is reported in the Karnak inscription that he declared:

I swear, as Re loves me, as my father Amon favors me, as my nostrils are rejuvenated with life and satisfaction, my majesty shall proceed upon this Aruna road! Let him of you who wishes go upon these roads of which you speak, and let him of you who wishes come in the following of my majesty![24]

As the Egyptian king took his place at the head of his army three days later, he led his troops successfully over the narrow pass into the plain beyond. There he met his enemies, who, only by abandoning their equipment, escaped and found protection within the great walled city of Megiddo. The account of the battle of Megiddo and of the flight of the enemy was inscribed thus:

Thereupon his majesty prevailed over them at the head of his army. Then they saw his majesty prevailing over them, and they fled headlong to Megiddo with faces of fear. They abandoned their horses and their chariots of gold and silver, so that someone might draw them up into this town by hoisting on their garments. Now the

[23] *ANET*, 235.   [24] *ANET*, 235.

people had shut this town against them, but they let down garments to hoist them up into this town. Now, if only his majesty's army had not given up their hearts to capturing the possessions of the enemy, they would have captured Megiddo at this time, while the wretched enemy of Kadesh and the wretched enemy of this town were being dragged up hastily to get them into their town, for the fear of his majesty entered their bodies, their arms were weak, for his serpent-diadem had over-powered them."[25]

The siege of the well-fortified city of Megiddo lasted for seven months, after which it surrendered to Thut-mose III. An inventory of the loot which fell to the Egyptians when the city finally succumbed, along with the length of time required to bring it into submission, is a measure of its importance:

> List of the booty which his majesty's army carried off from the town of Megiddo: 340 living prisoners and 83 hands; 2,041 horses, 191 foals, 6 stallions, and . . . colts; 1 chariot worked with gold, with a body of gold, belonging to that enemy 1 fine chariot worked with gold belonging to the Prince of Megiddo . . . , and 892 chariots of his wretched army—total: 924; 1 fine bronze coat of mail belonging to that enemy, 1 fine bronze coat of mail belonging to the Prince of Megiddo, and 200 leather coats of mail belonging to his wretched army; 502 bows; and 7 poles of *meru*-wood, worked with silver, of the tent of that enemy.[26]

Thut-mose III's account of this strategic victory at Megiddo is one of the earliest military histories which has been preserved.

In the year 609 B.C. another Egyptian Pharaoh went up to Megiddo and there slew Josiah, the king of Judah. Of this event there is but the briefest report in the Bible: "In his

25 *ANET*, 236-237.   26 *ANET*, 237.

Fig. 12. Egyptian attack upon a Canaanite fortress.

days Pharaoh-necoh king of Egypt went up against the king
of Assyria to the river Euphrates; and king Josiah went
against him; and he slew him at Megiddo, when he had

seen him. And his servants carried him in a chariot dead from Megiddo, and brought him to Jerusalem. . . ."[27]

Twenty-five centuries later this same pass at Megiddo was the scene of another decisive battle—this time it witnessed the end of the campaign of General Edmund H. H. Allenby, who took Palestine from the Turks in World War I. Words from the official record of the advance of the Egyptian Expeditionary Force, published by His Majesty's Stationery Office, tell of the advance over the same pass and the march into Nazareth, where the enemy's supreme commander in Palestine, Liman von Sanders, was surprised and routed. It is the entry for September 20, 1918: "Pressing all night in parallel columns, the 4th Cavalry Division on Megiddo . . . the Plain of Esdraelon was reached before dawn. . . . Yilderim Army Group Headquarters were captured in Nazareth with numbers of valuable documents, and the enemy commander, Marshal Liman von Sanders Pasha, himself only just made his escape in time. . . . An eyewitness asserts that at the first alarm he ran, clad only in pyjamas and armed with an electric torch, from his sleeping quarters to near Our Lady's Well shouting for the driver of his motor car in which he made off."[28]

In May of 1925, with the accounts of these three important battles in mind—he had himself translated the account of the first from hieroglyphs into English years before—James Henry Breasted, the director of the Oriental Institute of the University of Chicago, persuaded John D. Rockefeller, Jr. to sponsor yet another "attack" upon Megiddo. The plan was to level it to the ground, recording its archaeological secrets layer by layer. Rockefeller agreed to finance the excavation for a five-year period, and by the end of the summer Clarence S. Fisher, the director of the new undertaking, had started to build an expedition house near the ancient site.

[27] II Kings 23:29-30.
[28] *A Brief Record of the Advance of the Egyptian Expeditionary Force under the Command of General Sir Edmund H. H. Allenby*, 1919, opp. pl. 43.

The components of a successful archaeological expedition are many—not the least of which is the vision of those who do the planning. Certainly, Breasted's contribution of enthusiasm was as essential a part of the excavation as that taken by any who actually dug there in the long period from 1926 to 1939.

While seeking to find support for the work of the Oriental Institute, Breasted had written to an old friend, F. T. Gates, asking for his help. Gates replied that he could see no valuable light for contemporary civilization—with its needs in the middle 1920's—lying under Eastern soil. His refusal was frank: "Megiddo and all its neighbors are curious, but no longer vital. Civilization can save them up like other choice dainties of its luxurious table, for times of leisure."[29]

To this refusal Breasted countered in a prophetic tone: "Coming generations will hold ours responsible if we fail to save from destruction the vast body of records which we have inherited from the Ancient Near East, many of which have come down and almost reached our eager fingers, only to be snatched away and to perish at the hands of modern vandalism."[30] It was this necessary ingredient of urgency which made possible the gaining of financial support for this most extensive of all Palestinian excavations.

In most excavations which had been made up until the beginning at Megiddo, the excavator had been content to dig trenches or to cut away part of the ancient mound of accumulated debris. The Megiddo Expedition planned to demolish layer by layer the entire thirteen acres of the mound, laying bare each city for thorough study before proceeding to its predecessor lying immediately below it.

This aim called for a long-range program. Clarence Fisher began by building a large expedition house—the most completely equipped yet known in Palestine. Living

---

29 Charles Breasted, *Pioneer to the Past*, New York, 1943, p. 378.
30 *ibid.*, pp. 378-379.

quarters in a stone building with a double roof, a garage for three cars, work rooms, offices for recording, a well-equipped photographic darkroom, Delco lighting system, Frigidaire equipment, an oil cooking-range and other equipment donated by Sears Roebuck and Co.—all were built or installed to make Megiddo a center where scholars could work in comfort the year around. As Breasted once wrote, in this operation to recover the original evidence for the conquest of civilization the machinery and inventions of modern man must be "brought to bear upon a quest for the true story of man's rise from a dim and as yet only fragmentarily discernible past."[31]

With adequate funds at its disposal the Megiddo Expedition purchased Decauville dump-cars, railway track, tubular steel chutes, a telephone to connect the expedition house with a booth on the top of the tell, and a meteorological balloon 10 feet in diameter, for taking aerial photographs of the excavation; and for the recreation of the staff, a tennis court. Never before had an expedition had a more auspicious start, with adequate finances, well-laid plans, an experienced director in the person of Clarence Fisher, who was a genius for recording accurately and efficiently all that might come to light, and a mound which had witnessed so much of human struggle.

The first battle of the Megiddo Expedition was with the Anopheles mosquito. The first staff to be assembled was laid low by malaria. But gradually, by draining the swamps, spraying the pools with Paris green and oil, and installing screens and nets, the fight against malaria was won. Because of ill health Fisher was forced to give up the directorship after two years and was succeeded by P.L.O. Guy, who carried on and enlarged upon the first director's plans.

It was in 1928 that a most important discovery began to come to light. In a stratum—it was the fourth from the top

31 *The Oriental Institute, Third Edition of the Handbook*, Chicago, 1931, p. 2.

and belonged to about the time of Solomon—Guy came upon a large compound composed of five units of stables (Fig.13). In front of the southern stable compound was an enclosed courtyard or parade ground 180 feet square, with a lime-plaster floor. In the center of it was a large cistern or water tank which could hold enough water for each of the 150 horses stabled there to have 18½ gallons of water.

The remains of buildings were recognized as stables by rows of stone pillars alternating with stone mangers. The pillars had served not only as supports for the building but as tethering posts for the horses. Holes for the halters were conveniently cut just above the tops of the mangers and "almost invariably on the side toward the central passage." Each stable was designed for 30 horses and was arranged with two rows of stalls separated by a central pas-

Fig. 13. The stables at Megiddo with hitching-posts and mangers in place.

sageway for grooms. The stalls were paved with rubble to prevent the horses from slipping. The plan was amazingly similar to that of a modern barn.

As work progressed on the north side of the mound, a second complex of stables was found in the same stratum. The excavators estimated that all told the capacity of the stables was approximately 450 horses. A possible total of 150 chariots could be accommodated in the adjacent areas.

Such a complex of easily-identifiable buildings would be archaeological news at any site. But at Megiddo, in a stratum which was inhabited at the time of Solomon, it was a remarkable confirmation of a reference in the Bible with which the discovery seemed to be connected. In I Kings 9:15-19 there is a list of cities built, or rebuilt, by Solomon: Hazor, Megiddo, Gezer, Beth-horon the nether, Baalath, Tadmor in the wilderness, and the "cities for his chariots, and the cities for his horsemen [probably horses]." At the end of the tenth chapter of I Kings there appears a listing of Solomon's chariots and horses (rather than "horsemen" as in the English translations) and a business memorandum on the trade in which he engaged. The passage reads:

> And Solomon gathered together chariots and horsemen; and he had a thousand and four hundred chariots, and twelve thousand horsemen, that he bestowed in the chariot cities, and with the king at Jerusalem. . . . And the horses which Solomon had were brought out of Egypt; also out of Keveh, the king's merchants buying them of the men of Keveh at a price. And a chariot came up and went out of Egypt for 600 shekels of silver, and a horse for 150; and so for all the kings of the Hittites, and for the kings of Aram, did they bring them out by their means.[32]

Once the identification of these remains at Megiddo became certain, it was recognized that similar buildings discovered long before at Tell el-Hesi and at Taanach also

[32] I Kings 10:26-29.

served as stables for horses. Taken together, these discoveries supplied an interesting note on the economic history of the period of Solomon.

After the clearing of the Solomonic city at Megiddo, work
was carried on until the entire accumulation of debris had
been penetrated to virgin soil. The grand plan to lay bare
the entire area of the mound had to be abandoned, but a
considerable portion was cut away to the period of the
founding of the first city on the site. In all, the excavators
could count twenty strata of occupation at Megiddo, reaching back in time to approximately four thousand years before Christ.

The wealth of historical and cultural data gathered during more than a decade of excavation at Megiddo, at a cost
of probably well on toward a million dollars, will remain

Fig. 14. An ivory carving from Megiddo depicting a prince or king cele-
brating a victory.

a lasting monument to the fruitful cooperation of pro-
moter, philanthropist, and a host of scholars who made
possible the recovery.

The most valuable museum pieces from Megiddo came
to light after eleven years of digging. They were pieces of
carved ivory—382 different objects were catalogued—found
in what may well have been the treasure room of a palace.
The assortment included playing pieces, a model pen-case,
cosmetic dishes or spoons, and some pieces inscribed in
Egyptian hieroglyphs with a text which mentions the Philistine city of Ashkelon. The collection of such diverse ob-

jects in a single room, arranged helter-skelter and mingled with fragments of gold jewelry and alabaster, has given rise to the serious conjecture "that ivory collecting was a hobby" of the prince or king who dwelt in the palace.[33]

The most important piece of this large collection contains a unique portrayal of royal life in Canaan (Fig. 14). On his sphinx throne sits a bearded king drinking from a bowl, waited upon by an attendant and a musician—a portrayal of the kind of ease suggested by the prophet Amos, who calls down woe upon those "that thrum on the psaltry . . . that drink wine in bowls." Behind the throne, two servants are depicted bringing food and drink. The other half of the scene pictures the victory: a soldier with shield and spear, two bound and stripped captives, and the chariot, perhaps that of the king himself. This is indeed a collector's item, an object of art, and at the same time a document of the social history of Canaanite life.

JERUSALEM UNDERGROUND

A promising archaeological site must meet certain requirements. First, the mound should be identifiable with some ancient city. Secondly, there should exist in literary remains or tradition some references to the place throughout the various phases of its history. And thirdly, there should be a deposit of ancient debris which is unencumbered by modern buildings or cemeteries, so as to be easily accessible for digging.

quote

On the first two counts Jerusalem leaves nothing to be desired. Mentioned 644 times, by actual count, in the Old Testament, it is the most important city in biblical history. In addition to the names of its kings, its conquerors, its prophets and priests, and its most important buildings mentioned in the Bible, there are numerous references to it in extra-biblical writings extending over the area from Assyria in the east to Egypt in the south. No city in the

[33] G. Loud, *The Megiddo Ivories*, Chicago, 1939, p. 2.

entire Near East has so rich a documentation in literature. Moreover, the identification of the modern city with the ancient has never been lost.

But this continuous identification with its past has robbed the archaeologist, in our day at least, of the chance of learning its secrets. Buildings sacred to three major faiths and the busy life of thousands of people crowded into the present walled town have made it impossible to dig in the most important areas. Furthermore, those areas which do offer themselves for excavation have proved singularly unproductive of both information and treasure, partly because of the bungling of piecemeal digging and partly because of the almost continuous occupation of the site by eager settlers who have moved in quickly after each destruction and rebuilt the city.

Despite the difficulties of getting at the remains of ancient Jerusalem, British, German, and French archaeologists have, for almost a century, persistently sought to locate its ancient walls and buildings. Army officers from England were the first to dig. A philanthropic English lady, Miss Burdett Coutts, with a desire to improve the sanitary conditions of the Old City, financed a "survey" which developed into the first "archaeological" enterprise in 1864. By means of shafts and tunnels Captain Charles Warren mined through masses of debris to get at the foundations of the early city walls. It was eventually determined that the ancient city of David lay to the southeast of the present walled city. Here, upon a spur of one of the many hills of the ancient Jerusalem, most of the digging has been done.

The outstanding discovery of almost a century of work at Jerusalem was made not by the many teams of western archaeologists, but by a native boy who had the bad luck to fall into a stream of water. In the month of June 1880, a pupil of Herr Conrad Schick, a German architect who had lived in Jerusalem for many years, was playing with some of his friends. On this hot summer day he waded

36

into a pool of water to the south of the Old City and made his way up a tunnel from which the pool was fed. His foot slipped and he fell into the cold water. On rising to the surface he noticed on the wall of the tunnel what looked to him like letters cut into the stone. After returning to school, he told his story to Herr Schick, who retraced the boy's steps and found that the wall of the tunnel did indeed have upon it six lines of writing in ancient Hebrew (Fig. 15). A text, a little larger than the page of a modern newspaper, had been engraved on a smoothed portion of the wall.

When this discovery was made in 1880 the existence of the tunnel had long been known and it had, in fact, been explored, measured, and surveyed by archaeologists. Forty-two years earlier the American explorer Edward Robinson had laboriously—clad, as he records, only in a pair of wide Arab drawers—made his way, sometimes lying at full length and dragging himself along by his elbows, through this rock-cut tunnel for a distance just short of one-third of a mile. He found that the tunnel was a conduit for the water from a copious spring to the north, leading over an S-shaped route to what he believed to be the pool of Siloam mentioned in the Bible.

Again, on a cold December day in 1867, Captain Charles Warren made the journey through the passage, remaining for nearly four hours in the water, crawling at times through a passage no more than 16 inches high, in which the water ran to a depth of one foot. He recorded his ordeal: "I was particularly embarrassed: one hand necessarily wet and dirty, the other holding a pencil, compass, and field-book; the candle for the most part in my mouth."[34] Sometimes, when observing, his mouth was under water. Under such conditions he may be excused for not noticing the inscription.

Word of the discovery of the Hebrew inscription was promptly passed on by Herr Schick to the scholarly world.

[34] *The Survey of Western Palestine: Jerusalem*, London, 1884, p. 355.

FIG. 15. The Siloam tunnel cut through the rock of Jerusalem. In the wall of this tunnel was inscribed an account of how the cutting was made.

Professor A. H. Sayce and others copied it by candlelight; a squeeze was made of it and casts made from the squeeze. By a treatment of dilute hydrochloric acid the incrustation which had filled in the letters was removed, and translation began to take shape through the combined efforts of a number of scholars.

The first part of the inscription seems to be missing, but what is left is intelligible:

> . . . when the tunnel was driven through. And this was the way in which it was cut through:—While . . . were still . . . axes, each man toward his fellow, and while there were still three cubits to be cut through, there was heard the voice of a man calling to his fellow, for there was an overlap in the rock on the right and on the left. And when the tunnel was driven through, the quarrymen hewed the rock, each man toward his fellow, axe against axe; and the water flowed from the spring toward the reservoir for 1,200 cubits, and the height of the rock above the heads of the quarrymen was 100 cubits.[35]

Who could have been responsible for this public works enterprise, an undertaking sufficiently important to have been celebrated by a commemorative inscription? In the Book of Kings there is a short summary of the works and deeds of Hezekiah, king of Judah during the perilous days of the siege of Jerusalem by Sennacherib. Tersely it concludes: "Now the rest of the acts of Hezekiah, and all his might, and how he made the pool, and the conduit, and brought water into the city, are they not written in the book of the chronicles of the kings of Judah?"[36] And even more explicit is the reference in Chronicles to Hezekiah's provision for Jerusalem's water supply in time of siege: "This same Hezekiah also stopped the upper spring of the waters of Gihon, and brought them straight down on the west side of the city of David."[37]

It soon became apparent that this equation of the tunnel

[35] *ANET*, 321.   [36] II Kings 20:20.   [37] II Chr. 32:30.

with the conduit of Hezekiah was indeed valid and that there had been found under ancient Jerusalem a construction which is mentioned in the Bible.

Ten years after the inscription was discovered the rock surface on which it was carved was cut out of the wall by a vandal. The pieces—for it had been broken as it was removed—were found some months later in the possession of a Greek citizen of Jerusalem, who claimed that he had bought them for 35 napoleons from an Arab, whose name he could not remember. Turkish officials immediately confiscated the pieces and sent them off to Istanbul, where they remain until this day.

The last chapter in the story of the recovery of Hezekiah's tunnel is connected with one of the most bizarre archaeological expeditions ever undertaken in the Holy Land, where, as it has been said by Sir Mortimer Wheeler, "more sins have probably been committed in the name of archaeology than on any commensurate portion of the earth's surface."[38]

For twenty years after it had been robbed of its commemorative plaque, the tunnel remained very much as it had been, half silted up and with many of the revealing details of its construction hidden. In 1909, Captain Montague Parker and a staff of English engineers, with a capital reputed to be about £25,000, began to explore the region around the upper entrance of the tunnel in search of the Ark of the Covenant and the original manuscript of the Law of Moses, which they believed to be hidden there. In this endeavor they were guided by an imaginative Finn, Walter Juvelius, who thought that he had found the key to the location of this ancient treasure through the application of cryptography to the writings of the prophet Ezekiel. Both the English and German archaeologists were kept out of the area of excavation by the treasure-hunters. The Palestine Exploration Fund felt obliged to advertise in

[38] Sir Mortimer Wheeler, *Archaeology from the Earth*, Oxford, 1954, p. 16.

its *Quarterly Statement* that it disavowed any connection with this "English party of amateurs on Ophel," while the German scholar Gustaf Dalman published exposés in German and in English. For some reason, however, the French were allowed to follow the course of the digging. When the episode was ended—Parker in a final bold attempt to find his treasure entered the Harem area by night, was betrayed by a disgruntled watchman whom he had not bribed sufficiently, and was forced to flee to his yacht anchored off Jaffa—the French Dominican Père H. Vincent was able to salvage much of the evidence and to publish it in the only account of the results of this strange expedition ever given to the public.

Along with the discovery of further details of the water system of ancient Jerusalem, the Parker mission completely excavated, surveyed, and measured, more accurately than had ever been done before, the tunnel of Hezekiah.

The length of the "1200-cubit" tunnel was found to be

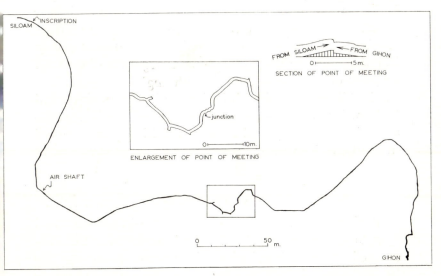

FIG. 16. Plan of Hezekiah's tunnel cut for a distance of 1200 cubits through rock to bring water from the spring Gihon outside the city wall to the Siloam pool within.

1,749 feet; its average height was 5 feet 11 inches; the fall in elevation from the one end to the other was 7 feet 2 inches; and details of the meeting of the two gangs of workers near the center of the tunnel became clear from the cuttings near the floor at the mid-way point (Fig.16). From the changes in directions at some distance from the junction, it has been surmised that when the two gangs were about 98 feet apart they first heard the blows of the others' pickaxes and were guided by these sounds to the point of meeting. When the break-through was finally made, the level of the southern portion of the channel was but about one foot higher than that of the northern portion. In all, about 850 cubic yards of rock had been mined, the removal of which would have taken, Vincent estimated, from 190 to 200 days. There was room for only one man to work at a time at the head of the cutting. For the southern gang, there was a single air-shaft at about 460 feet from the starting point; but for those working from the northern end, there was no supply of fresh air except for that which seeped in from the entrance itself. The problem of just why the builders took this S-shaped course over a distance of 1,749 feet instead of a straight line remains to this day a mystery. But that the two gangs met so successfully is one of the wonders of ancient engineering skill.

The Siloam tunnel with its inscription in good biblical Hebrew is one of the most trustworthy links between archaeological discovery in Palestine and history as recorded in the Old Testament.

SCROLLS FROM CAVES OVERLOOKING
THE DEAD SEA

Readers of *The New Yorker* magazine in the spring of 1955 found that almost half of the issue for May 14th was devoted to an archaeological discovery made eight years before in Palestine. A book-length article spread over seventy-six pages, written by Edmund Wilson, dealt with "The Scrolls from the Dead Sea." Through radio, television, and books, this discovery of ancient manuscripts became, in a very short time, more widely known than any single result of Palestinian archaeology in the sixty-five years since Petrie went to Tell el-Hesi in 1890 to begin the first scientific excavation.

The scrolls became a sensation for several reasons. The soil of Palestine had yielded indestructible materials from biblical times, such as pottery, stone, metal, and ivory, but no leather or parchment. Even though perishable writing materials had survived in the dry climate of Egypt for thousands of years, before the finding of the Dead Sea Scrolls no sober scholar would have dreamed of finding in Palestine, where the winters are wet, ancient writings on leather which had lasted through many centuries.

That among the surviving scrolls should have been manuscripts and fragments of biblical books, copies which are older by a thousand years than the Hebrew manuscripts that were known and used in making translations into modern languages, was another cause for amazement. These new discoveries should enable one to by-pass the errors and changes of copyists and bring the modern reader closer to what the original ancient writer had said. So recently as a decade before the first discovery of the scrolls, Sir Frederic Kenyon, an authority on biblical manuscripts, had given up hope of finding any copies of the Bible as old as those discovered in 1947. He had written: "There is, indeed, no probability that we shall ever find manuscripts of the Hebrew text going back to a period before the formation of the text which we know as Massoretic."[39] But the improbable had come to pass.

The first discovery of scrolls was ironical, in that, like the discovery of the Siloam inscription, it was made by a native boy, and not by any one of the hundreds of scientific explorers and excavators. In the spring of 1947, so the story can be pieced together from somewhat conflicting

[39] Sir Frederic Kenyon, *Our Bible and the Ancient Manuscripts*, London. 1939, p. 48.

reports, a fifteen-year-old shepherd, Muhammad adh-Dhib, "Muhammad the Wolf," first came upon a cave in the cliff about a mile from the shore of the northwest corner of the Dead Sea. Although the cave is just eight miles directly south of Jericho, it had not been noticed in modern times. Inside the cave there were several jars, most of them broken, but some of them containing scrolls of leather wrapped in linen cloth. Muhammad and his friends took their curious finds to Bethlehem, where they eventually passed into the hands of merchants, who in turn disposed of them in two lots. One collection of five scrolls (two later turned out to be parts of one document) was acquired by the Metropolitan-Archbishop Athanasius Yeshue Samuel of the Syrian Orthodox Monastery of St. Mark in Jerusalem. The other lot of three scrolls fell into the hands of Professor E. L. Sukenik of the Hebrew University in Jerusalem.

What were these scrolls? The larger of the two collections, that purchased by Archbishop Samuel, contained four important works: (1) the Book of Isaiah, a leather scroll about 24 feet long, with fifty-four columns of text, which according to Millar Burrows, who first compared it with the standard but much later Hebrew text of Isaiah, is "by and large the same as that of our familiar Book of Isaiah, with many more or less important differences in details";[40] (2) a commentary on the Book of Habakkuk; (3) a Manual of Discipline, a book of rules governing the Jewish sect to which the library belonged—thought to be the Essenes; (4) an Aramaic document, a "Genesis Apocryphon," which was generally referred to as the "Lamech Scroll," before it was unrolled in 1955.

This collection of ancient documents, after having been seen by a number of people, none of whom considered them very important, came in February of 1948 to the American School of Oriental Research in Jerusalem, where three of them were photographed by John C. Trever. On

[40] Millar Burrows, *The Dead Sea Scrolls*, New York, 1955, p. 21.

March 15th, Trever received from William F. Albright, to whom he had sent some sample photographs of the documents, an opinion confirming his belief that the scrolls were genuine and ancient and asserting that this was "the greatest manuscript discovery of modern times."[41]

The second lot of scrolls was acquired by E. L. Sukenik. On November 29, 1947, Sukenik bought from an antiquity dealer in Bethlehem "several bundles of coarse parchment ... along with two earthenware vessels in which the Beduin said the scrolls had been stored."[42] Later he added to his collection. This material contained a part of a manuscript of the Book of Isaiah; a scroll of "The War of the Sons of Light with the Sons of Darkness," more than nine feet long when unrolled; and a collection of "Thanksgiving Psalms."

The material from the first discovery of scrolls has now been published and the non-biblical texts are available in translation. But this first discovery has been followed by a series of important new discoveries. To be sure, no large manuscripts have come to light, but hundreds of portions and fragments of scrolls have come from the general area in which the first discovery was made.

Not until almost two years after the first manuscripts were taken from the cave by Bedouins did archaeologists have the opportunity to excavate carefully. The result of this belated search under scientific control, in which the work was done painstakingly with penknives, brushes, tweezers, and fingers, was the finding of several hundred fragments of inscribed pieces of leather, a few fragments of papyrus, pieces of linen wrappers for the scrolls, and broken pottery which once belonged to about fifty jars and their covers. Enough evidence came out of the cave to demonstrate that it had been a repository for an ancient library in the late first century A.D.

---

[41] *Biblical Archaeologist*, vol. 11, 1948, p. 55.

[42] E. L. Sukenik, ed., *The Dead Sea Scrolls of the Hebrew University*, Jerusalem, 1955, p. 14.

FIG. 17. A member of the international team of scholars working at the Palestine Archaeological Museum in Jerusalem with the fragments of scrolls from the caves near the Dead Sea.

Fragments of manuscripts by the hundreds continued to pour into the Palestine Archaeological Museum in Jerusalem. By January 1956 ten other manuscript-bearing caves had been discovered in the same area, which had now come to be known as Qumran. The lion's share of the discovery was made by Bedouin Arabs who looted the caves for this new type of "treasure" and sold it to the archaeologists; the latter, too, dug the caves and salvaged the less conspicuous evidence. From Cave 4, the most prolific, there have been identified fragments of about 330 documents, which now fill 420 plates of glass, between which the fragments are mounted (Fig. 17).

When Père Roland de Vaux and G. Lankester Harding excavated the first cave in 1949, their attention had been drawn to an ancient ruin, Khirbet Qumran, on a high terrace overlooking the Dead Sea at a point about a quarter of a mile to the south of the cave (Fig. 18). In 1851, F. de Saulcy had paid it a visit and suggested the famed Gomorrah as its identification. With more caution, others had labeled it as a Roman fort. On their way from the cave in 1949, Harding and de Vaux stopped long enough to make surface explorations and to open two tombs, but found nothing which indicated a connection with either the manuscripts or the cave in which they had been found.

It is difficult to imagine a less likely place for human habitation than Khirbet Qumran. Shut in between the steep cliff of the Judaean mountains to the west and the lifeless Dead Sea to the east, it lies in a barren waste scorched by the sun and devoid of vegetation most of the year.

Not satisfied with the hurried examination of two years before, de Vaux and Harding returned to dig Khirbet Qumran in 1951 and remained at the task for five seasons. To their surprise, the ruins were not a Roman fort, nor, in fact, an ordinary Palestinian town with city walls, streets, and houses, but an utterly unique structure. Covering an

Fig. 18. Khirbet Qumran partly excavated.

area of about one and a half acres were the ruins of a kind of Jewish "monastery" which flourished in this forsaken spot during parts of the first century B.C. and the first century A.D. And, what was an even greater surprise, it was the site of the very sectarian settlement which had produced the scrolls which had come from the nearby caves. Rarely have excavators had the good luck to have in their hands a contemporary literary document like the "Manual of Discipline," the description of the community life of the group, to aid them in interpreting the archaeological evidence which they uncovered.

As the excavation proceeded, the mystery of how a large group of people could live in this desert place was cleared up. By an elaborate system of canals and plastered reservoirs the water which rushed down the steep hills during the rainy season was caught and stored. Purified in a large settling basin, it was stored in at least seven large cisterns located advantageously for the work which had to be done by the members of the community. In addition, there were two baths which were supplied with water from the canal —a commentary on the emphasis which the group placed in their rule of discipline on ritual purity.

Five campaigns of careful work at Qumran have yielded a profile of its archaeological history. In Israelite times a small settlement occupied the terrace during the eighth and seventh centuries, and it was probably called the City of Salt, mentioned in Joshua 15:62. The site was abandoned for four centuries, probably until sometime in the reign of John Hyrcanus (135-104 B.C.), when it was replanned and rebuilt to serve the needs of the Qumran community. During the time of Alexander Jannaeus (103-76 B.C.) further development of the building took place, and these buildings served the community until the time of the severe earthquake of 31 B.C. Cisterns and walls were cracked and a fire was started which turned the buildings into ruins. Not until the time of Herod Archelaus (4 B.C.-A.D. 6) was the community restored for the second period of its habitation. Another violent destruction took place in A.D. 68, when the Roman X Legion attacked the settlement. Roman soldiers made use of the site as a military fortress for a period at the end of the first century, and it was occupied only briefly during the Second Jewish Revolt.

The largest room in the buildings, measuring 72 feet by 14 feet 9 inches, was assumed by de Vaux to have been the meeting room of the community, probably the place where the ceremonial meals, mentioned in the scrolls, were held. This first hypothesis was strengthened by the finding in an adjoining room of more than 1,080 earthenware dishes— among them 210 plates, 708 bowls, and 75 goblets. Obviously, de Vaux had come upon the pantry of the kitchen. Toward the west end of the long meeting room was a circular paved surface which well might have been the place occupied by the president of the assembly.

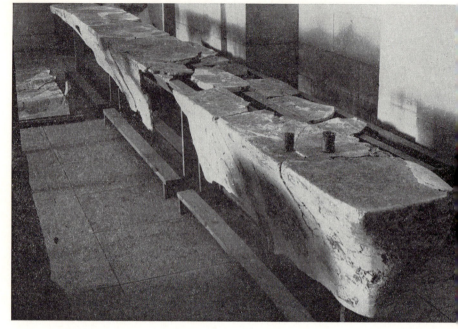

FIG. 19. Copy desk from Qumran as reconstructed from fragments.

Among the shops in which members performed their various tasks, was the most complete pottery-making installation yet found in a Palestinian excavation. It was equipped with a basin for washing the clay, an emplacement for the potter's wheel, and two kilns, the furnaces for which were so located that they could catch the prevailing winds for draft.

The most distinctive detail of the equipment of this monastic community was the remains of a scriptorium, where manuscripts had been copied. From an upper story there had fallen fragments of a brick-like table about 16 feet long and 20 inches high and parts of one or two smaller tables (Fig. 19). The guess that these had served as copy desks was borne out by the discovery of two ink-holders, one of bronze and another of clay. One of them still contained dried ink.

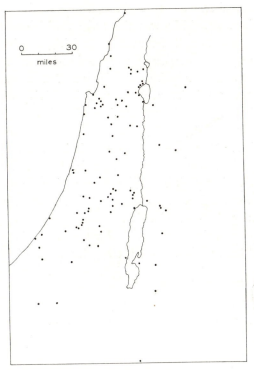

FIG. 20. Sites in Palestine, from Sidon in the north to Petra in the south, where excavations have been made.

In the course of a mere ten years there has emerged a picture of the life of a community of Jewish sectarians of the centuries before and after Christ, a picture generously documented by contemporary writings and by the actual remains of the community. The significance of this discovery—despite the bitter debates among scholars and the exaggerated claims and counterclaims which have been made in over-popularized accounts—lies in the light which it has already shed, even at this early stage in the study of the material, on the history of both Judaism and Christianity. And Qumran and its caves have provided us with the oldest copies of the Hebrew text of the Bible.

51

Tell el-Hesi was the site of the first scientific expedition in Palestine; Megiddo was the most ambitious undertaking; Jerusalem is still the most promising site in the land; and Qumran has achieved the distinction of having become the most widely known discovery. But the most impressive result of the archaeological activity of the past century is the total accumulation of evidence which has been uncovered and published by the scores of excavators in Palestine. On a recent map of this land, approximately the size of the State of Vermont or the Island of Sicily, can be counted ninety-nine ancient sites which have been subjected to excavation (Fig. 20). Of this number, twenty-five have been worked sufficiently to justify the labeling of them as major excavations. This is indeed an impressive achievement in the attempt to recover the land of the Bible.

CHAPTER 2

THE MAKING OF A MAP

PILGRIMS AND SOLDIERS

AT THE BEGINNING of the nineteenth century, no area of the earth's surface comparable in size to Palestine could claim to have received as much attention from the outside as the Holy Land. Pilgrims by the hundreds had written stories of adventures on their visits to its holy places. Many had drawn maps of their journeys, indicating the routes that they had taken to the shrines, and had filled in details of rivers, mountains, cities, and tribes, as they supposed them to have been from their reading of the Bible and the writings of Josephus, Eusebius, and Jerome.

An industrious bibliographer named Reinhold Röhricht has listed 1,561 published works of travels and pilgrimages made to Palestine before A.D. 1800, and more than three hundred maps of the whole or parts of the land drawn from the fourth through the eighteenth centuries.[1]

That Palestine was mapped so frequently throughout fifteen centuries is not strange. It was the *terra sancta* for the entire western world, and a pilgrimage provided the occasion for both an act of devotion and an adventure. But piety and curiosity were not the only reasons for the continued geographical interest. Palestine was not only the holy land; it was believed to be the exact center of the earth!

Jerome, the great biblical scholar of the fourth century, noted that the prophet Ezekiel had spoken of the land of Israel as "the navel of the earth" (38:12, Greek version) and of Jerusalem as having the countries "round about her" (5:5).[2] Relying upon the infallible authority of the

---

[1] *Bibliotheca Geographica Palaestinae*, Berlin, 1890, pp. 1-335, 598-629.

[2] Cf. A. D. White, *A History of the Warfare of Science with Theology in Christendom*, New York, 1899, vol. 1, pp. 99-100.

Scriptures, mapmakers showed the world as circular with Jerusalem at its very center. The maker of the thirteenth-century map of the world in the Hereford Cathedral expressed this orthodox view of world geography in a decorated map of the round world (Fig. 21), and Dante put the hint derived from Ezekiel in the thirty-fourth canto of the *Inferno*.

Yet, with all the map-making of fifteen centuries, Palestinian geography at the beginning of the nineteenth century relied principally on theology, pious legend, and guesswork. Travelers had followed well-worn paths and had had no means for checking directions or for measuring accurately the distances or angles. They had been content to accept uncritically traditions which guides and custodians of the shrines were eager to pass on to them. Ancient sites were indicated on their maps without references to the names of the modern places and the landmarks of the physical geography.

If one takes the latest and most detailed map of Palestine, that of the Cadastral Survey made in the 1930's, and looks for familiar biblical place-names, he will find such towns as Acre, Beersheba, Bethlehem, Gaza, Hebron, Jericho, Jerusalem, Nazareth, and Tiberius. Yet, on the present-day map of this land, so rich with history, he will not find Samaria, Bethel, Lachish, Anathoth, Gibeah, Megiddo, Beth-shan, or the more than six hundred other names which figure in the biblical history of the land west of the Jordan between Dan and Beersheba. The ancient names—except for the few more important towns—have either been lost sight of or obscured by the modern inhabitants of the land.

The gradual recovery in the last century and a half of the lost map of ancient Palestine has involved two things: an accurate survey of the land—its villages, ruins, mountains, valleys, and springs—and the finding of a sure method of identifying these observable features with the names which appear in the ancient biblical and extra-biblical sources.

FIG. 21. Thirteenth-century map of the world in Hereford Cathedral showing Jerusalem as the center of the world.

Neither religious devotion nor a crusade occasioned the first large-scale, modern map of the Holy Land. This map, printed on five large sheets, was the by-product of Napoleon Bonaparte's campaign through Palestine in 1799, by which he sought to protect his troops in Egypt from attack by the Turkish army in Syria. When Napoleon arrived in Alexandria, Egypt, on July 1, 1798, with an expeditionary force of 32,000 men, he was accompanied by a corps of geographical engineers, headed by M. Testevuide. The chief geographer was, however, soon assassinated during an insurrection in Cairo. He was replaced by his nephew, Pierre Jacotin, on whom there fell the responsibility for mapping the four-month campaign of 1799 in Palestine and Syria. During this short and hazardous expedition Jacotin accompanied the army and succeeded in surveying no less than a total of 426 places along the route and placing them on five large maps, which were published a few years later in Paris.[3]

Map-making during a hasty military campaign was no easy task. At times, one of the engineers wrote later, they were obliged to substitute weapons for surveying instruments and to fight for and conquer the terrain which they were to measure. There was not only the incessant danger of famine and disease but the possibility of falling into the hands of hostile Arabs. Not infrequently the surveyors had to take points of latitude and longitude which had been determined by earlier explorers. Areas which could not be reached by the geographers because of enemy occupation had to be supplied from older maps, or filled in from military reports of smaller expeditions, like the one which was sent to Tyre.

Jacotin's maps, covering a good part of the area from Gaza in the south to Sidon in the north, are indeed a remarkable achievement, especially when consideration is

---

[3] For the campaign of Napoleon see: *Description de l'Egypte*, 2nd ed., vol. 17, 1824, esp. pp. 594-609; and C. M. Watson, "Bonaparte's Expedition to Palestine in 1799," *Quarterly Statement of the Palestine Exploration Fund*, 1917, pp. 17-35.

taken of the adverse conditions under which the geographical engineers worked. While the results left much to be desired, exact measurements and astronomical observations had at long last been introduced to replace the older methods of route surveys. This work, on the scale of 1:100,-000, was the beginning of a base map on which ancient sites could eventually be plotted with accuracy.

THE FOUNDER OF PALESTINOLOGY: ROBINSON

Just forty years after Napoleon landed in Egypt, an American professor of biblical literature, Edward Robinson, visited Palestine for the first time. In a short visit of a little less than two and a half months, more was done to recover the map of ancient Palestine than had been accomplished by the combined visits of hundreds of predecessors. Robinson became the founder of modern Palestinology.

The account of his journey of 1838, *Biblical Researches in Palestine*, received from the Royal Geographical Society of London their Patron's Gold Medal, and was proclaimed by the German geographer Carl Ritter as "a classic in its own field—a production which has already set the geography of the Holy Land on a more fixed basis than it had ever had before."[4]

When Edward Robinson went to Palestine at the age of forty-four, he was already recognized as a competent scholar in the field of biblical studies. He had translated from German into English both a Hebrew lexicon and a Greek grammar, making them available to his American students. Not only did he know the biblical sources for Palestinian geography, but for fifteen years prior to 1838, including a four-year period of residence in Europe, he had combed the vast literature of former travelers.

In 1832 Robinson met a former pupil, the Reverend Eli Smith, an American missionary stationed at Beirut, and discussed with him the projected visit to Palestine. Smith

---

[4] Carl Ritter, *The Comparative Geography of Palestine*, trans. by W. L. Gage, vol. 2, New York, 1870, p. 70.

agreed to accompany him as an interpreter. Eli Smith's name is better known, perhaps, for the role which he played in the movement for Arab nationalism by bringing the first printing press with Arabic type to Syria, thus making possible the printing of textbooks in Arabic; he is none

FIG. 22. Edward Robinson, who made the first scientific explorations in Palestine.

the less distinguished as a contributor to the new epoch in Palestinian geography which Robinson's researches brought in.

Robinson differed from the earlier travelers to Palestine in that he possessed a greater knowledge of the literature, both biblical and modern. Also, he was highly skeptical of the tapestry of tradition which was woven about the holy places. The first of his general principles, he said, was "to avoid as far as possible all contact with the convents and the authority of the monks; to examine everywhere for ourselves with the Scriptures in our hands; and to apply for information solely to the native Arab population."[5] This may have been the New England Puritan speaking, but the method of inquiry served the purposes of objective scholarship. Eli Smith was useful to him in getting at the Arab population and in recording accurately the Arabic names for the places which they visited.

Did not the ancient names for the places on the land tend to preserve themselves in the modern Arabic names? Disciplined by a thorough knowledge of the groupings of ancient cities in the biblical texts, Robinson could detect in the sound of el-Jib, the ancient Gibeon; in el-Bireh, the biblical Beeroth; in Kefir, the Hebrew Chephirah; in Anata, Anathoth, the home of Jeremiah. Leaving the beaten paths of former travelers, Robinson and Smith discovered many formerly unknown sites and made scores of identifications of ancient places which have stood up under the more controlled methods of the archaeologist.

The expedition began on Monday, March 12, 1838, when the two Americans left Cairo for a month's journey through Sinai to Palestine. Their equipment included a large tent, two old muskets, a pair of pistols, the best maps available at the time, the Bible in English, Greek, and Hebrew, and five of the most important books on travels in Palestine. The only instruments were an ordinary surveyor's and two pocket compasses, a thermometer, telescopes, and measuring tapes. The two men kept separate journals, in which each recorded his notes independent of the other. Provisions consisted principally of rice and biscuits, coffee, tea, sugar, butter, dried apricots—"quite a luxury in the desert"—tobacco, for winning the favor of Arabs, wax candles, and a supply of charcoal. With some hired servants and camels to pack the provisions, they set out for Sinai.

Nothing of interest escaped the notice of the travelers. The temperature was usually recorded four times a day:

5 *Biblical Researches in Palestine*, Boston, 1874, vol. 1, p. 256.

at sunrise, 10:00 A.M., 2:00 P.M., and at sunset; the time
of arrival at and of departure from each point of interest
was scrupulously entered in the journals; directions of
important points were observed and recorded; prices of
commodities were set down; and notes about the customs of
Arab tribes were made.

Information picked up during evening talks with Arabs
became a part of the record. A certain Tuweileb told them
of pasturing his camels in an area where there was not a
drop of water for himself or them: "He drank the milk
of the camels," Robinson reported, "and they, as well as
sheep and goats, when they have fresh pasture, need no
water. In such case they will sometimes go for three or
four months without it. Others had told us that the camel
needs water once in every three days in summer, and every
five days in winter; but this is probably when the pastures
are dry, or when they are fed on provender."[6] As Albrecht
Alt, a later student of the geography of Palestine, wrote on
the occasion of the centenary of Robinson's first visit, his
work represents our most important source for the state of
settlement in Palestine a century ago. The wide curiosity of
Robinson and his careful record of what he saw and heard
are reflected on every page of his three volumes of *Biblical
Researches*.

Occasionally the scientific observer became the pilgrim.
Only once did he break the rule of resting on the Christian
Sabbath, a practice which "left upon the mind an impression that can never be forgotten."[7] When Robinson arrived
in the very precincts of Sinai, about which from the earliest
childhood he had thought and read with so much wonder,
he records that "although not given to the melting mood,
I could not refrain from bursting into tears."[8] Hebron
seemed to have stirred his emotions, for he wrote on arriving there of David: "In Hebron too he probably composed
many of his Psalms, which yet thrill through the soul and

[6] *ibid.*, p. 150.   [7] *ibid.*, p. 65.   [8] *ibid.*, p. 91.

60

lift it up to God."[9] These exceptions only prove the rule that he was primarily the objective scientist.

One month had been consumed in the trek across Sinai; in two and a half more months Robinson completed his journeys through Palestine. He reached Beirut so exhausted and weakened by the rigors and hazards of his travels that he was confined to his room for eight days.

At the beginning of the journey, he wrote, "I never thought of adding anything to the former stock of knowledge on these subjects; I never dreamed of any thing like discoveries in this field."[10] But in this short time he had laid a foundation of sound method upon which others were to build the science of Palestinian topography.

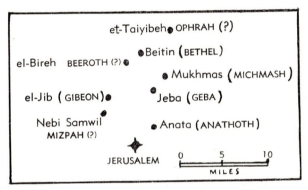

Fig. 23. On May 4 and 5, 1838, Edward Robinson visited eight places to the north of Jerusalem and identified them with names mentioned in the Bible. Only three of Robinson's identifications are questioned today; none has actually proved to be wrong.

Robinson made a second visit in 1852. On this journey he investigated anew certain points about which doubts had been expressed and explored some portions of the country which had not been included in the first visit. For a period of two and a half months he followed his former method, accompanied again for most of the time by his

9 *ibid.*, p. 214.   10 *ibid.*, pp. 31-32.

trusted companion and friend Eli Smith. The observations of this journey he published as *Later Biblical Researches in Palestine*, a similarly valuable compendium of information.

Robinson's place in the line of explorers of Palestine has been ably stated by a great geographer of this region, Père F. M. Abel, who wrote, a century after the trip of 1838, that although Robinson did not have the means for realizing his program completely, and although he left much to be done by those who followed him, "he still remains the authoritative precursor of contemporary exploration in Palestine."[11]

SURVEYING WESTERN PALESTINE

It may seem strange that a land as small as Western Palestine, so frequently visited by pilgrims and travelers over so many centuries, should have lacked an accurate map produced by theodolite, chain, and compass until 1880. Of the hundreds of maps which had been made before this time, most were based solely on route surveys, while the few more pretentious ones, such as Jacotin's five sheets, were inadequately prepared in the haste of coping with disease and hostile tribes.

The Palestine Exploration Fund map, published in 1880, the work of a team of British surveyors, located accurately about 9,000 names on the 6,000 square miles of Western Palestine.[12] Following Robinson's method of asking local inhabitants for names of towns, hills, ruins, rivers, and springs, they set down what they heard. All of this valuable information was plotted, to a scale of one inch to one mile, on twenty-six sheets, which when joined together extended 7 by 13 feet. There were five times as many places entered on this map as on the best previously available one,

[11] *Journal of Biblical Literature*, vol. 58, 1939, p. 372.
[12] *Map of Western Palestine in 26 Sheets from Surveys Conducted for the Committee of the Palestine Exploration Fund by Lieutenants C. R. Conder and H. H. Kitchener, R. E., during the Years 1872-1877*, London, 1880.

that of Van de Velde. In addition to the map itself the Survey published seven large volumes of explanatory memoirs, a useful collection of detailed information garnered by the surveying party during the six years spent in the field. As Sir Walter Besant wrote of the successful completion of this survey, nothing since the translation of the Bible into the Vulgar tongue can compare with this work for the illustration and right understanding of the historical portions of the Old and New Testaments.

This survey, completed at a cost of about £18,000, was supported entirely by public subscription. The Palestine Exploration Fund had been organized in 1865 with the ponderous title, "A Society for the Accurate and Systematic Investigation of the Archaeology, the Topography, the Geology and Physical Geography, the Manners and Customs of the Holy Land for Biblical Illustration."[13] At its first meeting the Archbishop of York had made it clear that all work should be carried out on scientific principles, that the body should abstain from controversy, and that it should not be conducted as a religious society. These provisions insured a wide base of support and a high quality of scientific results. The project of an accurate survey of the land was admirably suited to the objectives of the Fund.

The survey was commenced in January of 1872 by Captain R. W. Stewart, a royal engineer, and a staff of three assistants. Although Stewart was almost immediately attacked by fever while measuring the first base line in Esdraelon, the party was able in a half year to survey accurately about 500 square miles.

In July of 1872 a little Russian steamer brought to the port of Jaffa a twenty-four-year-old engineer, Lieutenant Claude Reignier Conder. He had come straight from his training at the Royal Military Academy at Woolwich and

13 F. J. Bliss, *The Development of Palestine Exploration*, London, 1906, p. 264.

a course at Chatham. It was under his direction that a large part of the survey of 6,000 square miles of Western Palestine was made.

That a thoroughgoing trigonometrical survey of Palestine was not made earlier is readily understandable when one reads the account of Conder's work in his two volumes, *Tent Work in Palestine*. Fever was a constant enemy, taking its toll in valuable time as one after another of the party fell ill; it finally claimed the life of the survey's archaeologist and linguist, C. F. Tyrwhitt Drake. Flies were a constant irritant: "With almost every breath," complained Conder, "we sucked in half a dozen of them; others were just small enough to get up one's nose; some yet smaller got into our eyes, and huge bluebottles bit through our clothes."[14] Then, on the occasion of a particularly heavy siege of fever, Conder received letters from the Fund in London complaining of the expense of the survey, "the last drop in the cup of my trouble."[15]

Difficulties with unfriendly tribes of Arabs reached a climax in the attack on the survey party at Safed. While the men were pitching the tents north of the village, an Arab sheikh seized Conder by the throat, but was twice knocked down. As Conder later told the story, "I hit out with each fist, and again knocked him off his legs. As he fell his intentions became clear, for in his hand was a hanjar, or knife, with a blade a foot long, which in another moment would have been sheathed in me, if I had not used the means of defense most natural to an Englishman."[16] A mob of three hundred persons then attacked the party with stones, and Conder was wounded by a blow on the forehead from a club studded with nails. After a defense of the camp for a half hour, the party fled just before the arrival of soldiers sent by the Governor. Not a member of the party escaped without injury, and the in-

14 C. R. Conder, *Tent Work in Palestine*, London, 1879, vol. 2, p. 70.
15 *ibid.*, p. 32.   16 *ibid.*, p. 192.

cident might well have cost all of them their lives. The Palestine Exploration Fund later got £270 damages from the attackers.

It fell to the lot of Lieutenant Kitchener (later Lord Kitchener) to complete the final 1,300 square miles of the survey, and, as Conder wrote later, to bring Palestine home to England, where "the student may travel, in his study, over its weary roads and rugged hills without an ache, and may ford its dangerous streams, and pass through its malarious plains without discomfort."[17] All of this actual surveying had been done in five years, at the cost of one penny per acre, and a party of sixteen men and sixteen animals had been maintained for an average cost of one shilling and six pence a day per man and one shilling per horse.

The editors of the great map of 1880 were not content merely to list the modern names for sites. They proposed identifications for places mentioned in the Bible and in the Apocrypha. Conder lists 622 ancient names and identified "with reasonable certainty" more than two-thirds, or 434. One hundred and seventy-two, he claims, were discoveries due to the survey. Understandably, not all these proposals have stood, but the achievement is truly monumental.

NEW SOURCES FOR AN ANCIENT MAP

Shortly after the completion of the great one-inch-to-one-mile map by Conder and Kitchener, new sources for the ancient topography of Palestine began to appear. From the point of view of those who had lived in Palestine they might be called enemy sources. Egypt for centuries had held her northern neighbor as a part of her Asiatic empire; later, Assyrian kings were successful in annexing portions of the land to their realm. The boastful records of Egyptian and Assyrian kings, as they were unearthed and under-

17 *ibid.*, vol. i, p. xvii.

stood, proved valuable for the geographer. Not only did these enemy sources supplement the records of the Bible, but they provided a control for interpreting the latter documents, many of which had been compiled for theological and polemical purposes. Further, in the new texts scholars had before them actual copies contemporary with the events they described.

Little did an Egyptian king, at about the nineteenth century B.C., suspect that his practice of a kind of "black magic" would supply scholars of the twentieth century A.D. with the names for a map of Palestine in this pre-biblical period. But it did. Extremely valuable topographical information was the gift of Egyptian superstition.

In 1926 there were published texts from broken fragments of pottery bowls which had come into the possession of the Berlin Museum. These inscribed sherds had been purchased at Thebes. The scholar who published them realized that they had been inscribed with "execration texts."

The Egyptian practice of execration seems to have involved the writing on bowls the names of enemies to be cursed. With the smashing of the pottery the curse was believed to become effective by sympathetic magic on the enemies themselves. Sometimes the object of the curse was stated in a blanket formula—not unlike that of modern legal language—as "All men, all people, all folk, all males, all eunuchs, all women, and all officials, who may rebel, who may plot, who may fight, who may talk of fighting, or who may talk of rebelling, and every rebel who talks of rebelling—in this entire land."[18]

On other fragments specific foreign rulers and their tribes and cities are mentioned. Shortly after the publication of the execration bowls, there were found at Sakkarah in Egypt similar texts written not on bowls but on fragments of clay figurines (Fig. 24). These also had been

[18] *ANET*, 329.

FIG. 24. Clay figurine of a bound prisoner inscribed with a curse. The figure was broken in an act which was intended to make the curse effective.

smashed to make effective the curse on the enemies which they represented. From these fragments come names which can be recognized as forms of ancient names of important towns in Palestine mentioned in the biblical texts from later centuries. Three are located in Transjordan: Laish, Ashtaroth, and Pella; eleven, which are identifiable, are in Palestine proper: Ashkelon, Jerusalem, Rehob, Beth-shan (?), Shechem, Aphek, Achshaph, Hazor, Tyre, Acre, Beth-shemesh. In addition to these fourteen biblical towns there are mentioned Zebulon, and probably Moab, as well as other unidentified Asiatic towns and peoples who were enemies of the Egyptian kings of the nineteenth and eighteenth centuries B.C.

Not merely towns, tribes, and rebellious people within Egypt itself were the object of this execration, but more indefinite forces which were felt to be a threat to peaceful life: "Every evil word, every evil speech, every evil slander, every evil thought, every evil plot, every evil fight, every evil quarrel, every evil plan, every evil thing, all evil dreams, and all evil slumber."[19]

A remnant of this same practice of execration can possibly be seen in a symbolic act which the prophet Jeremiah performed at Jerusalem. The prophet was commanded by the Lord to buy an earthen jar, or flask, and to break it in the sight of his audience, which had followed him to Topheth, with the pronouncement: "Thus saith the Lord of hosts: Even so will I break this people and this city, as one breaketh a potter's vessel, that cannot be made whole again. . . . Thus will I do unto this place, saith the Lord, and to the inhabitants thereof, even making this city as Topheth."[20]

The annals of the great Egyptian King Thut-mose III (about 1490-1436 B.C.), who for over a period of twenty years led campaigns into Asia almost every year, read like a gazetteer of Palestine and Syria (Figs. 25 and 26). Men-

[19] *ANET*, 329.   [20] Jer. 19:11-12.

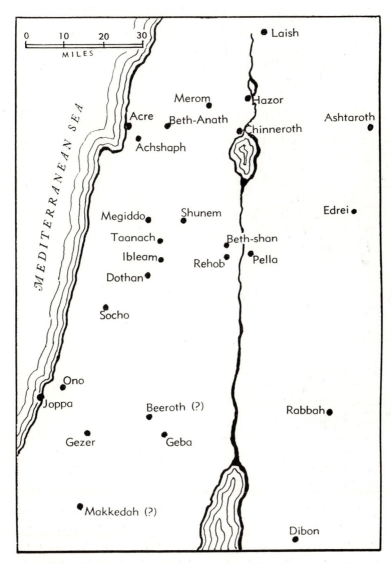

Fig. 25. Places in Palestine mentioned in the annals of
Thut-mose III (about 1490-1436 B.C.).

tioned are such well-known biblical towns as: Acre, Ash-taroth, Beeroth Beth-shan, Damascus, Dibon, Dothan, Geba, Gezer, Hamath, Hazor, Ibleam, Joppa, Laish, Megid-do, Merom, Pella, Rabbah, Rehob, Socho, Taanach, and many others.[21]

FIG. 26. A portion of a list of 115 names of places in Asia conquered by Thut-mose III. Each ring containing a name is surmounted by the upper part of a figure of a bound Asiatic.

In addition to topographical information, the Egyptian records of the New Kingdom occasionally give interesting details of adventures encountered by the king and his troops. A soldier, whose autobiography is painted on the walls of his tomb at Thebes, and who accompanied Thut-mose III on one of his Asiatic campaigns, describes an ele-phant hunt which the king conducted at Ni, a town to the south of Carchemish on the Euphrates:

[21] *ANET*, 242-243.

Again I saw another successful deed which the Lord of the Two Lands accomplished at Ni. He hunted 120 elephants at their mudhole. Then the biggest elephant which was among them began to fight before the face of his majesty. I was the one who cut off his hand [*sic,* for "trunk"] while he was still alive, in the presence of his majesty, while I was standing in the water between two rocks. Then my lord rewarded me with gold: . . . , and five pieces of clothing."[22]

It is likely that the subjects of Thut-mose III knew Palestine rather better from the popular tales which were told of his conquests than from the lists of conquered cities which he had engraved on public buildings. One of these tales, which has come down to us on a badly-broken papyrus, tells of the clever, but deceptive, stratagem by which an officer of the army of Thut-mose, General Thoth (or Thuti), took the Palestinian town of Joppa, the setting of the popular Hebrew tale of Jonah's encounter with the fish.

It seems from the broken beginning of the text that the Prince of Joppa had gone to the Egyptian camp and was conferring with General Thoth, the besieger of Joppa, to arrange some kind of terms. After they became drunken, Thoth said to the Prince of Joppa that he would deliver himself, his wife and children, over to the side of the Prince of the besieged city. Apparently in a convivial spirit the two commanders continued their conversations.

Then the Enemy of Joppa said to Thoth: "I want to see the great staff of King Men-kheper-Re [Thut-mose III] . . . if you have it today . . . bring it to me!"

And he did so and brought the great staff of King Men-kheper-Re and he laid hold of his cloak, and he stood upright, and said: "Look at me, O Enemy of Joppa! Behold the King Men-kheper-Re—life, prosperity,

FIG. 27. Gold bowl in the Louvre inscribed with the name of General Thoth of the army of Thut-mose III.

health!—the fierce lion, the son of Sekhmet! Amon gave him his victory!" And he raised his hand and struck the Enemy of Joppa on the forehead. And he fell down, made prostrate before him. And he put him in fetters. . . .

And he had the two hundred baskets brought which he had had made, and he had two hundred soldiers get down into them. And their arms were filled with bonds and fetters, and they were sealed up with seals. And they were given their sandals, as well as their carrying-poles and staves. And they had every good soldier carrying them, totaling five hundred men. And they were told: "When you enter the city, you are to let out your companions and lay hold on all the people who are in the city and put them in bonds immediately."

All this time, it seems, the charioteer who had driven the Prince of Joppa to the conference was waiting outside the Egyptian encampment.

FIG. 28. Syrian prisoners taken by Ramses II (1290-1224 B.C.). One of the bearded captives is shown with his hands bound in a shackle.

And they went out to tell the charioteer of the Enemy of Joppa: "Thus speaks your lord: 'Go and tell your mistress: "Rejoice, for Seth has given us Thoth, along with his wife and his children! See the vanguard of their tribute." You shall tell her about these two hundred baskets,' " which were filled with men with fetters and bonds.

Thus he went ahead of them to bring the good news to his mistress, saying: "We have captured Thoth!" And

FIG. 29. The double-walled fortress of Ashkelon in Palestine is being stormed by the soldiers of Ramses II. Storming ladders have been set against the wall and a soldier is hacking at a door with an axe.

they opened the locks of the city before the soldiers. And they entered the city and let out their companions. And they laid hold on the city, small and great, and put them in bonds and fetters immediately. So the mighty arm of Pharaoh—life, prosperity, health!—captured the city . . . .

It has come to a happy ending. . . .[23]

[23] *ANET*, 23.

The fortunate discovery by an Egyptian woman at Tell el-Amarna, in 1887, (see p. 193) of the correspondence between the kings Amen-hotep III and Akh-en-Aton and the governors of cities in Palestine and Syria has supplied the best glimpse of life in Palestine before the coming of the Hebrews led by Joshua. From the first part of the fifteenth century B.C. we have the bare lists of Palestinian cities which Thut-mose III carved in stone. Less than a hundred years later many of the names in this list come to life in the correspondence contained on the clay tablets found at Tell el-Amarna. Unlike the boastful inscriptions on the monuments at Karnak, these letters were never intended for publication. Reflected in them are intrigue, jealousies, feuds between local governors of Palestinian towns, and a wealth of detail about politics, trade and commerce, and warfare.

At typical chronicler of the age would have found these vignettes of life in Palestine and Syria at the beginning of the fourteenth century disappointing. There are no lists of cities, no dynasties of kings are listed. Rather, they present a series of kaleidoscopic views of the situation of the moment in such important places as Jerusalem, Gezer, Megiddo, and Tyre. For the historian these are more valuable than the work of the official chronicler.

Megiddo was an Egyptian city-state presided over by a certain Biridiya, a prince who bore, as did many other princes of nothern Palestine of the time, an Indo-Aryan name. Biridiya was threatened by Lab'ayu, the "lion-like," who was aggressively raiding his neighbors. Desperately, the prince of Megiddo beseeches the king of Egypt for reinforcements:

At the two feet of the king, my lord, and my Sun-god, seven and seven times I fall. Let the king know that ever since the archers returned [to Egypt?], Lab'ayu has carried on hostilities against me, and we are not able to pluck the wool, and we are not able to go outside the gate in the presence of Lab'ayu, since he learned that thou has not given archers; and now his face is set to take Megiddo, but let the king protect his city, lest Lab'ayu seize it. Verily, the city is destroyed by death from pestilence and disease. Let the king give one hundred garrison troops to guard the city lest Lab'ayu seize it. Verily, there is no other purpose in Lab'ayu. He seeks to destroy Megiddo.[24]

In the same file of correspondence is a letter from this Lab'ayu, protesting that he had to fight. He had been the innocent victim of aggression in the capture of his native town:

". . . I am slandered/blamed before the king, my lord." Further, when even ants are smitten, they do not accept it passively, but they bite the hand of the man who smites them. How could I hesitate this day when two of my towns are taken? Further, even if thou shouldst say: "Fall beneath them, and let them smite thee," I should still repel my foe, and the men who seized the town and my god, the despoilers of my father, yea I would repel them.[25]

In another letter the "lion-like" Lab'ayu protests—possibly too much—his innocence against certain specific charges which the Egyptian king has made against him. He acknowledges a letter which he has received:

I have heard the words which the king wrote to me, and who am I that the king should lose his land because of me? Behold, I am a faithful servant of the king, and I have not rebelled and I have not sinned, and I do not withhold my tribute, and I do not refuse the requests of my commissioner. Now they wickedly slander me, but let the king, my lord, not impute rebellion to me!

. . . .

24 *ANET*, 485.   25 *ANET*, 486.

Further, the king wrote concerning my son. I did not know that my son associates with the 'Apiru, and I have verily delivered him into the hand of Addaya. Further, if the king should write for my wife, how could I withhold her? If the king should write to me, "Plunge a bronze dagger into thy heart and die!", how could I refuse to carry out the command of the king?[26]

The Egyptian king was not solely concerned with politics in Palestine, as can be seen from the following letter sent by the king to Milkilu, the Prince of Gezer. It contains an inventory of the products which Egypt exported to Asia and an order that they be paid for with fine concubines:

Thus the king. Now I have sent thee this tablet to say to thee: Behold, I am sending to thee Hanya, the commissioner of the archers, together with goods, in order to procure fine concubines [i.e.] weaving women: silver, gold, linen garments, turquoise, all sorts of precious stones, chairs of ebony, as well as every good thing, totalling 160 deben. Total: 40 concubines: the price of each concubine is 40 shekels of silver. So send very fine concubines in whom there is no blemish. And let the king, thy lord, say to thee, "This is good. To thee life has been decreed." And mayest thou know that the king is well, like the sun-god. His troops, his chariots, his horses are very well.[27]

The animation which the map of Palestine received by the discovery of the Amarna correspondence from the beginning of the fourteenth century B.C. is even more graphic a century later in the bas-reliefs on the walls of the great hypostyle hall at Karnak.

King Seti I (about 1302-1291 B.C.), setting for himself the recovery of the Asiatic empire which Egypt had lost during the Amarna revolution, made expeditions into Pal-

[26] *ANET*, 486. [27] *ANET*, 487.

estine and Syria. The records of these campaigns consist
not only of a listing of towns in that area at the end of the
fourteenth century, but of pictures of important battles
by which Syria was brought again under the sway of Egypt.
This contemporary documentation—most of it can still
be seen on the north exterior wall of the great hall at Karnak—records such details as clothing of the enemy, weapons, city walls and fortifications.

From one bas-relief, that of the taking of Yanoam, we
can see the fortress surrounded by a forest and encircled
by a moat for added protection (Fig. 30). Lining the cren-
elated walls of the city the besieged inhabitants stand in
surrender. Outside the fortress a horseman and an infantry-

Fig. 30. The soldiers of King Seti I (1302-1290 B.C.) capturing the walled
town of Yanoam somewhere in Palestine-Syria. The fortress is situated in a
wooded region and surrounded by a moat. Below, the Syrians hold their
hands on their heads in a gesture of surrender to the Egyptian king.

man are transfixed by enemy spears, while Syrians in the forest hold their hands over their heads in a gesture of surrender.

Sometime around 1100 B.C., soon after the Philistines and the Tjeker had settled along the Palestinian coast and while the Israelites were struggling to get a hold in the hill country, an Egyptian official named Wen-Amon visited the seaport of Dor, which lies just a few miles to the south of Mt. Carmel. The adventure he had there is recounted on a papyrus which is now the property of the Moscow Museum. The Dor episode in the tale is but one incident among many which Wen-Amon had in the long journey that took him from Tanis in the Delta to Dor, to Tyre, to Sidon, to Byblos, to Cyprus, and then back to Egypt.

Wen-Amon had been sent by the priests of Thebes to fetch wood from the Lebanon for building a barque for the Egyptian god Amon-Re. At Tanis he was sent by the ruler of the Delta in a ship toward his destination at Byblos. But at Dor, which belonged to the Tjeker, he was robbed. His account of dealings which he had with Beder, the prince of Dor, is so full of personal detail that we might speak of it as the earliest adventure story of a visit to the Holy Land.

> I reached Dor, a town of the Tjeker, and Beder, its prince, had 50 loaves of bread, one jug of wine, and one leg of beef brought to me. And a man of my ship ran away and stole one vessel of gold, amounting to 5 deben, four jars of silver, amounting to 20 deben, and a sack of 11 deben of silver. Total of what he stole: 5 deben of gold and 31 deben of silver.
>
> I got up in the morning, and I went to the place where the Prince was, and I said to him: "I have been robbed in your harbor. Now you are the prince of this land, and you are its investigator who should look for my silver. Now about this silver—it belongs to Amon-Re. . . .

And he said to me: "Whether you are important or whether you are eminent—look here, I do not recognize this accusation which you have made to me! Suppose it had been a thief who belonged to my land who went on your boat and stole your silver, I should have repaid it to you from my treasury, until they had found this thief of yours—whoever he may be. Now about the thief who robbed you—he belongs to you! He belongs to your ship! Spend a few days here visiting me, so that I may look for him."

I spent nine days moored in his harbor, and I went to call on him, and I said to him: "Look, you have not found my silver. Just let me go with the ship captains and with those who go to sea!" But he said to me: "Be quiet! . . ."²⁸

At this point the speech of Beder breaks off abruptly. It is clear that Wen-Amon went to Tyre, and possibly called at Sidon. When the text begins again, we see Wen-Amon in a tent on the seashore at Byblos, with his god Amon-of-the-Road and silver which he had seized from some of the Tjeker whom he had encountered.

And the Prince of Byblos sent to me, saying: "Get out of my harbor!" And I sent to him, saying: "Where should I go to? . . . If you have a ship to carry me, have me taken to Egypt again!" So I spent twenty-nine days in his harbor, while he spent the time sending to me every day to say: "Get out of my harbor!"²⁹

The change in the fortunes of Wen-Amon at Byblos came about because of the prophetic activity—not unlike that attributed to Saul when he prophesied before Samuel (I Samuel 19:24)—of a court page, who revealed to the Prince that the god Amon had truly sent Wen-Amon.

Now while he was making offering to his gods, the god seized one of his youths and made him possessed. And he said to him: "Bring up the god! Bring the messenger

²⁸ *ANET*, 26.   ²⁹ *ANET*, 26.

who is carrying him! Amon is the one who sent him out! He is the one who made him come!" And while the possessed youth was having his frenzy on this night, I had already found a ship headed for Egypt and had loaded everything that I had into it. While I was watching for the darkness, thinking that when it descended I would load the god also, so that no other eye might see him, the harbor master came to me, saying: "Wait until morning—so says the Prince." So I said to him: "Aren't you the one who spend the time coming to me every day to say: 'Get out of my harbor'? Aren't you saying 'Wait' tonight in order to let the ship which I have found get away— and then you will come again to say: 'Go away!'?" So he went and told it to the Prince. And the Prince sent to the captain of the ship to say: "Wait until morning—so says the Prince!"

When morning came, he sent and brought me up, but the god stayed in the tent where he was, on the shore of the sea. And I found him sitting in his upper room, with his back turned to a window, so that the waves of the great Syrian sea broke against the back of his head.[30]

In this setting, with the Prince of Byblos sitting before a window from which Wen-Amon could see the surf of the Mediterranean, there takes place a long conversation which reveals much of the state of international relations between Egypt and Syria. Eventually, Wen-Amon gets his timber, but not until he had sent for and received from Egypt the following payment:

4 jars and 1 *kak-men* of gold; 5 jars of silver; 10 pieces of clothing in royal linen; 10 *kherd* of good Upper Egyptian linen; 500 rolls of finished papyrus; 500 cowhides; 500 ropes; 20 sacks of lentils; and 30 baskets of fish.[31]

On receipt of this payment, the Prince sent three hundred men to cut and three hundred cattle to deliver the timber at the harbor. Finally, Wen-Amon sailed for Ala-

[30] *ANET*, 26. [31] *ANET*, 28.

shiya, probably Cyprus, where he met with more adversity. We may assume, although the papyrus breaks off at this point, that Wen-Amon must have returned to Egypt to tell his tale.

SURFACE EXPLORATION FOR POTTERY

Ten years after the publication of the Palestine Exploration Fund's great map, Flinders Petrie demonstrated by his careful excavation of the "mound of many cities," Tell el-Hesi, the value of the humble potsherd for dating ancient remains. As we have seen, he claimed that, by means of his knowledge of pottery forms, he could ride over ruins and determine their age without even dismounting. Thirty years, however, passed before this new technique discovered by Petrie contributed much to the making of an accurate map of ancient Palestine.

During these three decades additional excavations, particularly those at Gezer and at Samaria, had greatly enlarged the data for an accurate knowledge of the characteristic pottery forms for the major periods in Palestine's long history. Furthermore, the excavations had proved that the artificial mound—called a *tell* in Arabic—with which the land was dotted, was, in fact, the accumulation of layers of ancient walled cities.

The true nature of a tell had not been recognized by the earlier explorers. When Robinson visited Tell el-Hesi, he had noted that "we could discover nothing whatever, to mark the existence of any former town or structure,"[32] even as he stood on top of no less than eight superimposed cities. When Conder finished the Survey of Western Palestine, he wondered about these mounds which he had so carefully charted on his map. Noting that they generally stand beside springs of water and that sun-dried bricks had been found in some of them, he guessed that they had been ancient brick factories!

[32] *Biblical Researches in Palestine*, Boston, 1874, vol. 2, p. 48.

On April 4, 1921, a small party of five men, three Americans accompanied by two Arabs who drove two donkeys loaded with equipment, set out from Jerusalem for a walking tour of the regions of Samaria and Galilee. The leader of the group was the thirty-year-old acting director of the American School of Oriental Research, William F. Albright. For more than three weeks they left the well-traveled paths and climbed over tells and ruins, living simply on native fare of unleavened bread, cheese, eggs, and leben.

For almost two years Albright had been studying the results of excavations in Palestine, paying special attention to the types of pottery dug from the various levels of its ancient cities. Why could not the information which broken jar-handles, rims, and bases bore for dating prove useful in fixing reliably ancient biblical sites on the modern map? There were hundreds of tells strewn with fragments of this relatively indestructible material. Even where the ancient deposits had been covered over by more recent layers of accumulation, rains had frequently washed loose bits of the earlier debris from the sides of the mound and left them at the base ready to be picked up by the explorer.

Albright retraced the steps of the earlier explorers in search for pottery. Now, not only did a location of a site on the modern map have to agree with the information given in the written sources—and these had greatly increased since the days of Robinson—it had to produce pottery which belonged to the periods to which the ancient sources testified. If the pottery for the ancient periods was lacking, the proposed identification was wrong.

"It is surprising," Albright wrote later, "how little of this very necessary work has been done hitherto. Except for a survey of Petrie's and a trip of Macalister's there is hardly an account published of the pottery material strewn on every ancient site in Palestine. . . ."[33]

[33] *Bulletin of the American Schools of Oriental Research*, no. 9, 1923, p. 6.

For the ten years that Albright was in Palestine during the 1920's, he pursued his method relentlessly. Other scholars interested in topographical research, including Albrecht Alt from Germany and the French Dominican Père H. Vincent, collaborated in the refinement of topographical knowledge. Long-standing equations of ancient sites with modern place-names were dropped or transferred when the history written in pottery was contradictory. New entries on the map made their appearance.

A common sight in Palestine during the 1920's and afterward was a group of scholars roaming the countryside and picking up bits of broken pottery as though it were valuable ore. These bits were stuffed into pockets or bags and carried back to Jerusalem to be looked at and debated by the experts. The age of prospecting for biblical cities had arrived. The map of ancient Palestine was being redrawn.

The less known region beyond the Jordan provided the most fertile field for this kind of exploration. In this extensive desert region an American, Nelson Glueck, worked for years almost singlehanded.

Glueck had gone to Palestine as an assistant to Albright in the excavation of a mound in the south called Tell Beit Mirsim. He was impressed by the way in which the results for dating the periods of occupation, which Albright obtained from his surface exploration, tallied with the results of careful excavation. By collecting hundreds of fragments of pottery Albright had estimated, before he had dug a spadeful of earth, that the place had been inhabited from about 2000 B.C. to 600 B.C. After four successive campaigns of laborious digging at Tell Beit Mirsim, Albright was convinced, as Glueck facetiously remarked, that his earlier estimate was mistaken. It had been inhabited from 2200 B.C. to 586 B.C.! If surface pottery, Glueck argued, could give dates that so closely approximated the results from systematic excavation, why not apply this easier technique to the archaeologically unknown land of Transjordan?

Beginning in 1932, Nelson Glueck worked, off and on, in the desert of Transjordan until 1947, visiting and recording the evidence from more than one thousand different ancient settlements. Collecting the evidence in carefully labeled bags, he deposited them for future reference in the Museum at Amman and in the Smithsonian Institution at Washington. Five large volumes filled with detailed notes on his journeys, and drawings and photographs of the pottery make the evidence even more widely accessible. Not all of Glueck's work was done on the ground. At times he took to the air to photograph from above the ancient settlements in the areas of Gilead, Moab, and Edom.

EXCAVATING FOR A MAP

Obviously, the most reliable means for determining the location of ancient sites on the map is systematic excavation. Careful excavation should provide a profile of the occupation history of the ancient site, revealing the periods of occupation, the gaps when the mound was deserted, and evidences for destructions. In many cases this profile, when set over against the history of an ancient town, as it is known from written sources, provides convincing proof for the site's identification.

In a few cases, the discoveries in the course of excavation have been more decisive. After Robinson's visit in 1852 to Beisan in northern Palestine, he was convinced, despite a rather unusual contraction in the modern name, that the place was to be identified as the ancient Beth-shan, to whose walls the bodies of Saul and his sons had been fastened by the Philistines. Slightly more than seventy years later, the American excavators found there an inscribed stela of the Egyptian King Seti I. In the text the king tells how he sent "the first army of the Re, (named) 'Plentiful of Valor,' to the town of Beth-shan."[34] The finding of the

[34] *ANET*, 253.

name of Beth-shan in the mound at Beisan was one further proof that Robinson had been right in his guess.

The discovery of the word "Lachish" in the text of the famous letter found at Tell ed-Duweir (see p. 16) strengthened earlier guesses that Lachish was to be placed at this site on the modern map. Long before it was excavated systematically, Gezer was identified with the modern Tell Jezer, when Clermont-Ganneau discovered on the outskirts of the tell boundary stones inscribed with the name of Gezer in Hebrew.

The fortunate discovery, in 1956, of the ancient name of the modern site of el-Jib, just eight miles north of Jerusalem, is an example of how excavation may terminate a lengthy debate over an identification.

Franz Ferdinand von Troilo, a Silesian nobleman, was the first modern traveler to record the suggestion that the Arab village of el-Jib was the location of the biblical Gibeon. He visited the village in 1666. In the following century, Richard Pococke, an Irish bishop, visited the Holy Land and, looking down on el-Jib from Nebi Samwil to the south, judged it to be ancient Gibeon. Exactly a century later, Edward Robinson spent forty minutes in el-Jib on May 5, 1838. From his careful study of the ancient sources, he concluded that "it is not difficult to recognize in el-Jib and its rocky eminence the ancient Gibeon of the Scriptures."[35]

But Robinson was not unaware of a difficulty in the identification. There is a statement by Eusebius. the Bishop of Caesarea, in his famous geographical work called the *Onomasticon*, that the location of Gibeon is four Roman miles west of Bethel. Since the village of el-Bireh, a town well to the north of el-Jib, qualifies as being about four Roman miles to the west of Bethel, Robinson took the reference on the part of the fourth-century Bishop of Cae-

<hr>

[35] *Biblical Researches in Palestine*, Boston, 1874, vol. 1, p. 455.

sarea to be a mistake and adhered to the identification
(Gibeon) which the sound of the modern "Jib" suggested
to his ear.

The first important voice to be raised against the el-Jib =
Gibeon equation was that of Albrecht Alt, who published
a learned article in 1926, by which he sought to settle some
of the problems of the ancient topography of the area to
the north of Jerusalem. Taking as trustworthy the note
given in the *Onomasticon*, Alt located Gibeon at Tell en-
Nasbeh and proposed that the biblical Beeroth had been
located at el-Jib. Other scholars of the German school took
up his view and supported it. More than a quarter of a
century later, Alt published some "New Considerations of
the Location of Mizpah, Ataroth, Beeroth and Gibeon."[36]
In spite of the objections of other geographers, he held to
the identification of el-Jib with Beeroth.

The answer to the long-debated question of el-Jib's
ancient name came suddenly and unexpectedly in 1956.
The first excavation of the site was carried on under the
direction of the writer for a brief period of ten weeks. In
the course of clearing the debris from a large, rock-cut pool
just inside the city wall at the north of the mound, there
were found two jar-handles and a portion of a third, inscribed with the name "Gibeon" in archaic Hebrew script
(Fig. 31).

While this discovery seemed to provide a satisfactory
answer to the question of identification, there was yet a
possibility that these three handles could have been brought
in ancient times from another city. Also, we were troubled
by the question as to why the owner of a jar should have
inscribed it with the name of his town.

We returned in 1957 to dig for a second season at el-Jib.
This time there appeared in the debris of the pool twenty-
four more handles inscribed with the name "Gibeon" and
the evidence that all of these handles had belonged to jars

---

[36] *Zeitschrift des deutschen Palaestina-Vereins,* vol. 69, 1953, pp. 1-27.

Fig. 31. One of the wine-jug handles inscribed with the name "Gibeon," which identified the modern site of el-Jib.

which were made expressly for wine which was exported from Gibeon. The name was, in fact, a part of the label which gave both the name and address of the maker of the wine.

The pool in which these and other inscriptions were found is itself an impressive and unique construction (Fig. 32). It is a cylindrical cutting in the solid rock with a diameter of approximately 35 feet and it extends downward to a depth of 33 feet. Beginning at the northwest, a spiral-stairway, approximately 5 feet wide and protected by a guard rail cut from the solid rock, leads downward spirally around the pool's edge. At the bottom of the pool the steps

Fig. 32. Pool at el-Jib in which were found the "Gibeon" jug-handles.

continue into a tunnel to a depth of 49 more feet, ending in a large underground chamber where water collects from the water-table deep beneath the hill on which the ancient Gibeon stood. A total of seventy-nine steps provided the citizens of Gibeon with access to one of the city's major water supplies.

With the identification of the site now firmly fixed as Gibeon, the reference in II Samuel 2:13 to the scene of the contest between the men of Joab and the men of Abner is particularly interesting. The text reads: "And Joab the son of Zeruiah, and the servants of David, went out; and they met together by the pool of Gibeon, and sat down, the one on the one side of the pool, and the other on the other side of the pool." Can it be that this impressive engineering feat, a rock-cut pool with steps leading down to the spring 82 feet below the surface, is the very landmark referred to as the scene of the contest between the men of Joab and the men of Abner?

Many handles which came from the pool were incised with the names of such biblical characters as Amariah, Azariah, and Hananiah. It is of no little interest that one of the men in the Bible who bore the name of Hananiah was the opponent of Jeremiah, and who, according to Jeremiah 28:1, "was of Gibeon."

There can be little doubt but that the excavations of el-Jib in 1956 and 1957 have placed ancient Gibeon firmly on the map.

The map of ancient Palestine has not yet been completed. A reliable method for placing ancient names on the land has been bequeathed by Robinson, Petrie, Vincent, Albright, Glueck, and others. From it, good results have been achieved. Work will go on as long as there are ancient tells in Palestine untagged with labels, and as long as ancient names in the growing literature from the ancient Near East have not been pegged down to modern sites.

CHAPTER 3

BAAL AND THE RELIGION OF CANAAN

THE FRENCH IN PHOENICIA

THE age-old religion of Canaan, a land extending in a narrow strip along the entire eastern coast of the Mediteranean, was known until about a century ago principally from the Old Testament. There, it is to be be seen through the eyes of zealously hostile Hebrew prophets, who condemned Canaanite religion without bothering to describe this rival system of religious practice. With the disappearance of the Canaanites and their religion, there were left only obscure allusions to their gods and sacrifices, references which had been full of meaning for the prophet's hearers, but which later readers found obscure.

While the picture of the religion of Canaan preserved in the Old Testament is vague, there are many references to it. "To go a whoring after" other gods, is a phrase as frank in its original Hebrew as it is in this older translation into Elizabethan English; it is the usual way of referring to participation in the rites for the Canaanite god Baal. Along with Baal, other deities are occasionally mentioned: the goddess Ashtoreth, to whom there was a temple at Beth-shan, where the armor of Saul was placed after his death; Chemosh, the god of the Transjordan Moabites, for whom Solomon erected a high place; Molech, the god to whom child sacrifice was made; and Dagon, the Philistine god of Ashdod. More frequently the pantheon of Canaan is referred to merely by the anonymous "other gods."

Vague also is the picture of how the Canaanites worshipped. From scattered references in the Bible we can piece together a picture of worship at high places, equipped with altars, standing pillars, and images of Asherah.

Idols were used, described as being of two kinds, molten images and graven images. The officiants at Canaanite shrines are named by two Hebrew words, the meanings of which translators have found difficult to convey in English. The word for the male functionary has been variously rendered by "sodomite," "temple prostitute," and "cult prostitute" in the Revised Standard Version. The female attendant is known by a term which has been translated as "cult prostitute," or "whore." Such was the language used to describe the personnel of the shrines of Israel's rivals.

These tantalizing references label, rather than describe, the objects and the personnel of the cult of Canaan. Yet the frequency with which these labels occur on the pages of the Old Testament makes it clear that the contest between Yahweh, the God of Israel, and Baal was a real and a long struggle.

The story of how this vague picture given in the Bible has, in the course of the last century, become clearer is largely the account of the work of French archaeologists in that area of ancient Canaan called Phoenicia. Even though their work has been supplemented and enlarged by the efforts of others, the credit belongs largely to the vision, the industry, and the luck of the French.

Archaeological activity in Phoenicia began in 1860 under the most auspicious, and yet somewhat unusual, circumstances. Toward the end of the month of May 1860, Napoleon III, Emperor of France, commissioned Ernest Renan to undertake an archaeological campaign in Phoenicia, a project of which the latter had long dreamed. By a "bizarre coincidence," wrote Renan later, on about the same day he received this commission from the Emperor there broke out in Lebanon a series of massacres—there was a total loss of 11,000 lives—which made it necessary for the French to send out an army of 6,000 men to maintain order. It was soon decided that the excavation which Renan had been commissioned to do should be carried on by the French army.

Thus it was that Ernest Renan, the first of an illustrious line of French scholars who were to contribute much toward an understanding of life in ancient Phoenicia, had French troops as laborers. To aid the archaeologist in supervising his operations—scattered along the coast at Ruad, Byblos, Sidon, and Tyre—a French naval vessel, the *Colbert,* was at his disposal. Rarely has an archaeological expedition had this kind of support from its government.

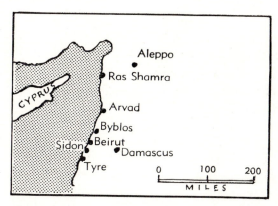

FIG. 33. Sites in the northern part of Canaan.

The explorer had been led to this beginning over a devious course. Renan was born in 1823 at Tréguier, Brittany, the son of a grocer and one-time seaman, who was mysteriously drowned when Ernest was five. Early in life he decided to study for the priesthood and did so well in school that he was awarded a prize for the continuance of his studies in Paris. At the age of twenty he entered upon his theological education at the Seminary of Saint Sulpice, where he sat under M. Le Hir for study in Hebrew, which he found his most absorbing subject. This special interest led him to take additional courses at the Sorbonne and at the Collège de France under the erudite Quatremère. In a short time his attention to philological science had persuaded him that the words of the Bible were full of errors

FIG. 34. Ernest Renan at the age of forty, shortly after he had returned from the first archaeological mission to Syria.

and that he could no longer accept the dogmas of Roman
Catholic theology. The doubts which came from his new
knowledge—he later remarked, "I am tempted to add to
the eight beatitudes a ninth: Blessed are the blind, for

they have no doubts"[1]—cut short his preparation for the priesthood.

It was not long before Renan had distinguished himself by taking the famous Prix Volney with an essay on "General History and Comparative System of the Semitic Languages," later to be published in an impressive volume. He was then but twenty-four. By the time of his departure for Syria, he had not only published books on Job—which a year later was placed on the Index—and on the Song of Songs, but had distinguished himself in the field of letters and had become a public figure through controversy.

The field of Phoenician archaeology had been particularly attractive to Renan because of the discovery at Sidon, just five years before his departure, of the great sarcophagus of Eshmunazar, a fifth-century king of Sidon (Fig. 35). This massive coffin of black basalt, measuring over 8 feet in length, has on its cover a fully preserved inscription of twenty-two lines, mentioning among other gods three Canaanite deities known from the Bible, Dagon, Baal, and Ashtoreth. The language of the text is remarkably similar to that of the Bible.

The inscription begins with a long curse upon anybody who disturbs the sarcophagus, "the long verbiage," as Renan remarked, "of a man of small mind, obsessed with silly terrors for the vat which contains his bones."[2]

I have been snatched away before my time. . . . I am lying in this casket and this grave, in a place which I myself built. Whoever you are, ruler and ordinary man, may he not open this resting-place and may he not search in it for anything, for nothing whatever has been placed into it!. . . Even if people goad you, do not listen to their talk, for any ruler and any man who shall open this resting-place . . . may they not have a resting-place with the

---

[1] L. F. Mott, *Ernest Renan*, New York, 1921, p. 337.
[2] A. Parrot, *Guide sommaire*, Le Département des Antiquités Orientales, Musée du Louvre, Paris, 1947, p. 54.

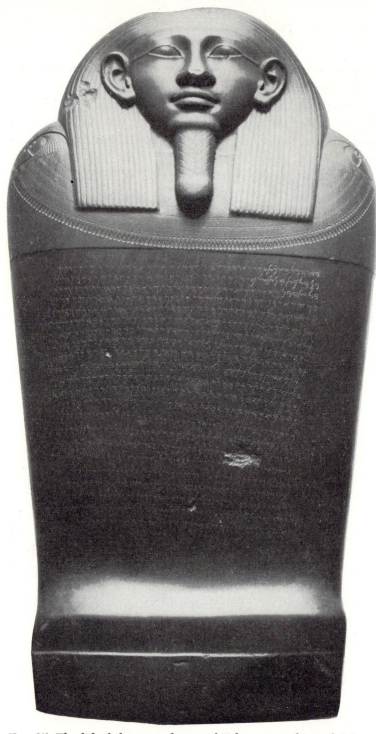

Fig. 35. The lid of the sarcophagus of Eshmunazar, king of Sidon.

shades, may they not be buried in a grave, and may they not have son and seed to take their place! . . . May they have no root down below and no fruit up on top. . . .[3]

Following this solemn and dire warning, Eshmunazar recounts the building program for which he and his family had been responsible.

We are the ones who built houses for the gods of Sidon in Sidon-by-the-Sea, a house for the Lord of Sidon and a house for 'Ashtart-Shem-Baal. Furthermore, the Lord of Kings gave us Dor and Joppa, the mighty lands of Dagon, which are in the Plain of Sharon, in accordance with the important deeds which I did.[4]

But Renan, although he dug at Sidon, was not so fortunate as to find anything as spectacular as the sarcophagus of Eshmunazar. His greatest hopes were for the campaign at Byblos. When he arrived, columns of marble and granite lay scattered about; there were exposed layers of debris of all periods; and there was a castle which travelers before him had, without exception, described as a monument of the Phoenician period. And to raise his hopes even higher, there were the traditions which made the city one of the most important religious centers of the ancient world. Had not the people of Byblos prepared the timber and stones for Solomon's temple in Jerusalem?

On Saturday, December 1, 1860, the Fourth Company of the Sixteenth Battalion "de chasseurs à pied" was established at Byblos, and by Monday had exchanged swords for tools. Renan worked for two months, but with disappointing results. He had come, he said, fifty years too late. Alas, the birth of a taste for Phoenician antiquities and the cupidity of the modern inhabitants of the place had combined to rob the site of its most valuable evidence. Bitterly he complained: "In order to find a ring worth several francs, remarkable tombs of style and grandeur have been

[3] *ANET*, 505.   [4] *ANET*, 505.

destroyed, for a piece of carved stone of the Roman period, ten inscriptions have been broken." Petty looters had destroyed forever the context of the objects, an example of how the "petty curiosity of the amateur is hostile to the great curiosity of the scholar."[5] Furthermore, the castle, so long thought to be of the Phoenician period, and perhaps of a date contemporary with Solomon, proved under careful scrutiny to belong to the Middle Ages.

[5] E. Renan, *Mission de Phénicie,* Paris, 1864, p. 155.

FIG. 36. An air view of the mound of ancient Byblos, the scene of French excavations since 1860.

FIG. 37. The sarcophagus of Ahiram of Byblos. The lid is inscribed with a curse on anyone who opens the casket. To the left of the scene sits King Ahiram on a sphinx throne before a table of offerings.

If the hopes of the pioneer in Phoenician archaeology failed to materialize during his two months of work in 1860-61, they were fulfilled sixty-two years later in the discovery of the remarkable inscribed sarcophagus of King Ahiram by Pierre Montet (Fig. 37). Like the casket of Eshmunazar of Sidon, it too bore the name of its owner and a solemn curse for the opener.

> If there be a king among kings and a governor among governors and an army commander up in Byblos who shall uncover this sarcophagus, let his judicial staff be broken, let his royal throne be upset! May peace flee from Byblos, and he himself be wiped out.[6]

More important, perhaps, than this earliest example of a Phoenician inscription—it is generally thought to belong to the tenth century B.C.—cut around the edges of the lid, is the scene carved around the four sides of the sar-

[6] *ANET*, 504.

cophagus. King Ahiram himself is shown sitting on a throne, with his feet on a triple-staged footstool. The throne of the king is of special interest because its side is in the form of a winged sphinx which is probably the cherub which the Old Testament describes as the motif of the decoration of the veil, the walls, and other religious objects of Solomon's temple. When the god of Israel is spoken of as He "who sitteth (upon) the cherubim," it is this throne from the symbolism of the land of Canaan which comes to mind. On an ivory inlay from Megiddo (see Fig. 14), of a slightly earlier period, there appears the same kind of Canaanite throne.

In this and other important discoveries in 1923, Montet also had the help of French soldiers of the army of the Levant, which had been put at his disposal by General Maxime Weygand, who was then the French high commissioner for Syria. Since then, the site of Byblos has proved to be, year after year, a veritable mine of inscriptions, artifacts, coins, and evidence for the close and frequent contacts between Egypt and Syria during many centuries. Nor have all its secrets yet been laid bare, despite the work of Maurice Dunand at the site over the last three decades. Rather than having come to Byblos fifty years too late, it might be said that Renan came too soon.

Six years after Renan returned from Syria, he proposed to the French Academy of Inscriptions a plan for publishing all the known Semitic inscriptions in a collection to be called by the Latin title of *Corpus Inscriptionum Semiticarum*. It is for this project, perhaps even more than for the distinction of being the pioneer in Phoenician archaeology, that Renan will be remembered. He later wrote, "Of all that I have done, it is the *Corpus* that I love the most."[7]

Renan made his proposal for the undertaking of this

[7] R. Dussaud, *L'œuvre scientifique d'Ernest Renan*, Paris, 1951, p. 126.

great work to the Academy on January 25, 1867. It was immediately given to a commission of distinguished scholars, which reported back that the project should be above the causes of interruption which affect all the works of individuals and proposed an elaborate scheme for publishing the inscriptions in ten books and an appendix. "France seems appointed," the report continued, "to give such a collection to the scholarly world."[8] Each text was to be given in photograph, in transcription into Hebrew letters, in translation into Latin, and with full commentary.

In the years since the first part of the *Corpus* appeared in 1881, this work has become a most important source for students of Canaanite culture, as can be seen from the ubiquitous references to it in the form of "*CIS*" scattered throughout the footnotes of any important work on the subject. Now, after three quarters of a century, the quarto volumes of this impressive publication fill a sizeable shelf, and more volumes are in preparation. Three large volumes contain over five thousand Phoenician inscriptions; a second part, containing Aramaic texts, has almost as many inscriptions; the part to which Hebrew inscriptions have been assigned has not yet been published; almost a thousand South Arabic inscriptions have been published in part four; and the fifth part, in which North Arabic texts appear, already contains over five thousand separate texts. Without doubt, the *Corpus* is a most impressive monument of Semitic scholarship.

The decipherment of the Phoenician script was accomplished more than two hundred years ago by a French abbé attached to the Cabinet des Médailles in Paris. Abbé Barthélemy worked on a four-line Phoenician inscription which had been found on Malta, more than 1,200 miles from the Phoenician coast. With the help of his knowledge of Hebrew and a three-line inscription in Greek below the Phoe-

---

[8] *Journal asiatique*, 6 séric, IX, 1867, p. 399.

nician, he was able to determine the values of the letters of the ancient Phoenician script and read the text.

A study of the Phoenician inscriptions has made it clear that the pantheon of Canaanite Palestine, as we know it from the Hebrew Bible, belongs to the same family of gods known in the cities of Tyre, Sidon, and Byblos, along the Phoenician coast. Many of the texts are on tombstones and contain the names of gods and goddesses to whom the stones are dedicated. Ashtart, or Ashtoreth as the name appears in the Bible, makes her appearance more than forty times in Phoenician and later Punic inscriptions; and the name occurs even more frequently as an element in personal names. The name Baal is common. The goddesses Anath and Asherah also appear in Phoenician texts.

One of the earliest discoveries of a Phoenician inscription was made at Marseilles, France, in 1845. The document, written possibly in the third or second century B.C., and perhaps at Carthage, lists the tariff of payments to be made to the priest by the worshiper for certain types of offerings. As in Leviticus (7:32), the part of the victim to be kept by the priest is carefully prescribed. The tariff for an ox is set as follows:

> For an ox, as a whole offering or a substitute offering or a complete whole offering, the priests shall have ten —10—silver pieces for each. In the case of a whole offering, they shall have, over and above this payment, meat weighing three hundred—300. In the case of a substitute offering, they shall have neck and shoulder joints (chuck), while the person offering the sacrifice shall have the skin, ribs, feet, and the rest of the meat.[9]

Similar payments and regulations are listed for a calf or stag, ram or goat, lamb or kid or young stag, and birds. But what happens when the worshiper is too poor to pay the rates fixed for the priests? The text continues:

[9] *ANET*, 502.

For any sacrifice which shall be offered by persons poor in cattle or poor in fowl, the priests shall have nothing whatever.[10]

Besides contributing to a knowledge of Canaanite religion, the inscriptions have augmented considerably the history of the kingdoms to the north of Israel, adding new materials for the reigns of Ben-Hadad and Hazael, and for the kings of Tyre and of Sidon.

MONUMENT OF MESHA, KING OF MOAB

A most spectacular enlargement of biblical history has come from a Canaanite inscription, called the Moabite stone, which turned up ninety years ago in the Arab village of Dhiban in Transjordan, about halfway along the east side of the Dead Sea (Fig. 38).

When we went to Dhiban in 1950, with an expedition of the American School of Oriental Research, to begin the first systematic excavation of this ancient Moabite city, we hoped that another such monument lay buried under the debris. But alas, five seasons of careful digging and sifting of the remains of the ancient city have yielded but one fragment of a Moabite inscription. And this was on a stone no larger than a biscuit, and contained one complete and five broken letters. Ironically this discovery was not made by any of the dozen archaeologists who have worked at the site, but by a casual visitor who had but an hour or so at the dig before catching a bus to take him back to Amman.

A missionary of the Church Missionary Society stationed at Jerusalem, the Rev. F. A. Klein, while traveling east of the Dead Sea in 1868, was the first European to see the famous slab of black basalt inscribed with an account of the wars and building program of Mesha, king of Moab. Shortly after his visit to Dhiban, some local Arabs, either out of fear that the stone was to be removed from their

[10] *ANET*, 503.

Fig. 38. The Mesha stone containing an account of the wars between Israel and the Moabites.

town or from a desire for greater profit through the sale of many pieces rather than of one stone, broke this important historical monument into many fragments. Fortunately a squeeze—a matrix made by placing soggy paper over the inscription, which retains when dry an impression of the writing carved in the stone—had been made before the destruction. Eight lines had also been copied. From the shambles of this priceless monument two large pieces and eighteen small fragments were eventually recovered, pieced together with the help of the squeeze and the copy, and placed in the Louvre in 1873 through the efforts of M. Clermont-Ganneau. There it remains to this day in the Crypte Sully alongside the framed copy of the eight important lines made by Selim el-Kari before the smashing.

The text, a long one of thirty-four lines, is written in the first person singular and begins with a somewhat boastful recital by Mesha, king of Moab, of his triumphs over the house of Omri, king of Israel. This information is of the greatest interest because of the account in the Book of Kings of Israel's war against Mesha, and of the extreme to which the Moabite king was pushed to raise the siege of the Israelites. Only when the king of Moab had offered his son, the heir to the throne, as a burnt offering upon the wall did the army of Israel, shocked and fearful, return to its own territory.

Mesha interpreted the success of his enemy, Israel, as a token of his own god's anger with his land.

As for Omri, king of Israel, he humbled Moab many years, for Chemosh was angry at his land. And his son followed him and he also said, "I will humble Moab." In my time he spoke thus, but I have triumphed over him and over his house, while Israel hath perished for ever![11]

In addition to the new information which the stone gives for the history of the ninth century—it actually raises more

[11] *ANET*, 320.

problems than it settles and historians have generally concluded that the Hebrew and the Moabite chroniclers
tended generally, and quite understandably, to ignore
their own losses and setbacks—there is reflected a glimpse
of Moabite theology. Mesha received his instructions for
battle from his god Chemosh. When his god gave him a
victory, he "devoted"—the same word is used in the inscription as appears in the Hebrew account of Joshua de-
voting the spoils of Jericho to Yahweh—all the inhabitants
of the town of Nebo (Moses' grave was on Mt. Nebo) to
his god Ashtar-Chemosh. The incident of the taking of
Nebo is described by Mesha:

> And Chemosh said to me, "Go, take Nebo from Israel!"
> So I went by night and fought against it from the break
> of dawn until noon, taking it and slaying all, seven
> thousand men, boys, women, girls and maid-servants, for
> I had devoted them to destruction for the god Ashtar-
> Chemosh. And I took from there the . . . of Yahweh,
> dragging them before Chemosh.[12]

In this brief passage we have the only mention of the
name of Israel's god, Yahweh, ever found outside Palestine
proper. And only in one other place outside the pages of
the Bible itself is Yahweh mentioned (pp. 15-17).

THE CANAANITE BIBLE FROM UGARIT

The discovery of a mass of new Canaanite literature in
a hitherto unknown script produced in scholarly circles of
the 1930's a sensation not unlike that made by the finding
of the Dead Sea Scrolls in the late 1940's and 1950's. The
new literature was a surprise on several counts. First, it
was from about the fourteenth century B.C., a period earlier by several hundred years than any previously known
Canaanite material; secondly, it was written in an alphabetic script quite unlike that used for other known Canaanite writings; and thirdly, the new texts were mytholog-

12 *ANET*, 320.

ical and legendary in content and poetic in form. Up until this time, no Canaanite mythology and no Canaanite poetry had come to light.

In the discoveries at Ras Shamra—the modern Arabic name for what was anciently called Ugarit—more light was thrown on the nature of Canaanite religion than had come from the entire preceding century of excavation and study. The impact of these finds from Ras Shamra was quickly felt in the circles of biblical research, particularly in the fields of Hebrew lexicography and poetry. Words and allusions long puzzling were cleared up by the new texts, and theories based on the assumption that there was no written poetry in the earliest periods of biblical history had to give way, or be modified, by this sudden appearance of an extensive library of poetry from the land of Canaan.

Again, it was the French who made the find of this important material—Syria had become a French protectorate in 1920—and who had a large share in its decipherment and interpretation.

One day in the spring of 1928, a Syrian peasant was plowing his field which stretched out along the edge of a small harbor for fishing boats on the north Syrian coast, called Minet el-Beida ("White Port"). His plow struck a large stone, which he proceeded to lift and found that it belonged to a tomb. Investigating further, the peasant found that the tomb contained pottery and that several of the smaller vases were intact. Word soon got to the Service des Antiquités, from which its director, Charles Virolleaud, promptly sent an assistant to inspect the find. Thus it was that a tomb so casually opened by a peasant led to the discovery of the cemetery, which in turn belonged to a low-lying mound less than a mile away, a tell which has turned out to be the most important Canaanite site yet found.

When spring came the following year, Claude F. A. Schaeffer, to whom the Académie des Inscriptions et Belles-Lettres had committed the archaeological mission, followed up the Syrian peasant's discovery with five weeks of scientific digging. Then, on May 9, 1929, Schaeffer left the necropolis and began work on the mound of the city.

Within less than a week the excavator found a library of ancient Ugarit, with inscribed tablets and a cache of seventy-four bronze weapons and instruments, including five axes on which there were inscriptions. Year by year, for eleven campaigns, until the outbreak of World War II, Schaeffer kept steadily at his work on this site; after the war he was there again unearthing what seems to be an almost inexhaustible supply of materials. The campaign of 1956 was the twentieth.

As it seems so often to happen, the most important find came at the very end of the campaign. In fact, just a day before the closing of the excavation of the necropolis, on May 14th, 1929, a large clay tablet covered with cuneiform characters and numerous smaller tablets similarly inscribed appeared in the corner of a room. These were promptly packed and sent off to Paris, where Virolleaud prepared them for publication in the archaeological journal *Syria*. By mid-April 1930, fifty of these texts in an unknown cuneiform script were presented to the scholarly world, along with observations by the editor that a total of twenty-six or twenty-seven signs seemed to be employed in the writing—actually it was later determined that there were thirty characters (Fig. 39)—and that the six signs on four

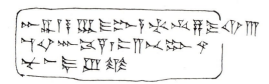

Fig. 39. The alphabet of thirty letters found on a small tablet at Ugarit.

identically-inscribed adzeheads may have been intended to represent the name of the owner. Furthermore, Virolleaud had noticed the same six signs on a clay tablet, but there they were preceded by a sign which he guessed to be the Canaanite preposition "to." All of these hunches proved later to be correct.

In Germany, Professor Hans Bauer at the University of Halle received by mail a copy of *Syria* and immediately set to work in an attempt to decode these enigmatic cuneiform signs. In a short time Bauer succeeded in finding the names for the deities, Baal, Asherah, Ashtart, El, and the words for the numerals "three" and "four." Within less than a month after his first decipherment on April 27, 1930, his results, including proposals for the values of seventeen of the signs, were communicated to the French Academy and shortly thereafter published in the German newspaper *Vossische Zeitung*.

During the spring of 1930, Père P. Dhorme, then in Jerusalem at the École Biblique, was working on the same fifty texts which had just appeared in *Syria*. Dhorme was well equipped for his task. Not only was he a trained Semitist but he had been so successful in solving enemy ciphers on the Salonika front during World War I, that the French Government had decorated him for his work in cryptology. The American archaeologist W. F. Albright, who was also in Jerusalem that summer, on seeing a copy of Bauer's article in a copy of the German newspaper belonging to Kurt Galling, borrowed it, and took it immediately to Dhorme at the French school. The latter saw that two of Bauer's values for signs were to be preferred to those he had arrived at on his own. Thus, he was able to correct his own tentative list in such a way as to carry the progress of decipherment beyond the point which Bauer had reached. By the end of September, he had published his table of alphabetic values in the French journal *Revue Biblique*.

In the meantime, Virolleaud, utilizing the results of his colleagues and new documents which had come from the second campaign at Ras Shamra—about eight hundred lines of text—made rapid progress and succeeded in determining the values for twenty-six of the signs. Thus, when M. Virolleaud on the 24th of October, 1930, communicated his results to the French Academy—in less than a year and a half after the first tablets had been taken from the ground—this completely new and hitherto unknown script could be said to have been deciphered.

The speed of this accomplishment stands in sharp contrast to the long and slow progress in deciphering both Egyptian hieroglyphs and Akkadian cuneiform and, for both of the latter, scholars had had the aid of bilingual texts. The achievement of reading Ugaritic so quickly may be credited to scholarly cooperation across national boundaries and to the generosity of the French in publishing so promptly the first discoveries.

From this spectacular and sudden beginning there has arisen since 1930 an entirely new branch of Semitic studies, now called Ugaritic after the ancient name of the town where the texts were found, a discipline which has acquired a grammar, a lexicon, and a long shelf of specialized studies on philology, history, and literature. Ugarit has supplied a Canaanite bible, texts amounting in quantity to about half the size of the Hebrew Book of Psalms.

Ancient Ugarit has yielded a rich variety of languages. Not only ancient Canaanite, but Sumerian, Akkadian, Hurrian, Hittite, Hieroglyphic "Hittite," Egyptian, and Cypriote—all of these languages have been found in its remains. In the writing of these languages no less than five different scripts were employed. Located as it was at the crossroads of the ancient world, Ugarit was indeed a polyglot city. There were merchants and soldiers in Ugarit as well as priests and scribes. A recent publication of over 250 Akkadian documents contains letters, economic documents, school exercises, and a large collection of juridical texts.

Before the discoveries of 1929 and 1930 practically nothing was known of the theological organization of the various gods and goddesses worshiped in Canaan. Now it is apparent that gods were not merely patrons of particular places, but that they were arranged in a highly-organized system, each having his function and authority. This pattern of relationship is not spelled out or diagramed but expressed in mythological terms.

Undisputed is the place of El, the Bull, Father Shunem, who dwells at the Sources of the Floods. His wife, the Mother of the Gods, is Lady Asherah of the Sea. Among their children are: Baal, the rain- and fertility-god, "the rider of the clouds"; the Maiden Anath, his sister; and Mot, the dreaded enemy of Baal.

One vivid episode in a long mythological poem has to do with Baal's obtaining permission from El for the building of a palace for himself. He and his sister Anath urge Asherah of the Sea to go on a journey to importune El for the desired palace. Lady Asherah starts on her mission.

> There, she is off on her way
>> Towards El of the Sources of the Two Floods
>> In the midst of the headwaters of the Two Oceans.
> She penetrates El's field and enters
>> The pavilion of King Father Shunem.
> At El's feet she bows and falls down,
>> Prostrates her and does him reverence.
> As soon as El espies her,
>> He parts his jaws and laughs.
> His feet upon the footstool he puts
>> And doth twiddle his fingers.
> He lifts up his voice and cries:
> "Why is come Lady Asherah of the Sea?
>> Why hither the Progenitress of the Gods?
> Art thou become hungry and faint,
>> Or art become thirsty and parched?
> Eat, pray, yea drink.
> Eat thou from the tables bread;
>> Drink from the flagons wine,
>> From the golden goblets blood of vines.
> See, El the King's love stirs thee,
>> Bull's affection arouses thee."[13]

[13] *ANET*, 133.

After this cordial reception at the palace of El, Lady
Asherah of the Sea comes to the point of her mission, the
need of Baal for a house.

> Quoth Lady Asherah of the Sea:
> "Thy decree, O El, is wise:
>   Wisdom with ever-life thy portion.
> Thy decree is: our king's Puissant Baal,
>   Our sovereign second to none;
> All of us must bear his gift,
>   All of us must bear his purse.
> But alas!
> He cries unto Bull El his father,
>   To El the King his begetter;
> He cries unto Asherah and her children,
>   Elath and the band of her kindred:
> Look, no house has Baal like the gods,
>   Nor court like the children of Asherah.
> The abode of El is the shelter of his son. . . ."[14]

El generously gives permission for the building of the
house for Baal; when the maiden Anath hears the news,
she hastens to inform Baal.

> Quoth the Kindly One El Benign:
> "Am I a slave, an attendant of Asherah?
>   Am I a slave, to handle. . . ?
> Or is Asherah a handmaid, to make bricks?
> Let a house be built for Baal like the god's,
>   And a court like the children of Asherah's!"

> Quoth Lady Asherah of the Sea:
> "Art great indeed, O El, and wise,
>   Thy beard's gray hair instructs thee,
>   . . . . to thy breast.
> Now, too, the seasons of his rains will Baal observe
>   The seasons of . . . with snow;
> And he will peal his thunder in the clouds,

14 *ANET*, 133.

Flashing his lightnings to the earth.
The house of cedar—let him burn it;
  Yea, the house of brick—remove it.
Be it told to Puissant Baal:
Summon weeds into thy house,
  Herbs into the midst of thy palace.
The mountains shall bring thee much silver,
  The hills a treasure of gold;
  They'll bring thee god's grandeur aplenty.
So build thou a silver and gold house,
  A house of most pure lapis lazuli."

The maiden Anath rejoices,
  Stamps with her foot so the earth quakes.
There, she is off on her way
  Unto Baal upon Zaphon's summit,
  O'er a thousand fields, ten thousand acres.
Laughing, the Maiden Anath
  Lifts up her voice and cries:

"Receive, Baal, the glad tidings I bring thee.
They will build thee a house like thy brethen's
  And a court like unto thy kindred's.
Summon weeds into thy house,
  Herbs into the midst of thy palace.
The mountains shall bring thee much silver,
  The hills a treasure of gold;
  They'll bring thee god's grandeur aplenty.
So build thou a silver and gold house,
  A house of most pure lapis lazuli."

Puissant Baal rejoiced.[15]

Worship at Ugarit employed not only a mythology rich
in its symbolism, the meaning of much of which escapes
even scholars who have labored for years with the texts,
but pictorial representation of the gods and goddesses.
Apparently, so well known were the deities which these

[15] *ANET*, 133.

FIG. 40. A Canaanite god seated on his throne
receiving an offering from a worshiper.

figures represented that there was no need for inscribed
labels. We can only guess as to which god was intended.

A scene of a devotee making an offering to a god seated
on an elaborate lion-footed throne, with his feet on a footstool, appears on a small, mottled stone exhibited in the
National Museum in Aleppo (Fig. 40). This god may well
represent El, the Bull, Father Shunem. The horned cap
and his elevation above the worshiper leave no doubt as to
the intention to represent a divine being. One of the god's
hands is raised in a gesture of benediction upon his devotee.

The image which is most likely to represent the rain-god

FIG. 41. The god of lightning, probably Baal,
on a stone found at ancient Ugarit.

Baal is on a stone slightly less than life-size (Fig. 41). The
god stands astride the mountain peaks, brandishing a club
and holding a lance represented in the form of forked
lightning. Below the point of a dagger, thrust through
his belt, is an inset, a figure, perhaps, of someone under
the protection of the deity. This "Baal of Lightning,"
as he is commonly called, seems to fit well the references
to the Puissant Baal in the poems.

A most dramatic episode in the Baal myth is the death

and resurrection of Baal, the god of rain and fertility. In this recital, students of ancient drama have seen a reflection of the changes in the season: the spring rains, followed by the summer drought, when all vegetation dies, and the renewal of vegetation shortly after the life-giving rains in the fall.

In the following lines, Anath takes the body of Baal, slain by Mot, and gives it burial with proper ceremonies.

> Then weeps she her fill of weeping;
> Deep she drinks tears, like wine.
> Loudly she calls
> Unto the Gods' Torch Shapsh.
> "Lift Puissant Baal, I pray,
> Onto me."
>
> Hearkening, Gods' Torch Shapsh
> Picks up Puissant Baal,
> Sets him on Anath's shoulder.
> Up to Zaphon's Fastness she brings him,
> Bewails him and buries him too,
> Lays him in the hollows of the earth-ghosts.
> She slaughters seventy buffaloes
> As tribute to Puissant Baal;
> She slaughters seventy neat
> As tribute to Puissant Baal. . . .[16]

Anath then makes her way to the supreme god El to tell him of the death of Baal.

> There, she is off on her way
> To El of the Sources of the Floods,
> In the midst of the Headwaters of the Two Deeps.
> She penetrates El's Field and enters
> The pavilion of King Father Shunem.
> At El's feet she bows and falls down,
> Prostrates her and does him honor.
> She lifts up her voice and cries:

[16] *ANET*, 139.

"Now let Asherah rejoice and her sons,
Elath and the band of her kinsmen;
For dead is Puissant Baal,
Perished the Prince, Lord of Earth."[17]

El proceeds to choose one of Lady Asherah's sons to
take the place formerly occupied by Baal. After passing
over a weakling, he chooses Ashtar to set on Baal's throne.
But he proves unequal to the position.

Loudly El doth cry
To Lady Asherah of the Sea:
"Hark, Lady Asherah of the Sea,
Give one of thy sons I'll make king."

Quoth Lady Asherah of the Sea:
"Why, let's make Yadi' Yalhan king."

Answered Kindly One El Benign:
"Too weakly. He can't race with Baal,
Throw jav'lin with Dagon's Son Glory-Crown!"

Replied Lady Asherah of the Sea:
"Well, let's make it Ashtar the Tyrant;
Let Ashtar the Tyrant be king."—

Straightway Ashtar the Tyrant
Goes up to the Fastness of Zaphon
And sits on Baal Puissant's throne.
But his feet reach not down to the footstool,
Nor his head reaches up to the top.
So Ashtar the Tyrant declares:
"I'll not reign in Zaphon's Fastness!"

Down goes Ashtar the Tyrant,
Down from the throne of Baal Puissant,
And reigns in El's Earth, all of it.[18]

After a large gap in the text, Anath proceeds to dispatch

[17] *ANET*, 140.   [18] *ANET*, 140.

the villain Mot, who had killed her brother Baal, in a significant ceremony.

> A day, even days pass by,
> From days unto months.
> Then Anath the Lass draws nigh him.
> Like the heart of a cow for her calf,
> Like the heart of a ewe for her lamb,
> So's the heart of Anath for Baal.
> She seizes the Godly Mot—
> With sword she doth cleave him.
> With fan she doth winnow him—
> With fire she doth burn him.
> With hand-mill she grinds him—
> In the field she doth sow him.
> Birds eat his remnants,
> Consuming his portions,
> Flitting from remnant to remnant.[19]

Following another missing portion of the text, there appears a triumphant hymn on the resurrected Baal, which contains a refrain emphasizing the return of plenty: "The heavens fat did rain, the wadies flow with honey."

> "That Puissant Baal had died,
> That the Prince Lord of Earth had perished.
> And behold, alive is Puissant Baal!
> And behold, existent the Prince, Lord of Earth!
> In a dream, O kindly El Benign,
> In a vision, Creator of Creatures,
> The heavens fat did rain,
> The wadies flow with honey.
> So I knew
> That alive was Puissant Baal!
> Existent the Prince, Lord of Earth!
> In a dream, Kindly El Benign,
> In a vision, Creator of Creatures,

[19] *ANET*, 140.

The heavens fat did rain,
The wadies flow with honey!"—
The Kindly One El Benign's glad.
His feet on the footstool he sets,
And parts his jaws and laughs.
He lifts up his voice and cries:
"Now will I sit and rest
And my soul be at ease in my breast.
For alive is Puissant Baal,
Existent the Prince, Lord of Earth!"[20]

Even a casual reading of these lines reveals a striking similarity to the poetic form of climactic parallelism found in the poetry of the Book of Psalms. A statement made in the first line of a couplet is repeated with slightly different nuance in the second. This poetic device, shared by Canaanite and Hebrew poetry, has led many scholars to see a clear case of borrowing on the part of the Hebrew poets from their alien neighbors. In a few cases the debt goes beyond poetic form, as for example the following two couplets in the Psalms:

For, lo, Thine enemies, O Lord,
For, lo, Thine enemies shall perish;
All the workers of iniquity shall be scattered.[21]

Thy kingdom is a kingdom for all ages,
And Thy dominion endureth throughout all generations.[22]

Similarly, the poet of the Baal Myth had written:

Now thine enemy, O Baal,
Now thine enemy wilt thou smite,
Now wilt thou cut off thine adversary.
Thou'lt take thine eternal kingdom,
Thine everlasting dominion.[23]

20 *ANET*, 140.
21 Ps. 92:10 in Hebrew; 92:9 in some English translations.
22 Ps. 145:13.   23 *ANET*, 131.

The concern of the poets of ancient Ugarit was not only with how the gods in their abode acted; there were stories of earthly heroes as well. In the two major epics, Keret and Aqhat, there is an occasional glimpse of what the author thought of the good life. There is, for example, the ideal of filial piety which emerges from the distant past of the fourteenth century B.C. in some lines from the Aqhat legend. In the Old Testament the obligation which offspring owe to parents is put in the command, to "honor thy father and thy mother." But in the Canaanite tale this duty is put picturesquely in a list of specific benefits one may reasonably expect from his son.

The passage appears in a poem of which one of the principals is Daniel, who is spoken of as "an upright" man, who sits before the gate, "judging the cause of the widow, adjudicating the case of the fatherless."[24] This Daniel is probably the hero of Hebrew tradition, the righteous man mentioned along with Job and Noah in the Book of Ezekiel and much later in the Book of Daniel. In the Canaanite tale, Daniel, desiring a son, propitiates the gods with appropriate sacrifices. To these, Baal responds by becoming the bearer of Daniel's petition to his father El. Baal describes the benefits which would come to Daniel from a son, as he prays:

> Wilt thou not bless him, O Bull El, my father,
>   Beatify him, O Creator of Creatures?
> So shall there be a son in his house,
>   A scion in the midst of his palace:
> Who sets up the stelae of his ancestral spirits,
>   In the holy place the protectors of his clan;
> Who frees his spirit from the earth,
>   From the dust guards his footsteps;
> Who smothers the life-force of his detractor,
>   Drives off who attacks his abode;
> Who takes him by the hand when he's drunk,

24 *ANET*, 151.

Carries him when he's sated with wine;
Consumes his funerary offering in Baal's house,
Even his portion in El's house;
Who plasters his roof when it leaks,
Washes his clothes when they're soiled.[25]

A similar obligation on the part of the son is recognized in some lines of an oracle in the Book of Isaiah, where Jerusalem is likened to the drunken parent. The prophet puts the simile:

There is none to guide her [Jerusalem]
Among all the sons whom she hath brought forth;
Neither is there any that taketh her by the hand
Of all the sons that she hath brought up.[26]

Aid in the time or condition of unsteadiness is what one may reasonably expect of a good child.

Fig. 42. A seven-headed dragon attacked by two gods. Three of the heads of the dragon are alive and fighting; four hang limp and defeated. Impression of a cylinder seal found at Tell Asmar in Mesopotamia.

In the Old Testament, there are some vestigial remains of a mythological conflict between Yahweh and fearful monsters. One such is a reference to a day when "the Lord with His sore and great and strong sword will punish leviathan the slant serpent, and leviathan the tortuous ser-

[25] *ANET*, 150. [26] Isa. 51:18.

pent; and He will slay the dragon that is in the sea."[27]
In a Psalm, God is addressed: "Thou didst shatter the heads
of the sea-monsters in the waters; Thou didst crush the
heads of leviathan."[28]

This graphic imagery of the triumph of Israel's god
over sea-monsters, leviathan, serpents, and dragons had
its precursor in Canaanite lore preserved at Ugarit. In a
fragment of the Baal myth, there is but the protasis of a
conditional sentence which shares with the Hebrew poetry
certain rare words:

> If thou smite Lothan [leviathan], the serpent slant,
> Destroy the serpent tortuous,
> Shalyat of the seven heads, . . .[29]

The prohibition by Hebrew prophet and lawmaker
against the making of idols suggests the prevalence of
idolatry in Canaan. From this clue one would naturally
look for the remains of Canaanite images in the debris
of the dozens of ancient sites which have been excavated
in Palestine-Syria.

The most frequently recurring "likeness of anything
that is in heaven above, or that is in the earth beneath,"
is the clay plaque of a nude female figure no larger than
a man's hand (Fig. 43a). These terracottas are far from being works of art. They are generally crude, but always emphasize, sometimes through exaggeration, the distinctively
feminine aspects of the human figure.

The widespread use of these objects is attested both by
the fact that they were sometimes mass-produced through
the use of a clay mold and by the great number of them
found in almost every major excavation of remains dating
from the eighteenth to the sixth centuries B.C. During
World War II, I was able to catalogue 294 of these objects
which had been published in excavation reports; if access
could have been had at that time to the museums of the
Near East, the number could have been greatly increased.

[27] Isa. 27:1.   [28] Ps. 74:13-14.   [29] ANET, 138.

Just what use these objects had remains a mystery to this day. Were they worshiped as a goddess? Were they charms to assist women in childbirth or as an aid to fertility? Or were they representations of the sacred harlots connected with Canaanite shrines? As yet one cannot be certain. But most opinion agrees that these objects served some vital religious or magical purpose in the practice of Canaanite religion.

FIG. 43a. Nude female figurine, made in a double mold, found at Megiddo.

FIG. 43b. Canaanite god made of bronze and covered with gold, found at Megiddo.

The male figure, which appears much less frequently, was made of metal rather than of clay, and was always represented clothed, and frequently portrayed in a seated posture (Fig. 43b). One of the best examples of these molten images comes from Megiddo. This small, ten-inch, gold-covered, bronze figure of the period of the Hebrew Judges may well represent a god, as he sits on his throne, wearing a high, conical headdress, earrings, and a long robe. The finding of this and other idols in Canaanite contexts of Palestinian soil gives perspective to the aniconic passion of the Hebrews in the midst of Canaanite idolatry.

SEX, FERTILITY, AND RELIGION

At one point at least the picture of Canaanite religion in the Old Testament and the discoveries of the past century converge: the cult of Canaan was concerned with fertility in field, flock, and family.

Ugaritic mythology pictures the gods as engaging in most human activities: they sacrifice, eat, make war, kill, build houses, relax and "twiddle their fingers," ride on beautiful jackasses. One text, of which only a fragment is preserved, has a graphic account of sexual union between Baal and Anath and seems to be followed by a description of the resulting fertility of the herds: "Calves the cows drop: an ox for the Maiden Anath and a heifer for Yahamat Liimmim."[30]

By a kind of sympathetic magic the union of gods, resulting, as it was believed, in the fertility of flocks and family, was effected, or at least stimulated, by similar actions among humans in the temples of the gods. Evidence for this ritual comes from a late, and possibly somewhat exaggerated, source in the writing of the the Greek Lucian of Samosata, who lived in the second century A.D. Under the thin veneer of the deities Aphrodite and Adonis may be recognized the older Canaanite personages of Ashtoreth and Baal. Wrote Lucian:

> But I also saw in Byblos a great temple of Aphrodite of Byblos, in which also the rites of Adonis are performed. I also made inquiry concerning the rites; for they tell the deed which is done to Adonis by a boar in their own country, and in memory of his suffering they beat their breasts each year, and wail, and celebrate these rites, and institute great lamentation throughout the country. But when they have bewailed and lamented, first they perform funeral rites to Adonis as if he were dead, but afterward upon another day they say he lives, and they

[30] *ANET*, 142.

cast dust into the air and shave their heads as the Egyptians do when Apis dies. But women such as do not wish to be shaven pay the following penalty: On a certain day they stand for prostitution at the proper time; and the market is open to strangers only, and the pay goes as a sacrifice to Aphrodite.[31]

The practice of sacred prostitution is probably the occasion for the invective of the prophet Hosea of the eighth century, who cried out: "They sacrifice upon the tops of the mountains, and offer upon the hills, under oaks and poplars and terebinths, because the shadow thereof is good; therefore your daughters commit harlotry, and your daughters-in-law commit adultery . . . and they sacrifice with harlots."[32]

A century later, the author of Deuteronomy, confronted with the age-old practice of sacred prostitution, wrote into this document of Israel's religious code a prohibition. But in place of mentioning outright the sodomite, or the male prostitute, he injected the opprobrious title of "dog" instead.

There shall be no harlot of the daughters of Israel, neither shall there be a sodomite of the sons of Israel. Thou shalt not bring the hire of a harlot, or the price of a dog, into the house of the Lord thy God for any vow; for even both these are an abomination unto the Lord thy God.[33]

While the picture of Canaanite religion from the literature and the monuments is admittedly sketchy, especially when contrasted with what is known of the neighboring religions of Egypt and Babylonia, certain facts have been established with a high degree of probability by the past hundred years of discovery. The pantheon is well documented from Greek, Phoenician, Hebrew, and Ugaritic

31 *De Dea Syria*, 6.   32 Hos. 4:13-14.   33 Deut. 23:18-19.

sources; in general it can be seen that the concern of the worshipers was for fertility and other benefits of nature. There was a highly-developed sacrificial system and a priesthood consisting of male and female temple servants; and there was a mythology expressed in a poetic form which

FIG. 44. Woman at the window, possibly the goddess Ashtart (or Astarte), ivory carving from Nimrud.

displays the parallelism long known to the Hebrew tradition in the Psalms. This century of excavation, decipherment, and research has, through many correspondences, established a basis for seeing Palestine and Syria as a unity in Canaanite times, and given to the partisan picture of Canaanite religion in Hebrew writings a new validity. The major share of the work in this recovery has been done by the French.

CHAPTER 4

ASSYRIA, ISRAEL'S ENEMY

LEARNING TO READ CUNEIFORM

IN THE ANNALS OF ARCHAEOLOGY the recovery of ancient Assyria stands out as a unique triumph. At the middle of the nineteenth century, two men, excavating along the upper Tigris River, discovered palace after palace of the Assyrian kings, richly documented with cuneiform inscriptions on their walls. At about the same time, the painstaking labors of two generations of scholars in deciphering cuneiform were crowned with success, so that the spectacular monuments from the Assyrian palaces could be placed almost immediately in the framework of written Assyrian history.

This achievement of discovery and decipherment provided a wealth of new material for understanding the history recorded in the Bible. Assyria and Israel had been in contact for centuries. Since to the biblical record of international relations could now be added the Assyrian side of the story, the history of ancient Israel no longer stood in the isolation of "sacred history." Thus it is fair to say that at the middle of the nineteenth century Israel had entered into the main stream of world history.

Before the discoveries of the 1840's and 1850's, Assyria appeared only as a long and menacing shadow casting itself over the pages of two centuries of biblical history. Generally it bears the vague label of "the King of Assyria," but in a few places the names of particular kings appear, as Tiglath-pileser, Shalmaneser, Sargon, Sennacherib, and Esarhaddon. The Prophet Isaiah, with characteristically vivid speech, described the approach of the King of Assyria as a disastrous flood, who "shall come up over all his channels and go over all his banks; and he shall sweep through Judah." Time and time again the flood swept over the two small kingdoms of Israel and Judah with terror and destruction in crises which aroused the Hebrew prophet to speak "the word of the Lord."

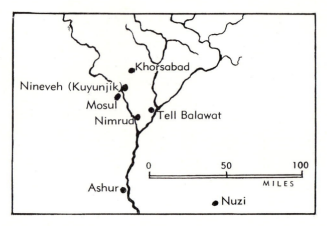

Fig. 45. Assyrian cities on the upper Tigris.

So well known were the names of Assyrian kings and so familiar the methods they used to impose their yoke on subject peoples, that biblical authors needed but mention the name Assyria to conjure up in the minds of their hearers a flood of tragic memories. Details, certainly, would have been superfluous. But with the fall of the Assyrian Empire and the passage of many centuries the history of Assyrian kings and their efficient and brutal means of warfare were all but forgotten. This oblivion into which Assyrian history had fallen remained until about a century ago, when Assyria was rediscovered and the vague shadow which it cast over the pages of the Old Testament was given reality.

Until a little more than a hundred years ago the thirty-nine kings of the two Hebrew kingdoms during the period of the divided monarchy were known only from the Bible and writings dependent upon it. Then from the earth of the region of the upper Tigris River there emerged records of the Assyrian kings mentioning Omri, Ahab, Jehu, Menahem, Hoshea, Pekah, and Hezekiah. Not only were these Israelite and Judaean enemies and subjects mentioned by name, but specific details of geography, dates, and amounts of tribute received were recorded in cuneiform.

This new perspective for biblical studies was achieved largely by four men of widely-differing backgrounds and interests. Henry C. Rawlinson was an English soldier, having seen service in India and Persia, and a student of oriental languages. Paul Botta, before distinguishing himself as an archaeologist, had been a ship's doctor on a voyage to California, a physician to Muhammad Ali in Egypt, and a consular official of France in Alexandria, Jerusalem, and Tripoli. Henry Layard's background for archaeology included work in a London law office, travels, and the British diplomatic service in a semi-official capacity. Among the four, only Edward Hincks, an Irishman, belonged to the clergy, the profession which for centuries had contributed most to biblical research. These were the men who set in motion the discipline of Assyriology as related to the Bible.

The records of ancient Assyria were written in a script and a language, the meanings of which had long since been forgotten. Decipherment and translation required several decades and the collaboration of British, French, and German scholars.

The key for deciphering the Assyrian inscriptions was supplied principally by a boastful text which the Persian King Darius had carved twenty-five centuries ago on the face of a mountain in Persia. That all might read, Darius had engraved at Behistun, on the main caravan route from Baghdad to Teheran, a record of his exploits in three languages, displayed at a height of 345 feet above the spring and 100 feet above the highest point to which a man can climb. To insure the preservation of this public record

FIG. 46. The trilingual inscription of Darius, king of Persia (521-486 B.C.), carved high on the side of the mountain at Behistun, was the "Rosetta Stone" for the decipherment of cuneiform. Here H. C. Rawlinson made the first successful copies of the inscriptions from 1835 to 1847.

against defacement he had, apparently on the completion of the work, taken the pains to sheer off the ascent to the inscription.

The first step toward decipherment called for physical courage. The texts in Old Persian, Elamite, and Akkadian —as they were later called—had to be copied. Credit for the first successful achievement of transferring these remote writings to paper belongs to Henry C. Rawlinson. At the age of seventeen, Rawlinson had left England for India in the service of His Majesty's government. Seven years later, in 1835, stationed near Behistun, he began to copy the Darius inscription (Fig. 46), and continued, off and on, to work at the project until 1847, when it was completed.

Risking his life to climb the rock at Behistun until he reached the bottom of the inscribed portion of the cliff, he continued by means of a ladder to copy even the top lines of the text. For this he had to stand on the topmost step of the ladder, steadying his body with his left arm and holding his notebook in his left hand while his right hand was employed with the pencil. "In this position," he later wrote, "I copied all the upper inscriptions, and the interest of the occupation entirely did away with any sense of danger."[1] This part of the work he did in 1844.

Three years later he returned to copy the more difficult area on which the Akkadian version appeared. When local goatherds who lived near the place pronounced the particular block unapproachable, a wild Kurdish boy, who had come from a distance, volunteered for a price to make the attempt. By means of ropes and a wooden peg driven into the rocks, the boy succeeded in reaching the text. At the direction of Rawlinson the boy, supported in a swinging seat like a painter's cradle, made a paper cast of the inscription. Since the days of Rawlinson, other and better copies of the inscriptions at Behistun have been made, but his copies were sufficient for deciphering the cuneiform writings.

1 *Archaeologia*, vol. 34, 1852, p. 74.

The decipherment of the Persian inscription, written in a cuneiform alphabetic script of forty-two characters, was achieved by the combined efforts of a dozen scholars, who by acute observation and brilliant deductions read and translated the text of Darius. With the publication of Rawlinson's "Memoir" in the *Journal of the Royal Asiatic Society* for 1846, it was apparent that Old Persian could at last be read with a relative degree of certainty.

Working on the assumption, which later proved to be correct, that the two other texts at Behistun were but versions of the Old Persian, scholars deciphered in a remarkably short time the Elamite and the Akkadian versions. For the latter, a wealth of new material had been reaching Europe in the late 1840's from the French and the English excavations on the upper Tigris, a circumstance which stimulated and aided the progress of decipherment.

Particularly noteworthy was the work of the Rev. Edward Hincks, the rector of the small parish of Killyleagh in County Down of Ireland, who reported his progress in papers read before the Royal Irish Academy. He was the first to publish a list of the values of the Akkadian characters. A milestone was reached when Rawlinson laid his translation of the Akkadian text at Behistun before the Royal Asiatic Society in the winter of 1850-51.

It was not, however, until the spring of 1857 that the general public was convinced that Akkadian cuneiform could be read. There had been so much debate among the few scholars who were working in the field of Akkadian that those outside this small circle were skeptical of the results of the alleged translations. It was W. H. Fox Talbot who conceived a plan to put an end to these doubts. Why not give a copy of the same text to four leading authorities, ask them to make independent translations into English, seal them and deliver to a reliable committee for comparison?

To the Royal Asiatic Society, Talbot sent a letter on

March 17, 1857, in which he argued: "Many persons have hitherto refused to believe in the truth of the system by which Dr. Hincks and Sir H. Rawlinson have interpreted the Assyrian writings, because it contains many things entirely contrary to their preconceived opinions."[2] He mentioned the reaction of many that if the system were as involved as the scholars asserted, the Assyrians themselves could never have read such a writing and continued: "It is well known that Sir H. Rawlinson has announced his intention of publishing translations of these lithographs [of a cuneiform text]. . . . Now, assuredly it will not add much to the authority of his translations if other scholars, after their publication, shall say that they are disposed to concur in them. . . . But it is evidently quite a different thing, when a translation has been prepared by another hand *before* the appearance of Sir H. Rawlinson's translation, and without any communication with him."[3] With this letter went Talbot's own translation in a sealed envelope.

Promptly the Royal Asiatic Society appointed a distinguished committee, including the Dean of St. Paul's, which sent lithographed copies of an inscription of Tiglath-pileser I to Dr. Hincks, Lieut.-Col. Sir H. Rawlinson, and Dr. Jules Oppert, a French scholar in the field of Akkadian studies. In a little more than two months the "examination papers" were all returned and a group of distinguished examiners sat in London, each holding one of the four translations in his hand. As one paragraph of a translation was read, three others checked the copies which they held. Each of the translations was read in this fashion, section by section.

Two members joined in a report on May 29th, to the effect that "the Examiners certify that the coincidences between the translations, both as to the general sense and

2 *Journal of the Royal Asiatic Society*, vol. 18, 1861, p. 150.
3 *ibid.*, p. 151.

verbal rendering, were very remarkable."[4] Two others issued reports reflecting the same general opinion, that the test had demonstrated that Akkadian could now be understood and reliably translated. The door was now open to a new approach to the study of the references to Assyria in the Bible.

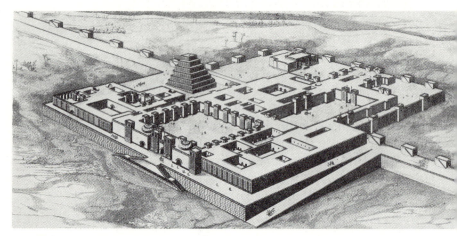

Fig. 47. A reconstructed drawing of the palace of Sargon II, king of Assyria (721-705 B.C.), at Khorsabad, first discovered by Botta in 1843. A later excavator found here 31 courts, 209 rooms, a ziggurat, and a temple—all built on a terrace from 46 to 59 feet high.

THE PALACE OF SARGON

The French were the first to discover the riches of the Assyrian kings buried beneath the mounds along the banks of the upper Tigris River. As early as 1842, the government of France appointed Paul Emile Botta, a son of a distinguished Italian historian, as its consular agent in Mosul, with instructions to make a collection of antiquities for France. Botta, then forty years old, a modest and generous man, arrived at his post and immediately set about his task by digging at Kuyunjik, just across the river from Mosul. There he dug for six weeks during the winter of

4 *ibid.*, p. 153.

FIG. 48. Sargon II making supplication to his god, on a wall painting found at Khorsabad, his capital.

1842-43, but with little success. Advised by a native of the village of Khorsabad, some fourteen miles away, of antiquities there, he moved to that village, and in a very short time found himself digging out the sculptured slabs of the palace of the great Assyrian King Sargon II.

For a year and a half Botta dug into the remains of the riches of Sargon II, producing a collection of Assyrian antiquities which became the nucleus of the Assyrian gallery at the Louvre. Surmounting great difficulties, he transported his treasures over land, river, and sea to Paris and later published them sumptuously in five volumes. Botta, the first excavator in Assyria, had the good fortune of hitting upon a site which was, in the next decade, to yield fabulous treasures from its palace of 31 courts and 209 rooms, the most celebrated of all the Assyrian palaces (Fig.

47). In it had lived the king who had destroyed the capital city of the little kingdom of Israel in 721 B.C.

The Assyrian King Sargon is mentioned by name only once in the Bible, and there he appears only as the king who sent his commander to take the city of Ashdod (Isaiah 20:1). But from the discoveries of Botta at Khorsabad it was soon apparent that it was none other than Sargon who was responsible for one of the principal events in the history of the people of Israel. For it was he who was the "king of Assyria," who "took Samaria, and carried Israel away unto Assyria, and placed them in Halah, and in Habor, on the river of Gozan, and in the cities of the Medes."[5] From this passage one could never have guessed that Sargon was this king of Assyria, especially since just three verses before Shalmaneser is mentioned. Shalmaneser had indeed gone up to Samaria and laid siege to it; but, toward the end of the three-year siege, Shalmaneser was succeeded by Sargon, and it was the latter who finally captured the capital of Israel's northern kingdom. The capitulation occurred in the year 721 B.C.

The text which Botta copied from the walls of the palace of Sargon at Khorsabad was promptly published in 1849-50. In it was detail which contributed additional information about this important event in the history of Israel.

> I besieged and conquered Samaria, led away as booty 27,290 inhabitants of it. I formed from among them a contingent of 50 chariots and made remaining inhabitants assume their social positions. I installed over them an officer of mine and imposed upon them the tribute of the former king.[6]

While this new text added to the biblical details, in another instance the biblical account of this event amplified the inscription of Sargon. In a summary of the events at the beginning of his reign, Sargon merely asserts of Samaria:

[5] II Kings 17:6. [6] *ANET*, 284-285.

Fig. 49. A portrait of Sargon II, the conqueror of Samaria in 721 B.C., wearing the royal Assyrian headdress. This was found in Sargon's palace at Khorsabad.

The town I rebuilt better than it was before and settled therein people from countries which I myself had conquered.[7]

The author of Kings is more explicit in describing the Assyrian policy of settling conquered and depopulated areas:

And the king of Assyria brought men from Babylon, and from Cuthah, and from Avva, and from Hamath and Sepharvaim, and placed them in the cities of Samaria

[7] *ANET*, 284.

instead of the children of Israel; and they possessed Samaria, and dwelt in the cities thereof.[8]

In the eleventh year of Sargon, 711 b.c., the Palestinian city of Ashdod revolted. The story of how Sargon moved speedily to squelch this uprising appears in a vivid passage of the Display Inscription carved on the walls of the palace at Khorsabad. It contains also the account of how the king of Ethiopia capitulated to the Assyrian might.

Azuri, king of Ashdod, had schemed not to deliver tribute any more and sent messages full of hostilities against Assyria, to the kings living in his neighborhood. On account of these acts which he committed, I abolished his rule over the people of his country and made Ahimiti, his younger brother, king over them. But these Hittites, always planning evil deeds, hated his reign and elevated to rule over them a Greek who, without any claim to the throne, had no respect for authority—just as they themselves. In a sudden rage, I did not wait to assemble the full might of my army or to prepare the camping equipment, but started out toward Ashdod only with those of my warriors who, even in friendly areas, never leave my side. But this Greek heard about the advance of my expedition, from afar, and he fled into the territory of Musru—which belongs now to Ethiopia—and his hiding place could not be detected. I besieged and conquered the cities Ashdod, Gath, Asdudimmu. . . .
The king of Ethiopia who lives in a distant country, in an inapproachable region, the road to which is . . . , whose fathers never—from remote days until now—had sent messengers to inquire after the health of my royal forefathers, he did hear, even that far away, of the might of Ashur, Nebo and Marduk. The awe-inspiring glamor of my kingship blinded him and terror overcame him. He threw [i.e. the Greek] in fetters, shackles and iron bands, and they brought him to Assyria, a long journey.[9]

---

[8] II Kings 17:24.   [9] *ANET*, 286.

The same campaign is referred to in the Book of Isaiah, where the Hebrew prophet advises Judah not to trust in Ethiopia, "their expectation."

In the year that Tartan [a title of Sargon's Commanding General] came unto Ashdod, then Sargon the king of Assyria sent him, and he fought against Ashdod and took it; at that time the Lord spoke by Isaiah the son of Amoz, saying: "Go, and loose the sackcloth from off thy loins, and put thy shoe from off thy foot." And he did so, walking naked and barefoot. And the Lord said: "Like as My servant Isaiah hath walked naked and barefoot to be for three years a sign and a wonder upon Egypt and upon Ethiopia, so shall the king of Assyria lead away the captives of Egypt, and the exiles of Ethiopia, young and old, naked and barefoot, and with buttocks uncovered, to the shame of Egypt. And they shall be dismayed and ashamed, because of Ethiopia their expectation, and of Egypt their glory. And the inhabitants of this coast-land shall say in that day: Behold, such is our expectation, whither we fled for help to be delivered from the king of Assyria; and how shall we escape?"[10]

THE BLACK OBELISK

On April 10, 1840, Austen Henry Layard, a twenty-three-year-old Englishman, entered the town of Mosul for the first time. He and his companion had spent the preceding winter wandering through Asia Minor and Syria, visiting the ancient seats of civilization. "We were both," he wrote later, "equally careless of comfort and unmindful of danger. We rode along; our arms were our only protection; a valise behind our saddles was our wardrobe, and we tended our own horses, except when relieved from the duty by the hospitable inhabitants of a Turcoman village or an Arab tent."[11] Thus they had traveled through areas

[10] Isa. 20.
[11] A. H. Layard, *Nineveh and Its Remains*, vol. I, London, 1854, p. 1.

where were some of the most spectacular ruins of antiquity.

The barren area beyond the Euphrates, with its desolate ruined mounds, fascinated Layard and made a much deeper impression on him than the temples of Baalbek and the theatres of Ionia. Particularly impressive was the mound at Nimrud, a short distance below Mosul, which he visited, and as he recalled later, "I formed the design of thoroughly examining, whenever it might be in my power, these singular ruins."[12]

Eventually the opportunity came for the traveler to become an archaeologist. Three years later Sir Stratford Canning, British Ambassador at Constantinople, gave Layard about £150 from his own private funds to carry on a two months' trial excavation at Nimrud. With this modest sum Layard left Constantinople by steamer for the Black Sea port of Samsun, and then hastened over land by post-horses to Mosul. This distance of over 600 miles he covered in twelve days.

Upon reaching Mosul in the autumn of 1845, he found the town and the area around it under the despotic rule of Muhammad Pasha, the Turkish governor, who had only one eye and one ear, and whose temper matched his villainous appearance. His cooperation could not be relied upon. If Layard were to succeed at Nimrud he would have to conceal his plan—at least for a while. So, he said, "on the 8th of November, having secretly procured a few tools, and engaged a mason at the moment of my depar ture, and carrying with me a variety of guns, spears, and other formidable weapons, I declared that I was going to hunt wild boars in a neighbouring village, and floated down the Tigris on a small raft constructed for my journey."[13]

After five hours on the raft, Layard and his three companions landed and were offered the hospitality of a miser-

---

[12] *ibid.*, p. 9.   [13] *ibid.*, p. 21-22.

Fig. 50. Three panels on the Black Obelisk, found by Layard at Nimrud. At the top is pictured Jehu, king of Israel, prostrating himself before Shalmaneser III, king of Assyria (858-824 B.C.). This is the only surviving picture of an Israelite king.

able Arab hovel belonging to a native named Awad. Lay-ard later wrote of his first night at the site which his labor was to make famous: "I slept little during the night. The hovel in which we had taken shelter, and its inmates, did not invite slumber. . . . Hopes, long cherished, were now to be realised, or were to end in disappointment. Visions of palaces underground, of gigantic monsters, of sculptured figures, and endless inscriptions, floated before me. After forming plan after plan for removing the earth, and ex-tricating these treasures, I fancied myself wandering in the maze of chambers from which I could find no outlet. . . . Exhausted, I was at length sinking into sleep, when hear-ing the voice of Awad, I rose from my carpet, and joined him outside the hovel. The day already dawned, he had returned with six Arabs, who agreed for a small sum to work under my direction."[14]

The fulfilment of his dreams came quickly. On this first day of work at Nimrud, with unprecedented luck, Layard hit upon walls lined with alabaster slabs bearing cunei-form inscriptions. Nor did his first good fortune fail him. In a very few months he had discovered tons of carved bas-relief from the palaces of Assyrian kings and had provided the British Museum with its principal Assyrian treasures.

The most important single monument for illustrating the Bible—and the only portrait we have of an Israelite king—is the Black Obelisk (Fig. 50). The credit for its discovery belongs to Austen Henry Layard.

In December of 1846, Layard was just about to abandon a trench 50 feet long which had yielded nothing of impor-tance. But, he thought, why not give one more day to this unproductive area? Having business in Mosul, the nearest important town, Layard gave orders to his workmen to continue until his return the following day, mounted his horse, and rode off. Scarcely had he left the mound when his workmen discovered the corner of a large, black stone

[14] *ibid.*, p. 25.

lying on the edge of the trench, some 10 feet below the surface. An Arab was dispatched without delay to overtake Layard. He returned in time to see one of his most spectacular discoveries completely exposed to view.

Layard wrote shortly afterward, but before the true significance of the monument was known: "Although its shape was that of an obelisk, yet it was flat at the top, and cut into three gradines. It was sculptured on the four sides; there were in all twenty small bas-reliefs, and above, below, and between them was carved an inscription 210 lines in length. The whole was in the best preservation; scarcely a character of the inscription was wanting; the figures were as sharp and well defined as if they had been carved but a few days before. The king [Shalmaneser III] is twice represented followed by his attendants; a prisoner is at his feet, and his vizier and eunuchs are introducing men leading various animals, and carrying vases and other objects of tribute on their shoulders, or in their hands. The animals are the elephant, the rhinoceros, the Bactrian or two-humped camel, the wild bull, the lion, the stag, and various kinds of monkeys."[15] Little did Layard suspect that the "prisoner" was soon to be identified by the inscription as Jehu, king of Israel.

The inscription of the obelisk was carefully copied and the monument crated for shipment to London. Buffalo-carts belonging to the local Pasha were pressed into service for carrying the crated antiquity to the river. Wrote Layard: "On Christmas day I had the satisfaction of seeing a raft, bearing twenty-three cases, in one of which was the obelisk, floating down the river. I watched them until they were out of sight, and then galloped into Mosul to celebrate the festivities of the season, with the few Europeans whom duty or business had collected in this remote corner of the globe."[16] But alas, it was a long time before the monument reached its destination in the British Museum.

[15] *ibid.*, p. 347.   [16] *ibid.*, p. 372.

The Black Obelisk and the other antiquities from Nimrud reached Basrah, the port at the head of the Persian Gulf, and there awaited some safe transport. A year after Layard had seen the obelisk depart from Nimrud, a sloop-of-war of the East India Company, the *Clive*, arrived in Basrah, stowed away some fifty cases in the driest and most sheltered position of the ship and transported them to Bombay. There, in the first part of 1848, the European community of Bombay took the liberty of opening Layard's cases, and displayed their contents to the public in the dockyard. A Dr. Buist was permitted to take casts of the Black Obelisk, and he lectured on the discovery before the Bombay Branch of the Royal Asiatic Society. The *Bombay Monthly Times* of May 20-June 18th published a report of the lecture. Thus it was that the first publication of Layard's find appeared in India.

Finally the cases of Assyrian antiquities were repacked at Bombay and shipped on H.M. brig *Jumna* on April 12, 1848. Some ten days later the *Jumna* was dismasted in a great storm, but was able to make Ceylon for refitting. Not until October 1848 did the obelisk reach England, after a journey of almost two years. There it was received by the keeper of Oriental Antiquities and unpacked in the presence of Layard himself.

Rawlinson was the first to offer a translation of the inscription on the Black Obelisk. He read it before the Royal Asiatic Society at the beginning of 1850, and others quickly added to it important points of detail. It was soon apparent that the monument contained the annals of a great Assyrian king, Shalmaneser III (858-824), who is not even mentioned by name in the Bible. Over the second row of panels is a clearly cut inscription as a label to the scene below it:

The tribute of Jehu, son of Omri; I received from him silver, gold, a golden *saplu*-bowl, a golden vase with

144

pointed bottom, golden tumblers, golden buckets, tin, a staff for a king, and wooden *puruḫtu*.[17]

The scenes depicting this tribute are in three panels, while the fourth shows the Assyrian king attended by two servants, standing before the Israelite Jehu, who prostrates himself at the head of the line of tribute bearers. From another inscription of Shalmaneser III it seems that this tribute was received in the eighteenth year of the king's reign, or 842 B.C. In all the colorful stories about Jehu in the Bible, no mention is made of this humiliating event of international importance.

Another important supplement to the history of Israel made its appearance in October of 1861, when J. E. Taylor, British Consul at Diyarbekir, discovered at Kurkh, a ruin lying beside the Tigris about 20 miles south of Diyarbekir, a large stela of Shalmaneser III (Fig. 51). It shows the king making a gesture of worship toward a row of divine emblems. Even though badly preserved, the inscription gives a detailed account of the defeat of Ahab by Shalmaneser III and of the tribute which the victor took.

In the sixth year of his reign (853 B.C.) the Assyrian King Shalmaneser III left his capital city of Nineveh on an expedition to the west. His march seems to have been unimpeded by any effective resistance until he came to the region of Hamath near the river Orontes. Here he met a coalition of twelve kings with strong forces, which the Assyrian scribe lists in considerable detail:

> I destroyed, tore down and burned down Karkara, his royal residence. He brought along to help him 1,200 chariots, 1,200 cavalrymen, 20,000 foot soldiers of Adad-'idri [i.e. Hadadezer] of Damascus, 700 chariots, 700 cavalrymen, 10,000 foot soldiers of Irhuleni from Hamath, 2,000 chariots, 10,000 foot soldiers of Ahab, the Israelite [list of allies follows]. . . . I slew 14,000 of their soldiers

---

[17] *ANET*, 281.

Fig. 51. A portrait of Shalmaneser III (858-824 B.C.), standing before the emblems of his gods. Inscribed on the face of the monument is an account of the battle of Karkar, in which Shalmaneser defeated Ahab the Israelite king, who is listed as having 2,000 chariots and 10,000 foot soldiers.

with the sword, descending upon them like Adad when
he makes a rainstorm pour down. I spread their corpses
everywhere, filling the entire plain with their widely
scattered, fleeing soldiers. During the battle I made
their blood flow down the *ḫur-pa-lu* of the district. The
plain was too small to let all their souls descend into

Fig. 52. Shalmaneser III ferrying tribute from the fortified town of Tyre,
situated on an island off the coast of Syria (above). Assyrians' chariots
advance from the Assyrian camp (lower left) to attack the town of Hazazu.
These scenes are on hammered and engraved bronze bands once attached
to the gates of a palace of Shalmaneser III.

the nether world, the vast field gave out when it came
to bury them. With their corpses I spanned the Orontes
before there was a bridge.[18]

This account of Ahab's participation in the battle of
Karkar is of great value for the history of Israel during
the reign of Ahab, since in the biblical sources no mention

[18] *ANET*, 278-279.

is made of the incident. Despite Shalmaneser's boastful claims of victory at Karkar, it seems from other records that the Assyrian victory was far from decisive. Shalmaneser was apparently checked in his advance, and Ahab with a considerable army had a part in the coalition of Syrian kings which forced the Assyrians to withdraw short of their main objectives.

TIGLATH-PILESER'S CONQUESTS IN PALESTINE

Austen Henry Layard's good fortune at Nimrud was not confined merely to the palace of Shalmaneser III. In addition he found sculptures which belonged to another As-

FIG. 53. A portrait of Tiglath-pileser III, king of Assyria (744-727 B.C.), who exacted tribute from Menahem, king of Israel, and from Ahaz, king of Judah.

syrian king—and one well known from the Bible. In 1853, just a few years after these monuments had been discovered, Layard wrote that the identity of the Assyrian king had been found "through a most important discovery, for which we are also indebted to Dr. Hincks. In an inscription on a bas-relief representing part of a line of war chariots, he had detected the name of Menahem, the king of Israel, amongst those of other monarchs paying tribute to the king of Assyria, in the eighth year of his reign."[19] The king, who had lived at Nimrud and whose palace Layard had found, was none other than Tiglath-pileser III, or Pul, as he is also called in the Bible (Fig. 53).

In the Old Testament the episode of Menahem's capitulation to Tiglath-pileser III in 738 B.C. is alluded to in the account of tribute he paid and of how he raised the amount of a thousand talents:

> There came against the land Pul the king of Assyria; and Menahem gave Pul a thousand talents of silver, that his hand might be with him to confirm the kingdom in his hand. And Menahem exacted the money of Israel, even of all the mighty men of wealth, of each man fifty shekels of silver, to give to the king of Assyria. So the king of Assyria turned back, and stayed not there in the land.[20]

Shortly after this capitulation to Tiglath-pileser III, Menahem died and was succeeded by his son, who reigned only a short two years before he was murdered by his captain, Pekah, who took the throne of Israel. Once again the biblical narrative tells of the invasion of the great Assyrian king:

> In the days of Pekah king of Israel came Tiglath-pileser King of Assyria, and took Ijon, and Abel-beth-maacah, and Janoah, and Kedesh, and Hazor, and Gilead, and Galilee, all the land of Naphtali; and he carried them captive to Assyria. And Hoshea the son of Elah made a conspiracy against Pekah the son of Remaliah, and smote him and slew him, and reigned in his stead.[21]

[19] A. H. Layard, *Discoveries among the Ruins of Nineveh and Babylon*, New York, 1856, p. 526.
[20] II Kings 15:19-20.   [21] II Kings 15:29-30.

When Layard excavated the palace of Tiglath-pileser III at Nimrud, he could not transport all the inscribed slabs to England. But, realizing the importance of the inscriptions, he made paper squeezes and brought them back to the British Museum. There they were stored. Two decades later George Smith, who was then interested in fragments of clay tablets from Nineveh, made comparisons

FIG. 54. Assyrian soldiers lead away the sheep and the inhabitants of the captured town of Astartu (?), probably the biblical Ashtaroth.

with the squeezes and came upon a startling cuneiform text. It was a summary of the campaigns of Tiglath-pileser III against Israel and mentioned the events which are described by the author of the Book of Kings. In 1870 he published the text in the third volume of Rawlinson's great *Cuneiform Inscriptions of Western Asia*. The inscription mentions the first "Exile" of Israel and gives the valuable information that Hoshea in his conspiracy had the backing of the Assyrian king.

As for Menahem I overwhelmed him like a snowstorm and he . . . fled like a bird, alone, and bowed to my feet. I returned him to his place and imposed tribute upon him, to wit: gold, silver, linen garments with multi-

colored trimmings, . . . great. . . . I received from him.
Israel . . . all its inhabitants and their possessions I led
to Assyria.

They overthrew their king Pekah and I placed Hoshea
as king over them. I received from them 10 talents of
gold, 1,000 [?] talents of silver as their tribute and
brought them to Assyria.[22]

FIG. 55. Assyrian soldiers of Tiglath-pileser III making use of a
siege-engine with battering-ram in their attack on the walled tower
of Gazru. This relief was found at Nimrud by Layard and a drawing of it published. The original has been lost.

Tiglath-pileser's attention was not limited to the northern kingdom of Israel; he boasts of tribute from the kings
of the south as well. On a clay tablet found at Nimrud
there is an inventory of booty:

I received the tribute of . . . Sanipu of Bit-Ammon,
Salamanu of Moab, . . . Mitinti of Ashkelon, Jehoahaz

22 *ANET*, 283-284.

of Judah, Kaushmalaku of Edom, . . . Hanno of Gaza consisting of gold, silver, tin, iron, antimony, linen garments with multicolored trimmings, garments of their native industries being made of dark purple wool . . . all kinds of costly objects be they products of the sea or of the continent, the choice products of their regions, the treasures of their kings, horses, mules trained for the yoke.[23]

From the Bible we are fortunate in having detail which supplements the Assyrian account of Jehoahaz—his name is sometimes shortened to Ahaz in the Bible—giving tribute to the king of Assyria. The reason he paid a "present" seems to have been that he wished to gain the Assyrian king's assistance against a nearer enemy, the king of Aram:

So Ahaz sent messengers to Tiglath-pileser king of Assyria, saying: "I am thy servant and thy son; come up, and save me out of the hand of the king of Aram, and out of the hand of the king of Israel, who rise up against me." And Ahaz took the silver and gold that was found in the house of the Lord, and in the treasures of the king's house, and sent it for a present to the king of Assyria.[24]

Layard's career as an archaeologist was as short as it was brilliant. In a little more than five years after his beginning at Nimrud, he considered his work in the Mosul area finished, and "on the 28th of April [1851] I bid a last farewell to my faithful Arab friends, and with a heavy heart turned from the ruins of ancient Nineveh."[25] And of this short period most of 1848 had been spent in England. Upon his retirement from the Assyrian field he was only thirty-four years old.

But in this brief period he had the good fortune to discover the most significant remains of four of the important

[23] *ANET*, 282.
[24] II Kings 16:7-8.
[25] A. H. Layard, *Discoveries among the Ruins of Nineveh and Babylon*, New York, 1856, p. 566.

kings of the Assyrian Empire: Ashurnasirpal II, Shalmaneser III, Sennacherib, and Ashurbanipal. With these discoveries he had documented in unique fashion, by picture
and by word, two and a half centuries of Assyrian history.
Not only had he published his finds promptly in a scientific fashion, but he had written a popular account of his
experience in *Nineveh and Its Remains,* which inside a
year's time had sold eight thousand copies, and which, as
he remarked in a letter to his traveling companion of some
years before, placed it "side by side with Mrs. Rundell's
Cookery."[26]

The fame of Layard, who recovered such spectacular
remains from the region of Nineveh, was party due to popular interest in the Old Testament. But as a later excavator
of Nineveh reflected, "one cannot help thinking that these
enormous Assyrian bulls had something very much in common with the ponderous, conservative philosophy of the
Mid-Victorian period, with its unshakable faith in this best
of all possible worlds, with its definite social castes duly prescribed by the Catechism, all doubtless to be maintained
in saecula saeculorum."[27] Nineveh, in the words of the
book of Jonah, was "an exceeding great city," but in 1851,
when Layard left Mosul, it possibly enjoyed a reputation
among as many people throughout the world as it had ever
had when it was the capital of the Assyrian kings.

Strangely enough, Layard left Mosul in the spring of
1851 without really knowing for certain whose palace it
was he had come upon in his second series of excavations.
The science of Assyriology was just being born out of the
study of inscriptions which Layard and Botta had made a-
vailable. Rawlinson, working in London during the summer
of that year, succeeded in making two amazing discoveries.
The scientific societies to which he usually reported were
closed but he could not contain his secrets. Excitedly Raw-

[26] A. H. Layard, *Autobiography,* London, 1903, vol. 2, p. 191.
[27] R. Campbell Thompson, *A Century of Exploration at Nineveh,* London, 1929, p. 41.

linson wrote to the *Athenaeum,* asking permission to publish "a most interesting and important discovery which I
have made within these few days."[28] He had discovered
that it was Sennacherib who had built the great palace at
Nineveh, and that there was a cuneiform text which stated
that the Judaean King Hezekiah had paid thirty talents
of gold, as well as other tribute to Sennacherib. And was
this not precisely the amount of gold which Sennacherib
set as tribute upon Hezekiah in Holy Writ?

The Assyrian King Sennacherib makes his appearance
in the Bible in connection with Isaiah, the prophet in the
days of Hezekiah, king of Judah. Beyond this one appearance on the scene of Judaean history as the dreaded conqueror of the villages about Jerusalem, little was known
until Layard's second excavation at Nineveh from October
1849 to April 1851. Here for over a year Layard uncovered
the rich deposit of a palace, laying bare seventy-one rooms
and almost two miles of sculpture and other evidence
which was to illuminate the reign of this powerful Assyrian
monarch.

A magnificent entrance, decorated with ten colossal
winged bulls with human heads, guarded the access to the
palace. But more important than the sculpture itself was
a series of inscriptions on the bulls which contained the
annals of six years of Sennacherib's reign. These Layard
carefully copied and showed to his friend Rawlinson upon
his return to England a little over a year later. And it was
the text of these inscriptions, when taken with texts on clay
cylinders, which enabled Rawlinson to announce so spec-
tacularly in 1851 his discovery of references to events in
the Bible. Eventually these inscriptions were sawed off
and taken to London. Two of the colossal winged creatures
actually remained in place on the mound at Nineveh until
1905. But since then they have found their way into the
lime-kiln of the natives and no longer exist.

[28] *The Athenaeum,* Aug. 23, 1851, pp. 902-903.

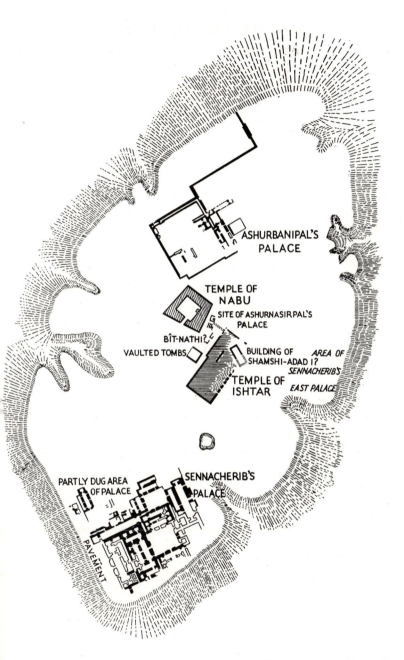

FIG. 56. The location of palaces and temples at ancient Nineveh.

SENNACHERIB AT JERUSALEM

The account of the third campaign of Sennacherib reads like a gazetteer of the eastern Mediterranean, with interesting footnotes on the problems created by rebellious rulers in certain cities. The king of Sidon, seeking to escape by sea, perished. His cities—Great Sidon, Little Sidon, Bit-Zitti, Zaribtu, Mahalliba, Ushu, Akzib, and Akko—although well supplied with food and water, capitulated. Over them Sennacherib set Ethba'al.

Submissive were the kings—they are said to have kissed the feet of Sennacherib—of Samsimuruna, Arvad, Byblos, Ashdod, Beth-Ammon, Moab and Edom. When the king of Ashkelon, Sidqia, resisted, he was deported with his family to Assyria and another pro-Assyrian king put in his place. It was necessary, the inscription continues, to lay siege to Beth-Dagon, Joppa, Banai-Barqa, and Azuru. Ekron presented a more difficult problem, since its citizens had overthrown the pro-Assyrian king and called to Egypt for help:

> The officials, the patricians and the common people of Ekron—who had thrown Padi, their king, into fetters because he was loyal to his solemn oath sworn by the god Ashur, and had handed him over to Hezekiah, the Jew—and he [Hezekiah] held him in prison, unlawfully, as if he [Padi] be an enemy—had become afraid and had called for help upon the kings of Egypt and the bowmen, the chariot-corps and the cavalry of the king of Ethiopia, an army beyond counting—and they actually had come to their assistance.[29]

In the plain of Eltekeh, Sennacherib defeated the Egyptians, then proceeded to conquer Eltekeh and Timnah and to assault Ekron. The rebellious officials and patricians of Ekron were killed and their bodies hung on poles surrounding the city (see Fig. 57)—a common Assyrian prac-

[29] *ANET*, 287.

tice. Padi, the former king, was returned from Jerusalem and set upon the throne.

Another rebel was Hezekiah, the Jew, king in Jerusalem:

> As to Hezekiah, the Jew, he did not submit to my yoke, I laid siege to 46 of his strong cities, walled forts and to the countless small villages in their vicinity, and conquered them by means of well-stamped earth-ramps, and battering-rams brought thus near to the walls combined with the attack by foot soldiers, using mines, breeches as well as sapper work. I drove out of them 200,150 people, young and old, male and female, horses, mules, donkeys, camels, big and small cattle beyond counting, and considered them booty. Himself I made a prisoner in Jerusalem, his royal residence, like a bird in a cage. I surrounded him with earthwork in order to molest those who were leaving his city's gate. His towns which I had plundered, I took away from his country and gave them over to Mitinti, king of Ashdod, Padi, king of Ekron, and Sillibel, king of Gaza. Thus I reduced his country, but I still increased the tribute . . . to be delivered annually.

> Hezekiah himself, whom the terror-inspiring splendor of my lordship had overwhelmed and whose irregular and elite troops which he had brought into Jerusalem, his royal residence, in order to strengthen it, had deserted him, did send me, later, to Nineveh, my lordly city, together with 30 talents of gold, 800 talents of silver, precious stones, antimony, large cuts of red stone, couches inlaid with ivory, *nîmedu*-chairs inlaid with ivory, elephant-hides, ebony-wood, box-wood and all kinds of valuable treasures, his own daughters, concubines, male and female musicians. In order to deliver the tribute and to do obeisance as a slave he sent his personal messenger.[30]

[30] *ANET*, 288.

The problem of reconciling this source with the several narratives in the Book of Kings, in Isaiah, and in Chronicles has challenged students of this segment of history for several generations. But one report, at least, in the Book of Kings, although abbreviated, seems to fit into the Assyrian account:

> And Hezekiah king of Judah sent to the king of Assyria to Lachish, saying: "I have offended; return from me; that which thou puttest on me will I bear." And

Fig. 57. The Assyrians made use of terror in their attacks by hanging citizens on stakes outside the town walls. From the walls of this town the defenders extend their hands in a gesture of surrender to the forces of Tiglath-pileser III.

the king of Assyria appointed unto Hezekiah king of Judah three hundred talents of silver and thirty talents of gold. And Hezekiah gave him all the silver that was found in the house of the Lord, and in the treasures of the king's house. At that time did Hezekiah cut off the gold from the doors of the temple of the Lord, and from the door-posts which Hezekiah king of Judah had overlaid, and gave it to the king of Assyria.[31]

The recovery of the main lines of Assyrian history came about suddenly. In the short span from 1843 to 1851, less than a decade, Khorsabad, Nimrud, and Nineveh yielded their most dramatic treasures. Even at this early period Assyriologists had not only been able to identify the great kings, Tiglath-pileser, Sargon, and Sennacherib, but they had also found records which dealt with some of the most important kings of Israel and Judah. Thus it was that by the middle of the nineteenth century Israel's history had moved out of the isolation which it had once enjoyed and had become a part of world history.

A successor to Layard, an excavator who came to Nineveh more than three quarters of a century later, R. Campbell Thompson, paid tribute to the earlier Assyriologists in this appropriate observation: "Champollion and Young solved the enigma of the Egyptian hieroglyphs, Schliemann was to excavate Troy, Arthur Evans was to reveal the palace of Minos to an unsuspecting world; but it is doubtful if any of these can quite equal the combined triumphs of the early Assyriologists of the middle of the last century, who not only uncovered palace after palace, but solved the riddle of the cuneiform on their walls."[32]

[31] II Kings 18:14-16.
[32] R. Campbell Thompson, *A Century of Exploration at Nineveh*, pp. 22-23.

CHAPTER 5

MYTH IN THE ANCIENT NEAR EAST

ALL MANKIND RETURNED TO CLAY

ONE OF THE MOST SPECTACULAR FINDS of biblical archaeology was recognized not at the site of a buried Near Eastern city, but in a small and poorly lighted room on the southwest staircase of the British Museum in London. Credit for the discovery belongs to George Smith, who at the time had never set foot on Near Eastern soil.

In the year 1872, while laboriously copying cuneiform signs from clay tablets in a large collection of more than 20,000 pieces which had come to the Museum from excavations at Nineveh, Smith came upon half of a tablet which had originally contained six columns of text. Casting his eye down the third column, he caught a reference to a ship resting on the mountains of Nisir, followed by an account of the sending forth of a dove and its finding no resting-place and returning. Could this be, by chance, a Babylonian account of the Flood? After searching thousands of fragments he succeeded in finding other portions of the same story, and by piecing them together he was able to make a translation. Certainly, the material was remarkably similar to the biblical story of the Flood.

When he shared his discovery with his superiors at the Museum, Birch and Rawlinson, they agreed that the exciting news should be read before the meeting of the Society of Biblical Archaeology at its December meeting. On December 3, 1872, a distinguished audience of scholars, theologians, and archaeologists—Mr. W. E. Gladstone, Dean and Lady Augusta Stanley, and Sir Henry Rawlinson were on the platform—heard the young assistant at the

British Museum make the announcement of one of the most important discoveries of the century.

"A short time back," Smith read, "I discovered among the Assyrian tablets in the British Museum, an account of the Flood; which, under the advice of our President, I now bring before the Society."[1] After a brief account of his labors and a translation of the text, he proceeded to the conclusion: "On reviewing the evidence it is apparent that the events of the Flood narrated in the Bible and the Inscription are the same, and occur in the same order."[2] This brief paper marks the beginning of a new epoch in our understanding of the character of the early stories in Genesis.

George Smith had come to Assyriology with no formal training. In fact, Assyrian antiquities were at first only a pastime with him. While apprenticed to the engraving firm of Messrs. Bradbury and Evans in London, where he sought to learn bank-note engraving, he spent his evenings reading the works of Layard and Rawlinson and his holidays—and even his dinner hours on the three days a week when the Sculpture Galleries of the British Museum were open to the public—haunting the exhibits of antiquities from Nineveh.

When the Keeper of Oriental Antiquities at the Museum, having noticed Smith's obvious dedication to the study of Assyrian remains, offered him a job of "repairer" of the inscribed tablets from Nineveh, Smith was easily persuaded to give up engraving and spend all his time with these more anciently inscribed materials.

At the time of his discovery of the Assyrian account of the Deluge, Smith had had approximately ten years of experience with cuneiform tablets. He had learned to decipher and to read the texts, and had already made other discoveries which he had published in the *Athenaeum* and in

---

[1] *Transactions of the Society of Biblical Archaeology*, vol. 2, 1873, p. 213.
[2] *ibid.*, p. 232.

a book of limited, scholarly interest. But with his announcement of the discovery of the Flood story, he became immediately world famous.

George Smith ended his paper on December 3rd with a guess that beneath the mounds of ancient Assyria there now "lay, together with older copies of this Deluge text, other legends and histories."[3] Sensing the news value of this sensational discovery and hopeful for more revelations of popular interest, the London *Daily Telegraph* proposed, immediately after Smith's lecture, the reopening of the excavations at Nineveh—and at the expense of the newspaper. If George Smith could get together this story from the scraps of tablets in the archives of the British Museum, could he not find even more important material in the library at ancient Nineveh itself?

Within less than two months after the announcement before the Society of Biblical Archaeology, Smith was on his way to Nineveh, with a grant of 1,000 guineas from the *Daily Telegraph*, a six months' leave from his work at the Museum, and high hopes of finding tablets which would fill in some of the gaps in the epic to which the Flood story belonged.

Work at Nineveh got under way by May 7th. A week later Smith sat down to examine some fragments of cuneiform inscriptions from the day's digging. As he brushed off the earth from one of these, he recognized that he had discovered a fragment containing seventeen lines which belonged to a missing portion of the first column of the Deluge tablet and which filled up the only serious gap in the story. In fact, in his paper read in London six months before, he had guessed that there were about fifteen lines missing at this point.

Immediately, Smith telegraphed the good news to his sponsor, the *Daily Telegraph*. When a copy of the paper reached Smith at Nineveh, he was surprised to read at the

---

[3] *ibid.*, p. 234.

end of the dispatch which he had sent the ominous words
added by the editors in London, "as the season is closing."
It was obvious that his patron was withdrawing from the

FIG. 58. A fragment of a large clay tablet from the library of Ashurbanipal
at Nineveh, inscribed with the Assyrian version of the Flood story.

field of archaeology, now that its objective seemed to have been accomplished. Smith soon returned home.

The trustees of the British Museum sponsored Smith in a second season of digging at Nineveh during the first part of 1874 and supplied him with £1,000. This time, Smith, single-handed, employed nearly six hundred men in a frantic race against the deadline for the expiration of the permit granted by the Turkish government. It was a scramble for tablets. Little else mattered. In less than four months of excavation on the two expeditions, Smith recovered over 3,000 inscriptions, as he remarked, "so rich were these mines of antiquities."[4]

In 1876, Smith began a third expedition but did not complete it. Ill fate attended him at every turn. His traveling companion on the trip from Constantinople to Baghdad died on the way. When the young excavator finally arrived at Nineveh, he found that no native would work on the site through the heat of July. Disappointed and tired, he set out for Aleppo in the worst of the summer heat. On the way he suffered an attack of dysentery which proved fatal. On August 19, at the age of thirty-six, he died and was buried in Aleppo.

The tablets which George Smith utilized in the making of his discovery of the Flood story came from the library of the Assyrian King Ashurbanipal, who reigned at Nineveh toward the end of the seventh century b.c. Since 1872, scores of new fragments of the Epic of Gilgamesh, to which the Flood story belongs, have come to light from excavations up and down the Tigris and Euphrates Rivers as well as from antiquity dealers who have been supplied from clandestine diggings. Not only have Ashur, Nippur, Kish, Ur, and Sippar yielded pieces, but the distant Hittite capital Hattusa in Anatolia has also produced fragments.

The most recent piece of this ancient literary document to make its appearance comes from the site of Megiddo in Palestine, where from 1926 to 1939 a staff from the Ori-

---

4 George Smith, *Assyrian Discoveries*, New York, 1876, p. 438.

ental Institute of the University of Chicago peeled off layer after layer of the mound. Recently, a shepherd, walking over a mound of the archaeologists' debris, picked up a cuneiform tablet. When it was read, it was found to contain forty lines of the Gilgamesh epic. Demonstrably, the story was known throughout the great triangle formed by Mesopotamia, Hittite Anatolia, and Palestine.

Since George Smith first offered a translation of a portion of the Babylonian story of the Flood in 1872, scores of scholars have labored both to better the translation of his text and to add new fragments to fill in the gaps. In the following translation taken from *Ancient Near Eastern Texts,* E. A. Speiser has acknowledged his debt to a long and distinguished line of scholars.

The episode of the Flood represents only one scene in the epic of Gilgamesh, one in which the hero of the Flood, Utnapishtim, recounts the story of how he escaped the general destruction of mankind. The great gods of the ancient city of Shuruppak (modern Fara) resolved to destroy mankind by a flood. The god Ea disclosed the divine decree by allowing Utnapishtim to hear the following advice:

> Man of Shuruppak, son of Ubar-Tutu,
> Tear down this house, build a ship!
> Give up possessions, seek thou life.
> Forswear worldly goods and keep the soul alive!
> Aboard the ship take thou the seed of all living things.
> The ship that thou shalt build,
> Her dimensions shall be to measure.
> Equal shall be her width and her length.
> Like the Apsu thou shalt ceil her. . . .

After a conversation between Utnapishtim and Ea, there follows the description of the building of the ship:

> The little ones carried bitumen,
> While the grown ones brought all else that was needful.

165

On the fifth day I laid her framework.
One whole acre was her floor space,
   Ten dozen cubits the height of each of her walls,
Ten dozen cubits each edge of the square deck.
I laid out the contours and joined her together.
I provided her with six decks,
Dividing her thus into seven parts.
Her floor plan I divided into nine parts.
I hammered water-plugs into her.
I saw to the punting-poles and laid in supplies. . . .

Measures of bitumen, asphalt, and oil were stowed away in the vessel.

Bullocks I slaughtered for the people,
And I killed sheep every day.
Must, red wine, oil, and white wine
I gave the workmen to drink, as though river water,
That they might feast as on New Year's Day.
I opened . . . ointment, applying it to my hand.
On the seventh day the ship was completed.
The launching was very difficult,
So that they had to shift the floor planks above and
   below,
Until two-thirds of the structure had gone into the
   water.

The loading of possessions, animals, family, and crafts-men now takes place:

Whatever I had I laded upon her:
Whatever I had of silver I laded upon her;
Whatever I had of gold I laded upon her;
Whatever I had of all the living beings I laded upon
   her.
All my family and kin I made go aboard the ship.
The beasts of the field, the wild creatures of the field,
   All the craftsmen I made go aboard. . . .

The time for the flood had arrived. The poet describes
in detail the approaching storm:

I watched the appearance of the weather.
The weather was awesome to behold.
I boarded the ship and battened up the entrance.
To batten down the whole ship, to Puzur-Amurri,
    the boatman,
I handed over the structure together with its con-
    tents.

When the first glow of dawn,
A black cloud rose up from the horizon.
Inside it Adad thunders,
While Shullat and Hanish go in front,
Moving as heralds over hill and plain.
Erragal tears out the posts;
Forth comes Ninurta and causes the dikes to follow.
The Anunnaki lift up the torches,
Setting the land ablaze with their glare.
Consternation over Adad reaches to the heavens,
Who turned to blackness all that had been light.
The wide land was shattered like a pot!
For one day the south-storm blew,
Gathering speed as it blew, submerging the moun-
    tains,
Overtaking the people like a battle.
No one can see his fellow,
Nor can the people be recognized from heaven.
The gods were frightened by the deluge,
And, shrinking back, they ascended to the heaven
    of Anu.
The gods cowered like dogs
    Crouched against the outer wall.
Ishtar cried out like a woman in travail,
The sweet-voiced mistress of the gods moans aloud:
"The olden days are alas turned to clay,
Because I bespoke evil in the Assembly of the gods.

How could I bespeak evil in the Assembly of the gods,
Ordering battle for the destruction of my people,
When it is I myself who give birth to my people!
Like the spawn of the fishes they fill the sea!"
The Anunnaki gods weep with her,
The gods, all humbled, sit and weep,
Their lips drawn tight, . . . one and all.
Six days and six nights
Blows the flood wind, as the south-storm sweeps the
 land.
When the seventh day arrived,
 The flood-carrying south-storm subsided in the
  battle,
Which it had fought like an army.
The sea grew quiet, the tempest was still, the flood
 ceased.
I looked at the weather: stillness had set in,
And all of mankind had returned to clay.
The landscape was as level as a flat roof.
I opened a hatch, and light fell upon my face.
Bowing low, I sat and wept,
Tears running down on my face.
I looked about for coast lines in the expanse of the
 sea:
In each of fourteen regions
 There emerged a region-mountain.
On Mount Nisir the ship came to a halt.
Mount Nisir held the ship fast,
 Allowing no motion.
One day, a second day, Mount Nisir held the ship
 fast,
 Allowing no motion.
A third day, a fourth day, Mount Nisir held the ship
 fast,
 Allowing no motion.

A fifth, and a sixth day, Mount Nisir held the ship
fast,
Allowing no motion.
When the seventh day arrived,
I sent forth and set free a dove.
The dove went forth, but came back;
Since no resting-place for it was visible, she turned
round.
Then I sent forth and set free a swallow.
The swallow went forth, but came back;
Since no resting-place for it was visible, she turned
round.
Then I sent forth and set free a raven.
The raven went forth and, seeing that the waters had
diminished,
He eats, circles, caws, and turns not round.
Then I let out all to the four winds
And offered a sacrifice.
I poured out a libation on the top of the mountain.
Seven and seven cult-vessels I set up,
Upon their pot-stands I heaped cane, cedarwood,
and myrtle,
The gods smelled the savor,
The gods smelled the sweet savor,
The gods crowded like flies about the sacrificer.[5]

After a council of the gods, Enlil went aboard the ship,
touched the foreheads of Utnapishtim and his wife, and
blessed them thus:

Hitherto Utnapishtim has been but human.
Henceforth Utnapishtim and his wife shall be like
unto us gods.[6]

It is no wonder that this ancient tale has been of interest to students of the biblical account of the Flood in chapters 6 to 9 of Genesis. The Babylonian gods resolve to destroy mankind by a flood; the Lord repents that he has

[5] *ANET*, 93-95.　　　　　　　[6] *ANET*, 95.

made man and decides to destroy him. The god Ea discloses the advice to Utnapishtim that he should build a ship; the Lord divulges his plan of destruction to Noah and orders him to make an ark. Both accounts give specifications for the ship; both tell of the loading of the vessel; and both record the duration of the flood.

Utnapishtim's ship comes to rest on Mt. Nisir; Noah's ark settles on Mt. Ararat. In both accounts the dove and the raven are sent out of the ship. Utnapishtim offers sacrifice, of which the gods smell the savor; Noah builds an altar, from which the Lord smells the sweet savor. Enlil confers immortality as a reward upon Utnapishtim; and God blesses Noah and makes a covenant with him.

While the points of agreement in the structure of the plots make it clear that the Hebrew version—probably originally two versions compressed into one—goes back to the Babylonian tradition, the religious concepts underlying the Hebrew account are strikingly different from those found in its predecessor. What we can say is that the Hebrew writers made use of traditions which were ready at hand as a means for presenting their own views about religion and life.

GILGAMESH, MOST SPLENDID AMONG HEROES

It is understandable that interest in the Gilgamesh epic has centered mainly on the story of the Flood in its eleventh tablet. But this concentration upon the part of the epic which is so obviously related to the Flood story in Genesis has led to the neglect of significant resemblances between Gilgamesh and other parts of biblical literature.

A notable exception to this neglect is the work of Peter Jensen, Professor of Semitic Philology at the University of Marburg. In the wake of earlier and important studies on the text of Gilgamesh, Jensen published, in 1906, a book of over a thousand pages in which he sought to prove that the character of Gilgamesh was the ancient prototype of the patriarchs of the Old Testament, its prophets and its liberators, as well as the central figure of the Gospels. Disturbed that his theories were not more widely noticed, Jensen wrote a monograph three years later under the title *Moses, Jesus, Paulus: Drei Varianten des babylonischen Gottmenschen Gilgamesch* (Moses, Jesus, Paul: Three Variants of the Babylonian God-Man Gilgamesh), a work which he labeled an "attack upon the theologians, an appeal to laymen." Following the extreme claims made in these two books, and in a third published in 1926, the question of possible parallels has not been pursued further. Gilgamesh suffered much harm at the hands of his friend Jensen.

The literary value of Gilgamesh as one of the world's great and earliest epics has not been unnoticed. In 1934, the American poet William Ellery Leonard noted the treatment of the central themes of "sex-love, combat, friendship, adventure, valour, loyalty, the mountain, the field, the forest, the wild beasts, the sea, the storm, the gods, the mysteries of birth and death,"[7] and set the epic in free rhythms. More recently, D. G. Bridson, of the British Broadcasting Corporation, paraphrased the translation of E. A. Speiser and, with a cast of actors and actresses, presented it over the BBC Third Programme on November 29, 1954.

The first tablet of the epic opens with the introduction of the central character of the story, Gilgamesh. He, like Odysseus, had seen and suffered much. In Uruk, which was his home, he had built the wall and the pure sanctuary of Ishtar, enduring monuments which all could inspect, the tokens of his greatness. Arithmetically, his greatness is described in terms of his being two-thirds god and one-third man.

In an arrogant way Gilgamesh has been oppressing those who lived in the famed Uruk, leaving not the son to his father, nor the maid to her mother. When the people of

---

[7] W. E. Leonard, *Gilgamesh*, New York, 1934, p. x.

Fig. 59. A colossal figure of a hero clutching a lion;
found at Khorsabad, the capital of Sargon II.

Uruk appeal to the gods of heaven for relief from this un-
seemly tyranny, the goddess Aruru, the creatress of Gilgamesh, is called upon to make his double to be his match.
Thereupon, she washes her hands, pinches off clay—in
Genesis the Lord God fashioned man out of the dust of
the earth—and creates the second principal character of
the epic, the valiant Enkidu.

Enkidu is an uncivilized man, in that he feeds on grass
and jostles with the animals at the drinking places. All his
body is shaggy with hair. His friends are the animals, of
whom he is the protector. A hunter who has been thwarted
in his fieldcraft by Enkidu, who tears up his traps, is advised to set a trap for Enkidu himself. He obtains a harlot-
lass from Gilgamesh, and the hunter and the harlot go to
the watering-place to await the arrival of the animals and
their friend Enkidu:

> The creeping creatures came, their heart delighting
>   in water.
> But as for him, Enkidu, born in the hills—
> With the gazelles he feeds on grass,
> With the wild beasts he drinks at the watering-place,
> With the creeping creatures his heart delights in wa-
>   ter—
> The lass beheld him, the savage-man,
> The barbarous fellow from the depths of the steppe:
> "There he is, O lass! Free thy breasts,
> Bare thy bosom that he may possess thy ripeness!
> Be not bashful! Welcome his ardor!
> As soon as he sees thee, he will draw near to thee.
> Lay aside thy cloth that he may rest upon thee.
> Treat him, the savage, to a woman's task!
> Reject him will his wild beasts that grew up on his
>   steppe,
> As his love is drawn unto thee."[8]

[8] *ANET*, 75.

The harlot offers herself to Enkidu, and for six days and seven nights Enkidu comes forth mating with the lass. The change which comes over his personality is immediate. The animals, his erstwhile companions, flee when he turns his face toward them. At this reaction,

> Startled was Enkidu, as his body became taut,
> His knees were motionless—for his wild beasts had gone.
> Enkidu had to slacken his pace—it was not as before;
> But he now had wisdom, broader understanding.[9]

A woman had tamed the wild man by the act of love, made him civilized. Now he is no longer a companion for the animals; he has been initiated into the life of humans. But this progress had been purchased at a price: no longer could he run as before! A different restriction—but nevertheless a curtailment of life and freedom—was placed on the first man, in the account in chapters 2 and 3 of Genesis, after his encounter with the woman and the discovery of sex.

There is an Old Babylonian version of this transformation of the wild Enkidu, written on a tablet which is at least a thousand years older than the version from Nineveh which we have been following. It tells in simple, but graphic, verse of the change which came over Enkidu:

> The milk of wild creatures
> He was wont to suck.
> Food they placed before him;
> He gagged, he gaped
> And he stared.
> Nothing does Enkidu know
> Of eating food;
> To drink strong drink
> He has not been taught.
> The harlot opened her mouth,
> Saying to Enkidu:

[9] *ANET*, 75.

"Eat the food, Enkidu,
As is life's due;
Drink the strong drink, as is the custom of the land."
Enkidu ate the food,
Until he was sated;
Of strong drink he drank
Seven goblets.
Carefree became his mood and cheerful,
His heart exulted
And his face glowed.
He rubbed the shaggy growth,
The hair of his body,
Anointed himself with oil,
Became human.
He put on clothing,
He is like a groom!
He took his weapon
To chase the lions,
That shepherds might rest at night.
He caught wolves,
He captured lions,
The chief cattlemen could lie down;
Enkidu is their watchman,
The bold man,
The unique hero![10]

Enkidu is brought into Uruk, where he engages Gilgamesh in combat. They grapple each other, butting like bulls, so that the walls shake. Since we see the two principals shortly afterwards as fast friends, we may surmise that each had recognized in this combat the heroic strength of the other.

The two friends, Gilgamesh and Enkidu, now embark on a hazardous expedition against the monster Humbaba —called in the older version Huwawa—who lives in the Cedar Forest. Enkidu hesitates before this fearsome undertaking, but Gilgamesh encourages him.

[10] *ANET*, 77.

FIG. 60. Contest scenes engraved on a cylinder seal for impressing wet clay. In the contest to the left a bearded hero subdues a water-buffalo; to the right, a bull-man fights with a lion.

> Only the gods live forever under the sun.
> As for mankind, numbered are their days;
> Whatever they achieve is but the wind!
> Even here thou art afraid of death.
> What of thy heroic might?
> Let me go then before thee,
> Let my mouth call to me, "Advance, fear not!"
> Should I fall, I shall have made me a name:
> "Gilgamesh"—they will say—"against fierce Huwawa
> Has fallen!" Long after
> My offspring has been born in my house.[11]

The elders of Uruk try to dissuade Gilgamesh from going, but with no effect. With a short prayer to Shamash and an unfavorable omen, he sets about his sorrowful task of preparing for the journey. The elders of Uruk commend Enkidu to Gilgamesh as a suitable companion.

So dangerous is the journey that even the goddess Ninsum, the mother of Gilgamesh, ascended the roof to offer incense to Shamash and to ask:

[11] *ANET*, 79.

FIG. 61. The god Shamash seated on his throne, as he appears at the top of the stela of Hammurabi. Before him is Hammurabi, king of Babylon.

> Why, having given me Gilgamesh for a son,
>   With a restless heart didst thou endow him?
> And now thou didst affect him to go
> On a far journey, to the place of Humbaba,
> To face an uncertain battle,
> To travel an uncertain road![12]

[12] *ANET*, 81.

FIG. 62. The Babylonian goddess Ishtar riding on a lion with her hand raised in benediction.

The expedition to the Cedar Forest is successful: the monster Humbaba is killed. Gilgamesh, the attractive hero, is proposed to by the goddess Ishtar with glowing promises of wealth and power in return for his favor. To these, Gilgamesh replies appropriately that he would have to give her oil for her body, clothes, her board and keep. Then, with sharply accelerated tempo, Gilgamesh hastens to hurl all kind of calumny at the lady making the proposal. Among other uncomplimentary things he calls her:

A back door which does not keep out blast
   and wind-storm . . .
A waterskin which soaks through its bearer . . .
A shoe which pinches the foot of its owner![13]

Enraged by these and other insults, Ishtar goes to the
god Anu and asks him to create the Bull of Heaven to destroy Gilgamesh. After the snorting bull has killed hundreds of men, Enkidu and Gilgamesh slay the bull and tear
out his heart. The enraged Ishtar utters a curse upon Gilgamesh. Whereupon, Enkidu tears loose the right thigh
and casts it in Ishtar's face with the words: "Could I but
get thee, like unto him I would do unto thee. His entrails
I would hang at thy side." Triumphantly the two heroes
embrace each other and ride through the market-street
of Uruk as Gilgamesh calls out:

   Who is most splendid among the heroes?
   Who is most glorious among men?

Antiphonally the lyre-maids of Uruk reply in a couplet,
the form of which brings to mind the song of the women
who came out to David after the slaughter of the Philistine (I Sam. 18:7):

   Gilgamesh is most splendid among the heroes,
   Gilgamesh is most glorious among men.[14]

After this triumph the two heroes lie down to sleep. Enkidu has a dream foreboding his death as a penalty for slaying
Humbaba and the Bull of Heaven. Soon afterwards, as he
lies on his deathbed, he reviews the events of his life from
the carefree days with the animals to becoming a famous
hero and companion of Gilgamesh. He recalls the harlot-
lass who lured him from his former ways and says:

   Come, lass, I will decree thy fate,
   A fate that shall not end for all eternity! . . .
   The shadow of the wall shall be thy station, . . .
   The besotted and the thirsty shall smite thy cheek![15]

13 *ANET*, 84.   14 *ANET*, 85.   15 *ANET*, 86.

The god Shamash hastens to remind Enkidu of the benefits which have come to him because of the harlot: not only food and drink, but the friendship of Gilgamesh, who will mourn him after his death:

> Why, O Enkidu, cursest thou the harlot-lass,
> Who made thee eat food fit for divinity,
> And gave thee to drink wine fit for royalty,
> Who clothed thee with noble garments,
> And made thee have fair Gilgamesh for a comrade?
> And has not now Gilgamesh, thy bosom friend,
> Made thee lie on a noble couch?
> He has made thee lie on a couch of honor,
> Has placed thee on the seat of ease, the seat at
>   the left,
> That the princes of the earth may kiss thy feet!
> He will make Uruk's people weep over thee and lament,
> Will fill joyful people with woe over thee.
> And, when thou art gone,
>   He will his body with uncut hair invest,
> Will don a lion skin and roam over the steppe.[16]

When Enkidu hears these words of Shamash his heart grows quiet. Soon, it seems, Enkidu dies.

The remainder of the epic has to do with Gilgamesh's long and fruitless quest for endless life. Enkidu's death has brought home to his friend the reality of death. As he weeps bitterly for Enkidu, he ranges over the steppe and reflects: "When I die, shall I not be like Enkidu?"[17] Goaded by grief and fear, Gilgamesh undertakes a long and dangerous journey to the place where lives Utnapishtim, the hero of the flood, that he might ask him about death and life.

At one stage of his journey Gilgamesh meets with Siduri, the ale-wife, who listens to his story of grief and then coun-

---

[16] *ANET*, 86.   [17] *ANET*, 88.

sels him to accept the fact of death and to enjoy life. Gilgamesh addresses Siduri:

"He who with me underwent all hardships—
Enkidu, whom I loved dearly,
Who with me underwent all hardships—
Has now gone to the fate of mankind!
Day and night I have wept over him.
I would not give him up for burial—
In case my friend should rise at my plaint—
Seven days and seven nights,
Until a worm fell out of his nose.
Since his passing I have not found life,
I have roamed like a hunter in the midst of the steppe.
O ale-wife, now that I have seen thy face,
Let me not see the death which I ever dread."
The ale-wife said to him, to Gilgamesh:
"Gilgamesh, whither rovest thou?
The life thou pursuest thou shalt not find.
When the gods created mankind,
Death for mankind they set aside,
Life in their own hands retaining.
Thou, Gilgamesh, let full be thy belly,
Make thou merry by day and by night.
Of each day make thou a feast of rejoicing,
Day and night dance thou and play!
Let thy garments be sparkling fresh,
Thy head be washed; bathe thou in water.
Pay heed to the little one that holds on to thy hand,
Let thy spouse delight in thy bosom!
For this is the task of mankind!"[18]

The advice of Siduri, the ale-wife, is not unlike that found in the Book of Ecclesiastes, "the words of Koheleth, the son of David, king in Jerusalem":

[18] *ANET*, 89-90.

Go thy way, eat thy bread with joy,
And drink thy wine with a merry heart;
For God hath already accepted thy works.
Let thy garments be always white;
And let thy head lack no oil.
Enjoy life with the wife whom thou lovest
All the days of the life of thy vanity.[19]

After crossing difficult mountains and sailing across the Waters of Death, Gilgamesh at last meets Utnapishtim, who discourses on the theme of the lack of permanency with specific reference to the transiency of life itself:

Do we build a house for ever?
Do we seal contracts for ever?
Do brothers divide shares for ever?
Does hatred persist for ever in the land?
Does the river for ever raise up and bring on floods?
The dragon-fly leaves its shell
That its face might but glance at the face of the sun.
Since the days of yore there has been no permanence;
The resting and the dead, how alike they are![20]

These gloomy reflections are apparently not sufficient to deter Gilgamesh from his search; he persists by asking Utnapishtim how it was that he achieved his deathless state. The reply is the long story of his salvation from the flood through obedience to the god Ea. At the conclusion of the recital of this story, Utnapishtim sets a test for Gilgamesh to try his heroism: "Up, lie not down to sleep for six days and seven nights." But the weak humanity of Gilgamesh is soon apparent:

As he sits there on his haunches,
Sleep fans him like the whirlwind.
Utnapishtim says to her, to his spouse:
"Behold this hero who seeks life!
Sleep fans him like a mist."[21]

[19] Eccles. 9:7-9.   [20] *ANET*, 92-93.   [21] *ANET*, 95.

After seven days of sleep Gilgamesh awakens, thinking that he has dozed but briefly until he is convinced by his host of his failure to meet the test. After a bath and a change of clothes, Gilgamesh is delivered into the hands of Urshanabi, the boatman, for return to his own city. At the departure of the disappointed hero, the wife of Utnapishtim intercedes to persuade her husband to reward him for his perilous journey. Thereupon, Utnapishtim reveals a hidden thing: a thorny plant at the bottom of the sea, if grasped, will assure life. By tying heavy stones to his feet, Gilgamesh descends to the deep and obtains the plant, which he calls "Man Becomes Young in Old Age." However, on the homeward journey, Gilgamesh stops for the night, and while he is bathing in a cool pool of water, a serpent snuffs the fragrance of the plant and carries it off. Immediately the serpent sheds its cast skin—a sure sign of the powers of the magic plant which Gilgamesh once had and has now lost.

Frustrated in his search, Gilgamesh returns to Uruk, the city from which he had set out on his useless quest. He now knows that "when the gods created mankind, death for mankind they set aside."

Although George Smith's tablets belonged to the seventh century, more recent research has demonstrated that the epic of Gilgamesh was composed shortly after 2000 B.C. by a Babylonian poet. The long life and the wide currency of the epic attest the vitality of this artistic statement of what may be called a pre-Greek philosophy.

CONFLICT AND CREATION

England's appetite for Babylonian legends had been whetted by George Smith's discovery of the story of the Flood on tablets which had come from the library of Ashurbanipal. The public did not have to wait long for an even more spectacular announcement from this youthful worker on the Ninevite tablets recovered by Layard, H.

Rassam, Loftus, and Smith himself. On March 4, 1875, a little over two years after his modest announcement of the Flood story, George Smith wrote a letter to his former patron, the *Daily Telegraph*, stating that he had recognized tablets of clay which "join or form parts of a continuous series of legends, giving the history of the world from the Creation down to some period after the Fall of Man."[22] A year later, Smith published a volume giving translations of the contents of about twenty fragments of the seven-tablet account of Creation.

These new discoveries were bound to give rise to religious controversy. A generation after the initial discoveries by Smith in England, a German Assyriologist, Friedrich Delitzsch, in 1902 was invited to give a private lecture, which he called "Babel and Bible," before the German Emperor at the Royal Palace in Berlin. In it, Delitzsch pointed to the similarities between biblical and Babylonian stories and emphasized the importance of Assyriology as a new tool for understanding the Bible. His purpose seems to have been to gain support for German expeditions into this field, which up until this time had been worked so successfully by the English and the French. He reminded the Emperor that it was "high time that Germany too should pitch her tent on the palm-crowned banks of the river of Paradise."[23]

As a result of the general interest in Assyrian discoveries and the extraordinary circumstance of the private lecture before the Emperor, the text was published far and wide, and "Babel and Bible" quickly became a subject of controversy not only in Germany but abroad. Typical of the storm of criticism which descended on Delitzsch was an article by the Rev. P. Wolff in the *Evangelische Kirkenzeitung*, for January 25, 1903, which ridiculed his pan-Babylonian views. "Following on the proofs which Delitzsch

22 George Smith, *The Chaldean Account of Genesis*, New York, 1876, p. 13.
23 F. Delitzsch, *Babel and Bible*, ed. C.H.W. Johns, New York, 1903, p. 71.

has already given," wrote Wolff, "we must expect that in his next Lecture he will point out that how profoundly inferior the views of Christendom regarding marriage are to the Babylonian, is shewn by the flight of the Saxon Crown-Princess. No Babylonian princess eloped with the tutor of her children."[24]

While many were concerned with the controversy and the irritation caused by Delitzsch's extreme and unguarded theological conclusions, a few scholars continued to search for pieces of tablets to fill in the breaks in the Babylonian account of Creation. In 1902, the same year of Delitzsch's controversial lecture, L. W. King succeeded in adding twenty-eight new fragments to the twenty-one which former scholars had utilized, and published a translation based on a total of forty-nine separate tablets and fragments. Since his day, new fragments recovered from excavations have made the recovery even more complete, although there are still gaps in the text of the Seven Tablets of Creation.

The Babylonian story of Creation is contained in a long poem which was recited in its entirety on the fourth day of the New Year's celebration each year. It begins with a picture of the earliest imaginable period of primordial time, when only the divine pair, Apsu, the fresh water, and Tiamat, the salt water, was existent. Nothing else had come into being.

> When on high the heaven had not been named,
> Firm ground below had not been called by name,
> Naught but primordial Apsu, their begetter,
> And Mummu-Tiamat, she who bore them all,
> Their waters commingling as a single body;
> No reed hut had been matted, no marsh land had
>   appeared,
> When no gods whatever had been brought into being,
> Uncalled by name, their destinies undetermined—
> Then it was that the gods were formed within them.[25]

[24] ibid., p. 224.   [25] ANET, 60-61.

In time, several generations of gods sprang from the first pair. Alienated from the older Apsu and Tiamat, the younger gods joined together, and, under the leadership of Ea, the wise earth- and water-god, succeeded in slaying the primordial Apsu, who had resolved to destroy his descendants. This act of violence the primordial Tiamat, the mother, determines to avenge by a well-planned attack on the gods. Much of the dramatic poem deals with the preparation for her attack and the choice and equipment of Marduk as a suitable champion to oppose this ancient goddess of the primordial chaos.

Fig. 63. The Babylonian god Marduk standing beside a horned demon, as portrayed on a piece of lapis lazuli found at Babylon.

Marduk, who was the principal god of the city of Babylon at the height of its power, is given the tokens of authority by the gods in assembly, which is described thus:

They held converse as they sat down to the banquet.
They ate festive bread, poured the wine,
They wetted their drinking-tubes with sweet intoxicant.

Fig. 64. An Assyrian god driving out a monster having a lion's head and body and the wings and claws of an eagle. This once stood at the door of a temple at Nimrud in about the ninth century B.C.

> As they drank the strong drink, their bodies swelled.
> They became very languid as their spirits rose.
> For Marduk, their avenger, they fixed the decrees.[26]

Having proclaimed Marduk's power, the gods then set a test to try it, a test which brings to mind the incident of the "fleece of wool" by which Gideon knew that he was chosen to save Israel from the Midianites.[27] The gods address Marduk:

> "Lord, truly thy decree is first among gods.
> Say but to wreck or create; it shall be.
> Open thy mouth: the cloth will vanish!
> Speak again, and the cloth will be whole!"
> At the word of his mouth the cloth vanished.
> He spoke again, and the cloth was restored.[28]

[26] *ANET*, 66.   [27] Judg. 6:36-40.   [28] *ANET*, 66.

187

FIG. 65. The god Ningirsu (or perhaps the king of Lagash) holds a net containing his captives. The Creation Epic recounts that the helpers of Tiamat were "thrown into the net, they found themselves ensnared." This is part of a stela from Tello, dating from the middle of the third millennium B.C.

Finally, the conflict between Tiamat and Marduk, for which much preparation had been made, began:

Then joined issue Tiamat and Marduk, wisest of gods.
They strove in single combat, locked in battle.
The lord spread out his net to enfold her,
The Evil Wind, which followed behind, he let loose
    in her face.
When Tiamat opened her mouth to consume him,
He drove in the Evil Wind that she close not her lips.
As the fierce winds charged her belly,
Her body was distended and her mouth was wide open.
He released the arrow, it tore her belly,
It cut through her insides, splitting the heart.
Having thus subdued her, he extinguished her life.

188

He cast down her carcass to stand upon it.
After he had slain Tiamat, the leader,
Her band was shattered, her troupe broken up;
And the gods, her helpers who marched at her side,
Trembling with terror, turned their backs about,
In order to save and preserve their lives.
Tightly encircled, they could not escape.
He made them captives and he smashed their weapons.
Thrown into the net, they found themselves ensnared;
Placed in cells, they were filled with wailing;
Bearing his wrath, they were held imprisoned.[29]

The dramatic triumph of the heroic Marduk over the villainous Tiamat and her band is a prelude to the process of creation. In the myth, the conflict is inseparable from creation, which follows immediately.

FIG. 66. An armed Hittite god, accompanied by another god, engages in combat with a serpent-dragon.

Two decades after Smith's announcement of the recovery of the Babylonian myth, Hermann Gunkel pointed out in a famous book, *Schöpfung und Chaos* (Creation and Chaos), that in the Bible there were some scattered references to a primeval conflict between Yahweh and mythological figures, bearing the names of Rahab, Leviathan, the dragon, and the serpent. The parallelism with Tiamat and

[29] *ANET*, 67.

"her helpers" is even more specific in that the "helpers of Rahab" are also mentioned, in Job 9:13, as bowing to Yahweh's anger. In Psalm 89:11, a song of praise is addressed to Yahweh in the words: "Thou didst crush Rahab, as one that is slain; Thou didst scatter Thine enemies with the arm of Thy strength." The dragon appears in a reference to the arm of Yahweh in Isaiah 51:9, where the poet asks: "Art thou not it that hewed Rahab in pieces, that pierced the dragon?" This same idea of the slaying of the monster appears, as we have seen above, in the literature from Ras Shamra, and may well be the prototype of the later legend of St. George and the Dragon. These pagan and mythological references to conflict, however, seem to have been scrupulously avoided by the author of the biblical account of Creation in the first chapter of Genesis.

When Marduk had vanquished the host of Tiamat, he turned to the rebellious goddess herself, whom he had bound up, and began the process of creation:

> The lord trod on the legs of Tiamat,
> With his unsparing mace he crushed her skull.
> When the arteries of her blood he had severed,
> The North Wind bore it to places undisclosed.
> On seeing this, his fathers were joyful and jubilant,
> They brought gifts of homage, they to him.
> Then the lord paused to view her dead body,
> That he might divide the monster and do artful works.
> He split her like a shellfish into two parts:
> Half of her he set up and ceiled it as sky,
> Pulled down the bar and posted guards.
> He bade them to allow not her waters to escape.
> He crossed the heavens and surveyed the regions.
> He squared Apsu's quarter, the abode of Nudimmud,
> As the lord measured the dimensions of Apsu.
> The Great Abode, its likeness, he fixed as Esharra,
> The Great Abode, Esharra, which he made as the firmament.

Anu, Enlil, and Ea he made occupy their places.
He constructed stations for the great gods,
Fixing their astral likenesses as constellations.
He determined the year by designating the zones:
He set up three constellations for each of the twelve
    months.
✧

In her belly he established the zenith.
The Moon he caused to shine, the night to him en-
    trusting.
He appointed him a creature of the night to signify
    the days:
✧

When Marduk hears the words of the gods,
His heart prompts him to fashion artful works.
Opening his mouth, he addresses Ea
To impart the plan he had conceived in his heart:
"Blood I will mass and cause bones to be.
I will establish a savage, 'man' shall be his name.
Verily, savage-man I will create.
He shall be charged with the service of the gods
    That they might be at ease! . . . ."[30]

The wise Ea suggests that one of the gods be handed
over as material for the creation of man. As they seek out
the most guilty among the forces of Tiamat, the gods reply:

"It was Kingu who contrived the uprising,
And made Tiamat rebel, and joined battle."
They bound him, holding him before Ea.
They imposed on him his guilt and severed his blood
    vessels.
Out of his blood they fashioned mankind.
He imposed the service and let free the gods.
After Ea, the wise, had created mankind,
Had imposed upon it the service of the gods—

[30] *ANET*, 67-68.

That work was beyond comprehension;
As artfully planned by Marduk, did Nudimmud create
    it— . . .[31]

Finally, after building a lofty shrine in Babylon, the gods
feast.

The great gods took their seats,
They set up festive drink, sat down to a banquet.
After they had made merry within it,
In Esagila, the splendid, had performed their rites,
The norms had been fixed and all their portents,
All the gods apportioned the stations of heaven and
    earth.[32]

The strongest link connecting this epic with the account
in the first chapter of Genesis is the order of events shared
by both. Before setting in parallel columns the correspondences, it must be pointed out that each contains elements
not shared by the other, such as the creation of animals,
fish, and fowl in Genesis, and the account of the building
of the temple of Esagila in the Babylonian story. But certain common elements in the two accounts can be matched
as follows:

BABYLONIAN	GENESIS
1. The primordial watery chaos of Tiamat and Apsu.	1. Existence of unformed earth and the deep.
2. Birth of Marduk, "Sun of the heavens."	2. Creation of light.
3. Fashioning of the sky from half of the body of Tiamat.	3. Creation of the firmament, the sky.
4. Squaring of Apsu's quarter (the earth?).	4. Gathering the water together to form the earth.
5. Setting up of the constellations.	5. Creation of lights in the firmament.
6. Making man for the service of the gods.	6. Creation of man to have dominion over animal life.
7. The divine banquet.	7. Resting of God on the seventh day.

[31] *ANET*, 68.

[32] *ANET*, 69.

The nature of the relationship between the account of Creation in Genesis and the Babylonian story, reaching back as it does into the early part of the second millennium B.C., is still far from certain. But the lengthy debate on the question, extending over eight decades, attests the importance of George Smith's discovery. No longer would one hold, as did Dr. John Lightfoot, vice-chancellor of the University of Cambridge, in the seventeenth century, that "heaven and earth, centre and circumference, were created all together, in the same instant, and clouds full of water," and that "this work took place and man was created by the Trinity on October 23, 4004 B.C., at nine o'clock in the morning."[33]

ADAPA'S LOST CHANCE FOR IMMORTALITY

If, as it seems from Smith's discovery of the Flood and the Creation stories, biblical writers knew the Babylonian traditions, how did the Hebrew writers learn of these legends of a distant culture and language? An answer was suggested, surprisingly enough, neither from Palestine nor from Mesopotamia, but by a discovery made far up the Nile.

In the fall of 1887—less than two decades after Smith's dramatic announcements—an Egyptian woman, living near Tell el-Amarna, about two hundred miles south of Cairo, found a cache of over three hundred clay tablets inscribed with strange characters. She proceeded to sell her discovery to a neighbor for 10 piasters. He in turn took them to the village and increased his investment a hundred fold by selling them for £10, it is reported. There, an official of the British Museum, E.A.W. Budge, was shown eighty-two of these tablets, which he quickly recognized as containing Babylonian cuneiform. He suggested an acceptable price, and they became the property of the British Museum.

[33] For this and similar views see A. D. White, *A History of the Warfare of Science with Theology in Christendom,* New York, 1899, vol. 1, p. 9.

The find could not long be kept a secret. An Egyptian who had come upon a particularly good specimen of these tablets—one about 20 inches long—hoping for a better market in a larger city, concealed it in his undergarments and proceeded to board the train for Cairo. But, as he stepped into the railway coach, the tablet slipped from his clothes, fell on the bed of the railway, and broke into many pieces. Villagers talked so freely of the poor man's misfortune that word of the discovery soon reached the ears of the Director of Antiquities, who set out to retrieve the collection, which by this time had fallen into many hands. His efforts served to accelerate the disposal of the loot, so that it was quickly scattered, never again to be collected—except in a publication twenty years later by the Norwegian Assyriologist J. A. Knudtzon.

Since the discovery in 1887, there have been achaeological excavations at Tell el-Amarna, but none has been as fortunate as that of the unknown Egyptian woman who made the first find of cuneiform tablets. Her collection is now scattered in London, Berlin, Paris, Istanbul, Leningrad, Brussels, Chicago, and New York, and, with the relatively meager discoveries of western archaeologists, the Tell el-Amarna documents now total approximately 377 tablets.

Cuneiformists were quick to see that this valuable collection of documents was a file of the Egyptian Foreign Office during the reigns of Amen-hotep III and Akh-en-Aton, the latter the highly individualistic and heretical Egyptian king who moved his capital from Thebes to Amarna and ruled his Asiatic empire from there. Letters from rulers in Byblos, Tyre, Megiddo, Gezer, Jerusalem, and other important towns, constitute a principal source for the history of Palestine and Syria during the early fourteenth century (see p. 75). It came as a surprise that the language of diplomatic correspondence between the Egyptian king and his governors in Syria and Palestine should

Fig. 67. King Akh-en-Aton and his wife Nefert-iti making an offering to the sun-god Aton. This bas-relief was once part of a balustrade of a temple at Tell el-Amarna, Akh-en-Aton's capital.

have been neither Canaanite nor Egyptian, but the Akkadian language (full of Canaanitisms) written in the
cuneiform script of Mesopotamia.

Among these letters was a text of an entirely different
nature: a portion of a myth already partly known from the
library of Ashurbanipal at Nineveh. How did this myth
become a part of the file? One can guess that it was a text
which had been used to teach Egyptian scribes how to
write Akkadian cuneiform correctly—possibly a "text-
book" written in Babylonia and brought to Egypt as a
model. Be that as it may, there is now no question as to
the wide diffusion of Babylonian mythological writings,
and one does not have to wonder any longer how people
in the intermediate area of Palestine could have been acquainted with cuneiform writings.

The text of the mythological tablet is of interest also for
the light it throws on some of the basic concepts underlying the story of "the fall of man" in the garden of Eden.
The principal character of the Babylonian myth is Adapa,
who, according to the text preserved from the Nineveh library, had been created by Ea, the patron god of Eridu.
"To him," the tablet reads, "he had given wisdom;
eternal life he had not given him."[34] Adapa's occupation
was to provide bread and fish for Ea's sanctuary at Eridu.
The tale, as we begin to read the tablet found in Egypt,
describes the capsizing of Adapa's fishing boat, his revenge
in breaking the wing of the "south wind," who had caused
the accident, and the consequent failure of the south wind
to blow over the land for a week. The lack of refreshing
breeze annoys the great god Anu, who summons Adapa to
heaven to account for his action:

The south wind blew and submerged him,
Causing him to go down to the home of the fish:
"South wind, . . . me all thy venom. . . .

[34] *ANET*, 101.

I will break thy wing!" Just as he said this with his
    mouth,
The wing of the south wind was broken. For seven
    days
The south wind blew not upon the land. Anu
Calls to Ilabrat, his vizier:
"Why has the south wind not blown over the land
    these seven days?"
His vizier, Ilabrat, answered him: "My lord,
Adapa, the son of Ea, the wing of the south wind
Has broken." When Anu heard this speech,
He cried, "Mercy!" Rising from his throne: "Let
    them fetch him hither!"[35]

Ea, the patron of Adapa, counsels him to seek by flattery
to ingratiate himself with the two gatekeepers, Tammuz
and Gizzida, and to refuse the food and drink which will
be offered him, for it will surely be the bread and the water
of death.

At that, Ea, he who knows what pertains to heaven,
    took hold of him,
Adapa, caused him to wear his hair unkempt, a
    mourning garb
He made him put on, and gave him this advice:
"Adapa, thou art going before Anu, the king;
The road to heaven thou wilt take. When to heaven
Thou hast gone up and hast approached the gate
    of Anu,
Tammuz and Gizzida at the gate of Anu
Will be standing. When they see thee, they will ask
    thee: 'Man,
For whom dost thou look thus? Adapa, for whom
Art thou clad with mourning garb?'
    'From our land two gods have disappeared,

[35] *ANET,* 101.

Hence I am thus.' 'Who are the two gods who from
    the land
Have disappeared?' 'Tammuz and Gizzida.' They
    will glance at each other
And will smile. A good word they
Will speak to Anu, and Anu's benign face
They will cause to be shown thee. As thou standest
    before Anu,
When they offer thee bread of death,
Thou shalt not eat it. When they offer thee water of
    death,
Thou shalt not drink it. When they offer thee a gar-
    ment,
Put it on. When they offer thee oil, anoint thyself
    therewith.
This advice that I have given thee, neglect not; the
    words
That I have spoken to thee, hold fast!" The mes-
    senger
Of Anu arrived there saying as follows: "Adapa the
    south wind's
Wing has broken, bring him before me!"[36]

The audience before Anu turns out to be as Ea has described it, but with one important exception: the proffered
food and drink are not the bread and water of death, but
of eternal life:

He made him take the road to heaven, and to heaven
    he went up.
When he had ascended to heaven and approached
    the gate of Anu,
Tammuz and Gizzida were standing at the gate of
    Anu.
When they saw Adapa, they cried, "Mercy!

[36] *ANET*, 101-102.

Man, for whom dost thou look thus? Adapa,
For whom art thou clad with mourning garb?"
"Two gods have disappeared from the land, there-
 fore with mourning garb
I am clad." "Who are the two gods who from the
 land have disappeared?"
"Tammuz and Gizzida." They glanced at each other
And smiled. As Adapa before Anu, the king,
Drew near and Anu saw him, he called:
"Come now, Adapa, wherefore the south wind's wing
Didst thou break?" Adapa replied to Anu: "My lord,
For the household of my master, in the midst of the
 sea
I was catching fish. The sea was like a mirror.
But the south wind came blowing and submerged me,
Causing me to go down to the home of the fish. In the
 wrath of my heart
I cursed the south wind." Speaking up at his side,
 Tammuz
And Gizzida to Anu a good word
Addressed. His heart quieted as he was . . .
"Why did Ea to a worthless human of the heaven
And of the earth the plan disclose,
Rendering him distinguished and making a name
 for him?
As for us, what shall we do about him? Bread of life
Fetch for him and he shall eat it." When the bread
 of life
They brought him, he did not eat; when the water
 of life
They brought him, he did not drink. When a garment
They brought him, he put it on; when oil
They brought him, he anointed himself therewith.
As Anu looked at him, he laughed at him:
"Come now, Adapa! Why didst thou neither eat nor
 drink?

Thou shalt not have eternal life! Ah, perverse
  mankind!"
  "Ea, my master,
Commanded me: 'Thou shalt not eat, thou shalt not
  drink.' "
"Take him away and return him to his earth."[37]

By heeding the advice of Ea, Adapa had missed his
chance to gain, in addition to wisdom, which he had been
given, the other prerogative of the gods, immortality. The
theme of this Babylonian myth, "man's squandered opportunity for gaining immortality," brings to mind the
Hebrew tradition of Adam, who was expelled from the
primeval garden "lest he put forth his hand, and take also
of the tree of life, and eat, and live for ever."[38]

The relationship between the stories of Adam and of
Adapa, although long debated, has never been determined
satisfactorily. Even though the Hebrew account of "the
fall" exhibits many distinctively Hebraic elements woven
firmly into its texture, few have failed to see striking and
basic elements which bear unmistakably the stamp of
Babylonian mythological thought. These elements the biblical writer used as a vehicle to serve his quite different
purposes. In both Adapa and Genesis there appears the
idea that the possession of wisdom and immortality by man
constitutes equality with the deity. In both, the man gets
the first, but misses the second. And in each narrative the
man is counseled by a supernatural voice to act in a course
which is contrary to his own interests, that of Ea in the one,
and the speech of the subtle serpent in the other. The idea
that man may obtain immortality by eating—the tree of
life in the one instance and the bread and water of life in
the other—is common to both.

Whatever the relationship of these two stories is, the discovery of this fragment of Babylonian mythology at Tell

el-Amarna makes clearer the pattern of ancient Near Eastern thought, which the Hebrew theologian knew and used. As early as the fourteenth century B.C., contacts existed between the widely-separated centers of Near Eastern culture.

FLOOD AND CREATION IN SUMER

In the last hundred years, the horizon of human history has been pushed back step by step to a remote antiquity. For many centuries Hebrew was considered, as Jerome called it, "the beginning of all human speech." But this notion of the antiquity of the Hebrew language disappeared with the discoveries of the nineteenth century, and the uniqueness of the Hebrew views of the primeval history of the Flood and of Creation also disappeared upon the discovery of the clay tablets in the famous library of Ashurbanipal at Nineveh. Soon the seventh-century Assyrian copies of these traditions were discovered to rest on versions earlier by a thousand years, texts written in the Old Babylonian period. More recently, even this early stage in the transmission of the familiar biblical cosmological ideas has been superseded by the discovery of the literature of a people who preceded the Semites of the Old Babylonian period in Mesopotamia. They were the Sumerians, a remarkably creative people who first—as far as we know at present—invented writing.

In terms of chronology, the Sumerian culture prevailed in lower Mesopotamia throughout a good part of the third millennium B.C. The language, written in a cuneiform script, was completely unlike the linguistic family to which Hebrew and Babylonian belonged. The Semitic invaders of Babylonia had borrowed the script of the Sumerians and had made it their own. Not only did the newcomers adopt the practice of writing with a stylus on clay tablets, but more specifically they took over myths and epic tales from those who had lived longer in the land. Frequently the

Fig. 68. Dudu, a Sumerian scribe from about the
twenty-fifth century B.C.

borrowers substituted their own gods—or at least the Semitic names for Sumerian gods—and translated the myths
and epics into their own Semitic language.

A good example of this borrowing is the Flood story.
Long known from the Hebrew version in Genesis, later
recognized in the Assyrian version of the eleventh tablet
of the Gilgamesh epic, and even later traced back by fragments of certain elements to the Old Babylonian period,
the story has recently been found written in Sumerian, a
language which antedates both Assyrian and Babylonian.

The clay tablet which contains the earliest account of
the Flood came from the first American excavation of a Sumerian site in Mesopotamia, the University of Pennsylvania's excavation at Nippur. Through four long campaigns, extending over the years 1889 to 1900, the excavators of Nippur were successful in recovering approximately
30,000 tablets and fragments—most of them written in the
Sumerian language. For over fifty years this remarkably
rich library of Sumerian materials—unfortunately split up
into three collections, one in Philadelphia, another in
Istanbul, and a third in Jena, Eastern Germany—has provided the source for much of our knowledge of Sumerian
mythology, as these tablets have gradually been copied and
translated. And yet, after more than a half century, scholars
are still "unearthing" a wealth of new material from these
collections long buried in museums.

The translation of the Sumerian flood story did not appear until fourteen years after the last of the four early
seasons of excavation at Nippur. In this version the hero of
the Flood is Ziusudra, the prototype of the biblical Noah
and of the Akkadian Utnapishtim. Ziusudra, a pious and
god-fearing king, stands by a wall, where he learns of the
decree of the gods "to destroy the seed of mankind." From
a fragmentary text, we can read of events with which we
are already familiar from later versions:

All the windstorms, exceedingly powerful, attacked
   as one,
At the same time, the flood sweeps over the cult-
   centers.
After, for seven days and seven nights,
The flood had swept over the land,
And the huge boat had been tossed about by the
   windstorms on the great waters,
Utu came forth, who sheds light on heaven and
   earth.
Ziusudra opened a window of the huge boat,
The hero Utu brought his rays into the giant boat.
Ziusudra, the king,
Prostrated himself before Utu,
The king kills an ox, slaughters a sheep.[39]

Allusions to Creation are also found in the earlier Sumerian mythology. The picture of the beginning is of a
primordial period when both heaven and earth were
united in a cosmic mountain. By the action of the air-god
Enlil, a separation was made between these two elements,
and man was created. As an introduction to an ancient
Sumerian poem puts it:

After heaven had been moved away from earth,
After earth had been separated from heaven,
After the name of man had been fixed;
After An had carried off heaven,
After Enlil had carried off the earth.[40]

Another Sumerian myth describes a paradise, the land
of Dilmun, which is pure, clean, and bright, where "the
lion kills not, the wolf snatches not the lamb."[41] In this
story there have been seen motifs which are parallel to

[39] *ANET*, 44.
[40] S. N. Kramer, *Sumerian Mythology*, Philadelphia, 1944, p. 37.
[41] *ANET*, 38.

those of the biblical paradise described in chapters 2 and 3 of Genesis.

In the new era which George Smith's brilliant discoveries in 1872 inaugurated, and which was carried on by scores of cuneiformists, views of the uniqueness of the plots of certain early Hebrew stories have fallen into discard—but not without bitter controversy—and have been replaced by a newer perspective. This new view, gained through the recovery of Assyrian, Old Babylonian, and Sumerian mythology, makes it possible to see more clearly the particular contribution which Hebrew writers made in their exposition of a truly radical monotheistic faith. What had once been taken blindly as factual history has, in the light of the last century of discovery and decipherment, been seen as the basic idiom of the world view of the ancient Near East, a system of cosmology truly authentic and indigenous to the world to which the Hebrew writers belonged.

CHAPTER 6

LAW AND WISDOM

HAMMURABI, THE KING OF JUSTICE

RARELY IN THE ANNALS OF ARCHAEOLOGY has the excavator been able to oblige his colleague the philologist by producing from the earth the very monument which the latter had suspected to have been in existence. One such extraordinary case was the discovery of the three large pieces of the famous Code of Hammurabi at Susa in December 1901 and January 1902 by Jacques de Morgan.

On the basis of the publication a few years earlier of clay tablets containing laws from the Old Babylonian period, Friedrich Delitzsch, in his famous lecture of 1902, "Babel and Bible," said: "After Hammurabi had succeeded in driving out of the country the Elamites. . . his first care was to enforce uniform laws throughout the land. He therefore prepared a great code which defined the civil law in all its branches."[1] Although Delitzsch did not then know it, the French had already discovered just such a "great code."

Credit for the finding of the Code of Hammurabi, which has thrown more light on life in ancient Babylonia than any other single monument, belongs to Jacques de Morgan. Trained as a mining engineer—he had mined gold in Transylvania and copper in the Caucasus Mountains—de Morgan had been drawn into the fields of geology and paleontology. At the age of thirty-four he was appointed as director of the Service des Antiquités in Egypt. While in Egypt he pursued his interest in the prehistoric periods and made such a contribution that it was later said, "it was

[1] *Babel and Bible*, ed. C. H. W. Johns, New York, 1903, pp. 34-35.

Jacques de Morgan who really created the prehistory of Egypt."[2]

FIG. 69. Air view of the mound of ancient Susa, where the stela of Hammurabi was found by de Morgan in 1901-02. The French have excavated here for over forty years.

After a few years in Egypt, de Morgan moved into yet another field of activity. In 1897, the French government organized the famous Délégation en Perse, having previously obtained from Nassr ed-Din, Shah of Persia, the exclusive right to carry on archaeological research in that country. The French Parliament generously alloted 100,-000 francs as an initial credit, and a sum of 130,000 francs as an annual payment to support the work. With this backing from the French government and with a staff of celebrated scholars, de Morgan began on December 18, 1897

[2] *L'Anthropologie*, vol. 34, 1924, p. 468.

FIG. 70. Part of the stela of Hammurabi, showing the laws inscribed in cuneiform. (cf. FIG. 61.)

to excavate the Elamite capital at Susa, the Shushan of the biblical Books of Esther and Daniel (Fig. 69).

The most famous of his many important discoveries at Susa was the finding of three large pieces of black diorite on which were inscribed about 250 laws of Hammurabi, one of the best known kings of Babylonia. The pieces were easily put together to form an impressive monument, which stood 7 feet 5 inches high, and which was covered with columns of cuneiform script (Fig. 70) and a scene of the king standing before the god Shamash (see Fig. 61).

Although it was no surprise that such a code of Baby-lonian laws existed, it was astonishing that it was found not within the bounds of ancient Babylonia, or in fact at the ancient Sippar, where it probably once stood, but far away in Susa—a distance from Sippar of some 230 miles as the crow flies. How did the monument get there? The best guess seems to be that an Elamite king, Shutruk-nahhunte, who is known to have raided Babylonia some five hundred years after the time of Hammurabi, carried off this im-pressive monument and other trophies as loot on the oc-casion of one of his raids. The guess is made plausible by the discovery of other Babylonian monuments at Susa which have the original inscription erased and an addition of texts of Shutruk-nahhunte engraved in its place. In fact, the Hammurabi monument itself has lost from five to seven columns of text at the bottom of the front side through erasure. Yet the defacer of this public monument did not replace the erased text with an inscription of the famous Elamite raider. Well might the curse which Ham-murabi wrote at the end of his laws have given pause to the Elamite king or his servant. It warns menacingly: "If that man did not heed my words which I wrote on my stela, and disregarded my curses . . . has altered my statutes, effaced my name inscribed (thereon), and has written his own name, (or) he has commissioned another (to do so) because of these curses—as for that man, whether king or lord, or governor or person of any rank, may the mighty Anum, the father of the gods, who proclaimed my reign, deprive him of the glory of sovereignty, may he break his scepter, may he curse his fate!"[3]

The speed with which this important document was published in scientific form was due largely to the choice by Jacques de Morgan of a brilliant Assyriologist, Père Jean Vincent Scheil, as a member of the team of the Délégation. So familiar was Scheil with cuneiform texts that he required only three months to translate and publish the famous Code of Hammurabi. By the end of the year 1902, less than one year after the discovery, the *editio princeps* of the Code had appeared in a folio volume of the *Mémoires* of the Délégation en Perse. This publication is an enduring monument to the genius, competence, and dispatch of Père Scheil.

The laws themselves are preceded by a lengthy prologue, in which Hammurabi, in the first person singular and with no false modesty, tells of his efforts as the wise shepherd of the people to make law prevail in his land and to promote the general welfare. To this task he has been called by the gods:

At that time Anum and Enlil named me
to promote the welfare of the people,
me, Hammurabi, the devout, god-fearing prince,
to cause justice to prevail in the land,
to destroy the wicked and the evil,
that the strong might not oppress the weak,
to rise like the sun over the black-headed people,
and to light up the land.[4]

In an epilogue, even more prolix than the prologue, the king recounts in verse the achievements of his reign in the promoting of the welfare of the land. That the strong might not oppress the weak and that justice might be dealt

---

[3] *ANET*, 178-179.   [4] *ANET*, 164.

the orphan and the widow, he said, "I wrote my precious words on my stela, and in the presence of the statue of me, the king of justice, I set it up in order to administer the law of the land, to prescribe the ordinances of the land, to give justice to the oppressed."[5]

From this epilogue we have a hint that the stela was inscribed and set up in a public place to serve more for the reassurance of the common man than as a source of reference for judges in deciding cases of law. Said Hammurabi, the king of justice:

Let any oppressed man who has a cause
come into the presence of the statue of me, the king
   of justice,
and then read carefully my inscribed stela,
and give heed to my precious words,
and may my stela make the case clear to him;
may he understand his cause;
may he set his mind at ease!
. . . .
I, Hammurabi, am the king of justice,
to whom Shamash committed law.
My words are choice; my deeds have no equal;
it is only to the fool that they are empty. . . .[6]

The more than 250 laws—the erased portion can be partly restored from legal texts found on clay tablets containing copies of the laws—which appear between the prologue and the epilogue constitute an important source for our knowledge of daily life in Babylonia at the time corresponding to the age of the Hebrew patriarchs. In Babylonian society there were three classes of citizens: the class composed of free men, the seigniors; the class of the commoners; and the slaves. The rights and responsibilities of each are fixed in the laws.

While the collection of laws has frequently been referred

[5] *ANET*, 178.   [6] *ANET*, 178.

to as a "code," it is apparent on careful scrutiny that some situations which would certainly have presented themselves in the daily life of ancient Babylonia are not covered at all. This observation has led to the recognition that Hammurabi's laws may not have been a statement of the common law of the time but rather a compilation of amendments to the existing law of the land.[7]

FIG. 71. A cuneiform tablet with its envelope. Thousands of these tablets have been found containing accounts of legal and business transactions.

The collection opens with laws dealing with the administration of justice, cases of unproved accusation, false testimony, and dishonest judges. Evidence for transactions, in the form of written contracts attested by witnesses, is

[7] G. R. Driver and John C. Miles, *The Babylonian Laws*, vol. 1, Oxford, 1952, pp. 41-45.

required for determining whether a man is the rightful owner of property or a thief. "If a seignior has purchased or he received for safekeeping either silver or gold or a male slave or a female slave or an ox or a sheep or an ass or any sort of thing from the hand of a seignior's son or a seignior's slave without witnesses and contracts, since that seignior is a thief, he shall be put to death."[8] This requirement for the documentation of business transactions accounts for the thousands of Babylonian business documents on clay tablets, many of which have found their way into museums around the world.

A longer collection of laws deals with offenses against property: theft of the property of the church or state, of property received for safekeeping, kidnapping—punishable by death—theft of a slave, and the harboring of a fugitive slave. The housebreaker is to be put to death in front of the breach which he has made and to be walled in. In case of a fire, the man who went to extinguish it and "cast his eye on the goods of the owner of the house," and appropriated them shall be thrown into the fire.[9]

In a feudal society, such as that which prevailed in the time of Hammurabi, laws about the tenure of fiefs, obligations of tenant farmers, and debts of farmers were necessary. Offenses connected with irrigation, sheep-herding, the cultivation of orchards and palm groves were defined. An obvious sense of fairness is evidenced by the law dealing with an irrigator's negligence which results in damage to a neighbor's field: "If a seignior, upon opening his canal for irrigation, became so lazy that he has let the water ravage a field adjoining his, he shall measure out grain on the basis of those adjoining his."[10]

Trade and commerce were regulated. Interest on both grain and money seems to have been charged at the rate of 20 per cent. The dealings of the traveling salesman who peddled his wares were subject to fixed laws. Retail trade

8 *ANET,* 166, §7.   9 *ANET,* 167, §25.   10 *ANET,* 168, §55.

in wine, carried on by women, had in the past been the source of injustice, and perhaps vice, to judge from the drafting of three laws which bear penalties of water ordeal, death, and burning for the offending woman:

> If a woman wine seller, instead of receiving grain for the price of a drink, has received money by the large weight and so has made the value of the drink less than the value of the grain, they shall prove it against that wine seller and throw her into the water.

> If outlaws have congregated in the establishment of a woman wine seller and she has not arrested those outlaws and did not take them to the palace, that wine seller shall be put to death.

> If a hierodule, a nun, who is not living in a convent, has opened the door of a wineshop or has entered a wineshop for a drink, they shall burn that woman.[11]

A man in debt might sell himself, his wife, his son, or his daughter into slavery for three years, but freedom must be reestablished in the fourth year;[12] in Hebrew laws freedom must be granted after six years of service.[13]

A considerable section of the collection is devoted to laws on marriage, family, and property. Regulated by law are such matters as slander, adultery, remarriage of a woman whose husband is long absent, and divorce. A man with a diseased wife, if he marries another wife, must continue to support the former wife as long as she lives.[14] The murderer of a husband, "they shall impale" on stakes.[15] Incest, inheritance, disinheritance (only after the judges have investigated the case), marriage of a sacral woman, adoption, and the nursing of infants are all provided for.

Two laws dealing with slander within the family are designed to protect both the woman and her husband:

11 *ANET*, 170 §§108-110.   12 *ANET*, 170-171, §117.
13 Ex. 21:2 and Deut. 15:12-18.   14 *ANET*, 172, §148.
15 *ANET*, 172, §153.

214

If a woman so hated her husband that she has declared, "You may not have me," her record shall be investigated at her city council, and if she was careful and was not at fault, even though her husband has been going out and disparaging her greatly, that woman, without incurring any blame at all, may take her dowry and go off to her father's house.[16]

If she was not careful, but was a gadabout, thus neglecting her house and humiliating her husband, they shall throw that woman into the water.[17]

Surgeon's fees for major operations on each of the three classes of society are set by law on the ratio of 10:5:2; penalties are imposed on a surgeon for failure in an operation. The builders of houses and of boats are held responsible to make their work strong and to make good any loss arising from poor workmanship. Other laws deal with agriculture, wages, rates, and slaves.

FIVE CODES OF CUNEIFORM LAW

During the first twenty years after the beginning of the new epoch which the discovery of the Code of Hammurabi inaugurated, other sizeable collections of laws from the ancient Near East made their appearance. They were not monumentally engraved on stelae but written on clay tablets, and were later in date than the impressive monument of black diorite of the Hammurabi period. Jacques de Morgan's famous stela from Susa remained the oldest and most extensive collection of ancient laws.

The Germans, who excavated at Ashur from 1903 to 1914, found tablets from the time of Tiglath-pileser I, king of Assyria in the twelfth century, B.C., containing what have come to be known as the "Middle Assyrian Laws." By 1920 these texts had been published.[18] A year later the Hittite laws, written in cuneiform, but not in the Se-

---

[16] *ANET*, 172, §142. [17] *ANET*, 172, §143.
[18] *Keilschrifttexte aus Assur verschiedenen Inhalts*, ed. O. Schroeder.

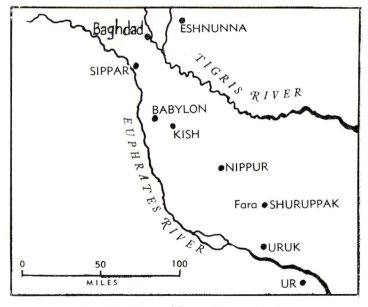

Fig. 72. Cities of lower Mesopotamia.

mitic language of Babylonia and Assyria, were published and soon afterwards translated. This new legal material, along with a wealth of clay tablets containing records of cases actually tried by the judges, provided the source for a detailed investigation of cuneiform law in the ancient Near East, extending from the time of Hammurabi onward, and over the wide area from Elam in the east to Anatolia in the west.[19] Numerous points of contact with biblical laws became apparent.

For almost a half century—forty-five years, to be exact—the Code of Hammurabi was the oldest known law code. But in 1947, an earlier code—older by a century and a half—was discovered, and in another five years two other pre-Hammurabi codes came to light, pushing back the evidence for codified cuneiform law to a point sometime before 2000 B.C. Thus, in a brief half century the horizon of an-

[19] A. Goetze, *Journal of the American Oriental Society*, vol. 69, 1949, p. 116.

cient Near Eastern law had been extended farther than men had ever dreamed in the nineteenth century.

The discovery that Hammurabi was not the first lawgiver came when Francis R. Steele, while making a catalogue of cuneiform tablets in the University Museum in Philadelphia, came upon four fragments which belonged to a single tablet, 11 by 9 inches in size, which had originally had ten columns of text on each side. The fragments had actually been "discovered" at Nippur, in southern Babylonia, several years before de Morgan's finding of the Code of Hammurabi. For half a century they had remained on museum shelves unread and unrecognized for what they were, parts of a Sumerian law code from the time of King Lipit-Ishtar of Isin. So fragmentary and so unprepossessing were they that they had been completely overlooked.

By carefully piecing together the fragments and by utilizing other pieces which had previously been published, Steele found that the tablet had originally contained not only a collection of laws—thirty-eight of which could be read in whole or in part—but that, like the Code of Hammurabi, the collection had been preceded by a prologue and followed by an epilogue. The similarity was even closer when the contents of the two were compared.

In the earlier code, as in Hammurabi, Lipit-Ishtar is called the "wise shepherd," whom Anu and Enlil had called "to the princeship of the land in order to establish justice in the land, to banish complaints, to turn back enmity and rebellion by the force of arms, and to bring well-being to the Sumerians and Akkadians."[20] Similarly, in the epilogue there is a correspondence in the curse which Lipit-Ishtar utters on him "who will commit some evil deed with regard to it, who will damage my handiwork, who will enter the storeroom and change its pedestal, who will erase its inscription, who will write his own name upon it or who, because of this curse, will substitute someone else for himself. . . ."[21] Furthermore, the mention of the "pedestal"

[20] *ANET,* 159.   [21] *ANET,* 161.

and the phrase, "I erected this stela," suggest that the law code which we chance to possess on a clay tablet was originally a monument like the stela of Hammurabi.

The laws of Lipit-Ishtar treat such subjects as hiring of boats, real estate, slaves, defaulting on taxes, inheritance and marriage, and rented oxen. Some of the laws find their almost exact parallel in the later code of Hammurabi; others are unique.

A second pre-Hammurabi collection of laws was published in 1948 by Albrecht Goetze. The new material is contained on two cuneiform tablets excavated by the Iraqi archaeologist Sayid Taha Baqir at the modern Tell Abu Harmal, a town which once belonged to the kingdom of Eshnunna, which flourished between the downfall of the Third Dynasty of Ur and the beginning of the Hammurabi period.[22]

After a short and poorly-preserved preamble, there appear sixty laws dealing with a wide variety of subjects. It has been estimated that all but about a quarter of these laws are reproduced more or less directly in the Hammurabi collection.[23] Some deal with totally different subjects, however. For example, the owner of a vicious dog, provided he has been warned by the authorities, is responsible for the injury done by the dog: "If a dog is vicious and the authorities have brought the fact to the knowledge of its owner, if nevertheless he does not keep it in, it bites a man and causes his death, then the owner of the dog shall pay two-thirds of a mina of silver."[24] But the principle of which this is an application is found in the later code.

One of the original features of this collection of laws of Eshnunna is that it begins with a statement of prices for certain basic commodities such as barley, oil, wool, salt, and copper, in terms of a silver standard. A list of wages follows. Thus it seems, as Albrecht Goetze has pointed out in his final publication of the text, that the legislator was

[22] A. Goetze, *The Laws of Eshnunna*, New Haven, 1956, pp. 1-4.
[23] G. R. Driver and John C. Miles, *The Babylonian Laws*, vol. 1, p. 9.
[24] *ANET*, 163, §56.

aware that fixed wages do not mean anything unless prices are likewise regulated.[25] Probably the prices of the several basic items of trade are the "ceiling prices" in the kingdom governed by the king of Eshnunna.

Exactly a half century after the discovery of the stela of Hammurabi at Susa, Samuel N. Kramer, while copying tablets in the Museum of the Ancient Orient in Istanbul, turned up a fragment of a code of King Ur-Nammu, who lived about three hundred years before Hammurabi. During the winter of 1952, Kramer received a letter from a former curator of the tablet collection at Istanbul calling his attention to a badly-broken tablet classified as a school tablet, but which he had long before thought to be a legal text. "If you have time," his friend wrote, "just try and copy it, it is badly broken."[26]

Kramer found the time, and soon saw that the Sumerian text contained a prologue and fragments of about seven laws, which had been promulgated, according to the prologue, by the famous King Ur-Nammu, the first king of the Third Dynasty of Ur, who began his reign about 2060 B.C. In the prologue, Ur-Nammu is described as the divinely appointed king of Ur, who established justice in the land and turned back evil and violence, and abolished "those who forcefully seized the oxen, seized the sheep, seized the donkeys."[27] He regulated, so it seems from the prologue, the weights and measures of the land in the interest of fair trade and instituted social reforms so that "the orphan was not given over to the rich, the widow was not given over to the powerful, the man of 1 shekel was not given over to the man of mina [i.e. 60 shekels]."[28]

The laws which remain on this badly-damaged tablet seem to deal with orchards, irrigation, witchcraft, fugitive slaves, and personal injuries, for which fines are imposed.

[25] A. Goetze, *The Laws of Eshnunna*, p. 32.
[26] *Orientalia*, vol. 23, 1954, p. 40.
[27] *Orientalia*, vol. 23, p. 46.
[28] *Orientalia*, vol. 23, p. 47.

FIG. 73. King Ur-Nammu of Ur, the promulgator of the oldest known law
code. In the upper register Ur-Nammu stands before a deity; in the second
register the king is twice shown in the act of offering a libation to a deity;
in third register the king carries a basket and surveying and building
instruments.

Most if not all the laws have their analogues in one or another of the codes from later periods.

While the general chronological relationship between the six cuneiform codes—Ur-Nammu, Eshnunna, Lipit-Ishtar, Hammurabi, Hittite, and Middle Assyrian—is relatively simple, the questions of borrowings and dependence are so involved and intricate that no clear-cut answer has yet emerged as to the genetic relationship between them. And when one asks what relationship the Hebrew laws of the Bible have to one or all of the cuneiform collections, very little can be said beyond the fact that there are certain correspondences and a number of differences.

Nevertheless the recent recovery of a half dozen codes older than the legal portions of the Bible is not without significance for an understanding of the biblical materials. The new discoveries in the field of ancient Near Eastern law have provided a perspective for study, interpretation, and evaluation of certain cultural and legal concepts, as well as of particular provisions, which is of great significance for the study of biblical law. The modern student is aware, as the student of a half century ago was not, of the intricate nature of the problems involved. We shall consider laws on four subjects—personal injury, rape, the goring ox, and deposited goods—to illustrate points of comparison and contrast.

Well known is the principle of Hebrew law called *lex talionis*, the law of retaliation, by which a similar injury is inflicted on the one who has produced the injury. In Exodus it is stated, "eye for eye, tooth for tooth, hand for hand, foot for foot, burning for burning, wound for wound, stripe for stripe,"[29] and in Leviticus, "and if a man maim his neighbour; as he hath done, so shall it be done to him."[30] This principle has generally been regarded as primitive, and consequently as representative of an early stage in the development of law.

29 Ex. 21:24-25. 30 Lev. 24:19.

In the Code of Hammurabi the law of retaliation also appears, where it applies to injuries inflicted by a man of the aristocracy, the seignior, upon another member of the same class:

> If a seignior has destroyed the eye of a member of the aristocracy, they shall destroy his eye.
>
> If he has broken another seignior's bone, they shall break his bone.
>
> . . . .
>
> If a seignior has knocked out a tooth of a seignior of his own rank, they shall knock out his tooth.[31]

These two points of view with regard to justice, that in the biblical codes and the principle of the Code of Hammurabi, seem remarkably close. In the Hittite Code, however, where similar injuries are specifically mentioned, a monetary fine has been substituted for the harsher retaliatory measure. The set penalties are preserved in two forms, an early and a later version:

> If anyone blinds a free man or knocks out his teeth, they would formerly give 1 mina [i.e. 60 shekels] of silver, now he shall give 20 shekels of silver and pledge his estate as security.
>
> If anyone blinds a free man in a quarrel, he shall give 1 mina of silver. If only his hand does wrong, he shall give 20 shekels of silver. . . .—If anyone knocks out the teeth of a free man, in case he knocks out 2 teeth or 3 teeth, he shall give 12 shekels of silver. . . .[32]

Since the Hittite laws are later than Hammurabi, one might be led to assume that in time the harsher provision of the *lex talionis* in the earlier period had given way to a more lenient attitude toward personal injury. But on

[31] *ANET*, 175, §§196, 197, 200.
[32] *ANET*, 189, §7, later version of §7 and §8.

looking at the pre-Hammurabi laws dealing with similar injuries, one finds the principle of imposing fines as penalties for injuries to the person. In the laws of Eshnunna the injuries are succinctly listed with the appropriate payments:

FIG. 74. Hittites, as depicted by the Egyptians of the time of Ramses II (1290-1224 B.C.). The shaved face and the long, curved nose are characteristic.

If a man bites the nose of another man and severs it, he shall pay 1 mina of silver. For an eye he shall pay 1 mina of silver; for a tooth ½ mina; for an ear ½ mina; for a slap in the face 10 shekels of silver.

If a man severs another man's finger, he shall pay 2/3 of a mina of silver.

If a man throws another man to the floor in an altercation and breaks his hand, he shall pay ½ mina of silver.

If he breaks his foot, he shall pay ½ mina of silver.[33]

When we turn to the oldest collection of laws, the Ur-Nammu Code, we find preserved in this Sumerian compilation set monetary payments for these offenses of personal injury, but in different amounts. Compensation for breaking a foot is 10 shekels, for severing a bone of another man a payment of 1 mina of silver is required, while "if a man

[33] *ANET*, 163, §§42-45.

has cut off with an . . . -instrument the . . . 'nose' of another man he shall pay 2/3 mina of silver."[34]

Hebrew law agrees in principle with Hammurabi; while Hittite, Eshnunna, and Ur-Nammu are similar in that they prescribe fines or compensation which are to be paid, to the injured person presumably.

In a comparative study of ancient Near Eastern laws, one law may make clear the reason for an analogous provision in another code where the law is less explicit. In the Hittite Code there appears a law having to do with rape in two different circumstances: "If a man seizes a woman in the mountains, it is the man's crime and he will be killed. But if he seizes her in her house, it is the woman's crime and the woman shall be killed."[35]

The reason for the difference in the responsibility in these two circumstances, the one in the mountain and the other in the town, becomes clear from the law concerning rape in the Book of Deuteronomy:

> If there be a damsel that is a virgin betrothed unto a man, and a man find her in the city, and lie with her; then ye shall bring them both out unto the gate of that city, and ye shall stone them with stones that they die: the damsel, because she cried not, being in the city. . . . But if the man find the damsel that is betrothed in the field, and the man take hold of her, and lie with her; then the man only that lay with her shall die. But unto the damsel thou shalt do nothing. . . . For he found her in the field; the betrothed damsel cried, and there was none to save her.[36]

In each of these laws the woman, whether married as in the Hittite Code, or engaged as in Deuteronomy, is given the benefit of any doubt which may have arisen over her

34 *Orientalia*, vol. 23, p. 48.
35 *ANET*, 196, §197.
36 Deut. 22:23-27.

willingness to become involved in an illegal act committed in the field or the mountain.

However, in the earlier codes of Hammurabi and of Eshnunna which deal with the case of the rape of a betrothed virgin—the case mentioned in Deuteronomy—the death penalty is prescribed for the man only. The law on the Hammurabi stela reads: "If a seignior bound the betrothed wife of another seignior, who had had no intercourse with a male and was still living in her father's house, and he has lain in her bosom and they have caught him, that seignior shall be put to death, while that woman shall go free."[37]

Similarly, the Eshnunna law states: "If a man gives bride-money for another man's daughter, but another man seizes her forcibly without asking the permission of her father and her mother and deprives her of her virginity, it is a capital offence and he shall die."[38]

A striking contrast is to be seen between two codes of cuneiform law and the biblical law, with regard to the penalty imposed on the owner of an ox, known to be dangerous, which kills a man. The two earlier cuneiform codes require a monetary payment, while the later Hebrew code sets death as the penalty for the owner of the offending animal. It is of interest that the drafting of the law in each of these three cases is strikingly similar.

The law of Eshnunna states:

> If an ox is known to gore habitually and the authorities have brought the fact to the knowledge of its owner, but he does not have his ox dehorned, it gores a man and causes his death, then the owner of the ox shall pay 2/3 of a mina of silver.[39]

In the Code of Hammurabi, the monetary compensation to be paid, presumably to the deceased man's family, is less:

37 *ANET*, 171, §130.   38 *ANET*, 162, §26.
39 *ANET*, 163, §54.

If a seignior's ox was a gorer and his city council made it known to him that it was a gorer, but he did not pad its horns or tie up his ox, and that ox gored to death a member of the aristocracy, he shall give ½ mina of silver.[40]

The law found in Exodus 21:29 specifies in the analogous situation that both the ox and the owner shall be put to death:

> But if the ox was wont to gore in time past, and warning hath been given to its owner, and he hath not kept it in, but it hath killed a man or a woman; the ox shall be stoned, and its owner also shall be put to death.

In the laws of Eshnunna there are two sections dealing with the case of the theft of property which has been given on deposit. Lacking evidence for burglary, the depositary is considered the thief. But in case the depositary has also lost some of his own property, either through the burglarizing of the house or its collapse, and declares so under oath, he is free of the responsibility to the depositor. The law reads:

> If a man gives property of his as a deposit to . . . and if the property he gives disappears without that the house was burglarized, the *sippu* [i.e., part of the house at or near the door] broken down or the window forced, he [the depositary] will replace his [the depositor's] property.
>
> If the man's [the depositary's] house either collapses or is burglarized and together with the property of the depositor which he gave him loss on the part of the owner of the house is incurred, the owner of the house shall swear him an oath in the gate of Tishpak [main god of Eshnunna] saying: "Together with your property my property was lost; I have done nothing improper or

[40] *ANET*, 176, §251.

fraudulent." If he swears him such an oath, he shall have no claim against him.[41]

The analogue in the Code of Hammurabi confuses the two principles of the Eshnunna law, the element of negligence and the simultaneous loss of property on the part of the owner of the house, in the following statement:

> If a seignior deposited property of his for safekeeping and at the place where he made the deposit his property has disappeared along with the property of the owner of the house, either through breaking in or through scaling the wall, the owner of the house, who was so careless that he let whatever was given to him for safekeeping get lost, shall make it good and make restitution to the owner of the goods, while the owner of the house shall make a thorough search for his lost property and take it from its thief.[42]

The law in this same situation found in Exodus might be said to be the most primitive. The clearance of the depositary from guilt, when no thief can be found, rests entirely on an oath or ordeal before God.

> If a man deliver unto his neighbour money or stuff to keep, and it be stolen out of the man's house; if the thief be found, he shall pay double. If the thief be not found, then the master of the house shall come near unto God, to see whether he have not put his hand unto his neighbour's goods.[43]

These few samples of the available material for a comparative study of four subjects of biblical law will suffice, I think, to illustrate the remarkable enrichment of understanding of ancient Near Eastern law in a little more than a half-century of discovery. No longer does the study of biblical law stand in sacred isolation.

[41] *ANET*, 163, §§36-37.   [42] *ANET*, 171, §125.   [43] Ex. 22:6-7.

ALL THE WISDOM OF EGYPT

A biblical writer described the great wisdom of King Solomon as excelling "all the wisdom of Egypt." What this claim implied could only have been guessed before the decipherment of Egyptian hieroglyphs and the recovery of the papyri on which the Egyptian wise men wrote their sayings. Now, however, the aptness of the reference to the wisdom of Egypt is documented by a wealth of instructions and precepts which attests the reputation which Egypt had for this type of literature.

The oldest example of Egyptian wisdom is a collection of wise sayings from about fifteen hundred years before the time of Solomon. It bears the name of Ptah-hotep, the vizier of a king of the Fifth Dynasty, and is addressed to his son, who is to succeed him as the king's chief counselor. Having reached the ideal age of one hundred and ten years,[44] Ptah-hotep looked back on a long and successful life in the king's service. What he had learned about wisdom and about the rules of good speech, he offered to his son. "There is no one born wise,"[45] he reminded him.

This document, like many of the proverbs in the Bible, is a guide for success. The chief end in life is the individual's attainment of the ostensible values of material life. In this robust philosophy of worldly success the vizier commends justice, for "wrongdoing has never brought its undertaking into port."[46] Besides, justice guarantees that a man may keep his wealth long enough to pass it along to an heir: "It may be that it is fraud that gains riches, but the strength of justice is that it lasts, and a man may say: 'It is the property of my father.'"[47]

Intellectual conceit and snobbishness are to be avoided: "Let not thy heart be puffed-up because of thy knowledge;

[44] According to biblical tradition (Gen. 50:26), Joseph, also a vizier of an Egyptian king, is said to have died at this same age.
[45] *ANET*, 412.   [46] *ANET*, 412.   [47] *ANET*, 412.

Fig. 75. An Egyptian scribe of the time of Ptah-hotep (Fifth Dynasty). In later times scribes were trained in school by copying the instructions and precepts of the wise men.

be not confident because thou art a wise man. Take counsel with the ignorant as well as the wise. . . . Good speech is more hidden than the emerald, but it may be found with maidservants at the grindstones. . . ."[48]

Table manners require that one take what is set before his nose. Do not pierce the host with many stares and "let thy face be cast down until he addresses thee, and thou shouldst speak only when he addresses thee. Laugh after he laughs."[49]

When on a mission for a superior, "be thoroughly reliable when he sends thee. Carry out the errand for him as he has spoken. Do not be reserved about what is said to thee, and beware of any act of forgetfulness. Grasp hold of truth, and do not exceed it. . . . Struggle against making words worse, thus making one great man hostile to another through vulgar speech."[50]

On women: "If thou desirest to make friendship last in a home to which thou hast access as master, as a brother, or as a friend, into any place where thou mightest enter, beware of approaching the women. It does not go well with the place where that is done. The face has no alertness by splitting it [possibly, he who has a wandering eye for the women cannot be keen]."[51]

Ptah-hotep does not fail to instruct his son on how to have peace at home: "If thou art a man of standing, thou shouldst found thy household and love thy wife at home as is fitting. Fill her belly; clothe her back. Ointment is the prescription for her body. Make her heart glad as long as thou livest. She is a profitable field for her lord. . . Let her heart be soothed through what may accrue to thee; it means keeping her long in thy house. . . ."[52]

Through long experience he had learned that for a petitioner "a good hearing is a soothing of the heart." Said he to the prospective vizier: "If thou art one to whom peti-

48 *ANET*, 412.   49 *ANET*, 412.   50 *ANET*, 413.
51 *ANET*, 413.   52 *ANET*, 413.

Fig. 76. An Egyptian nobleman and his wife of the Fourth Dynasty (2650-2500 B.C.) of the Old Kingdom.

tion is made, be calm as thou listenest to the petitioner's speech. Do not rebuff him before he has swept out his body or before he has said that for which he came. A petitioner likes attention to his words better than the fulfilling of that for which he came."[53]

During the time of troubles which beset Egypt at the end of the Old Kingdom, the age of the pyramids, instructions for material success began to be questioned. This period of disintegration of governmental authority toward the end of the third millennium B.C. is well documented by the sayings of wise men and social prophets, whose writings were popular enough to circulate in much later times.

A graphic picture of conditions in the land in the age following the Pyramid Age is given by a "prophet," Ipu-wer, who had the temerity to appear at the palace of the Egyptian king, describe the topsy-turvy state of affairs, and denounce the king for his evasion of responsibility.

According to Ipu-wer, anarchy was apparent everywhere, even extending to the looting of the royal tombs:

Behold now, something has been done which never happened for a long time: the king has been taken away by poor men.

Behold, he who was buried as a falcon now lies on a mere bier. What the pyramid hid has become empty.[54]

The secrets of both church and state have been exposed to common view:

Why really, magic is exposed. Go-spells and enfold-spells are made ineffectual because they are repeated by ordinary people.

Why really, public offices are open, and their reports are read.

. . . .

[53] *ANET*, 413.   [54] *ANET*, 442.

Why really, the writings of the scribes of the mat have been removed. The grain-sustenance of Egypt is now a come-and-get-it.[55]

Not only were the secrets of the land laid bare, but the ancient social groupings have been dissolved and the former roles have been reversed:

Behold, nobles' ladies are now gleaners, and nobles are in the workhouse. But he who never even slept on a plank is now the owner of a bed. . . .

. . . .

Behold, he who knew not the lyre is now the owner of a harp. He who never sang for himself now praises the goddess of music. . . .

Behold, the bald-headed man who had no oil has become the owner of jars of sweet myrrh.

Behold, she who had not even a box is now the owner of a trunk. She who looked at her face in the water is now the owner of a mirror. . . .[56]

In contrast to this forthright condemnation of anarchy by the prophetic Ipu-wer, with its nostalgic remembrance of the better days of the Old Kingdom, is a more intro-spective document of the same general period. It is in the form of an argument between a man and his own soul over the wisdom of suicide. Poignantly the man who is weary of life asks some rhetorical questions:

To whom can I speak today?
One's fellows are evil;
The friends of today do not love.
To whom can I speak today?
Hearts are rapacious:
Every man seizes his fellow's goods.

[55] *ANET*, 442.   [56] *ANET*, 442.

To whom can I speak today?
　The gentle man has perished,
　But the violent man has access to everybody.[57]

In these circumstances this lonely and sensitive man contemplates suicide.

Death is in my sight today
　Like the recovery of a sick man,
　Like going out into the open after a confinement.
Death is in my sight today
　Like the odor of myrrh
　Like sitting under an awning on a breezy day.
Death is in my sight today
　Like the odor of lotus blossoms
　Like sitting on the banks of drunkenness.
Death is in my sight today
　Like the passing away of rain,
　Like the return of men to their houses from
　　an expedition.
Death is in my sight today
　Like the clearing of the sky,
　Like a man fowling thereby for what he knew not.
Death is in my sight today
　Like the longing of a man to see his house again,
　After he has spent many years held in captivity.[58]

The breakdown of ancient social institutions was accompanied by a distrust of the formulas of success which the wisdom of the Old Kingdom had set forth. Skepticism extended even to religion. Since the tombs of the most venerable men of the past had not been able to hold their bodies in peace and safety, and since not one of the ancients had returned from the after-life, men became skeptical of the cornerstone of Egyptian faith, the belief in a future life of felicity. The "Harper" in his song advocated

[57] *ANET*, 406.　　[58] *ANET*, 407.

the enjoyment of life in the here-and-now. You can't take it with you, he said in effect:

> I have heard the words of Ii-em-hotep and Hor-
> dedef,
> With whose discourses men speak so much.
> What are their places now?
> Their walls are broken apart, and their places are
> not—
> As though they had never been!
> There is none who comes back from over there,
> That he may tell their state,
> That he may tell their needs,
> That he may still our hearts,
> Until we too may travel to the place where they
> have gone.
> Let thy desire flourish,
> In order to let thy heart forget the beatifications for
> thee.[59]

The song ends with a refrain:

> Make holiday, and weary not therein!
> Behold, it is not given to a man to take his property
> with him,
> Behold, there is not one who departs who comes
> back again![60]

The instruction for King Meri-ka-Re (end of the twenty-second century B.C.) contains much of the utilitarian wisdom which was characteristic of the Pyramid Age. But in addition, there are new emphases, values which suggest a change in thinking about life, to match the social and political changes which had taken place with the breakdown of the old order. "Do justice whilst thou endurest upon earth. Quiet the weeper; do not oppress the widow. . . . Be on thy guard against punishing wrongfully."[61] "Enrich thy house of the West; embellish thy place of the necropolis, as

---

[59] *ANET*, 467.   [60] *ANET*, 467.   [61] *ANET*, 415.

an upright man and as one who executes the justice upon which men's hearts rely. More acceptable is the character of one upright of heart than the ox of the evildoer."[62] This is not unlike the word of the biblical prophet Samuel in I Samuel 15:22: "To obey is better than sacrifice."

In the days of the Egyptian Empire, when the kings of the New Kingdom reached out and held the towns of Palestine and Syria in subjection, the writing of wisdom was popular. As John A. Wilson has pointed out,[63] the older instructions for success continued to be written, but new emphases made their appearance. Success in material terms was subordinated to right relations with others. The benefits of life came to men, not so much from their own efforts, but as the gifts of the gods.

Toward the end of the Empire period a certain Ani set forth instructions to this son. The section on the correct treatment of mother and wife is instructive in showing the change from the earlier attitude, which Ptah-hotep of the Old Kingdom expressed when he said that a wife is a profitable field for her lord.[64] Ani instructed his son:

> Double the food which thou givest to thy mother, and carry her as she carried thee. She had a heavy load in thee, but she did not leave it to me. Thou wert born after thy months, but she was still yoked with thee, for her breast was in thy mouth for three years, continuously. Though thy filth was disgusting, her heart was not disgusted, saying: "What can I do?" She put thee into school when thou wert taught to write, and she continued on thy behalf everyday, with bread and beer in her house.
>
> When thou art a young man and takest to thyself a wife and art settled in thy house, set thy eye on how thy

62 *ANET*, 417.

63 H. and H. A. Frankfort, John A. Wilson, Thorkild Jacobsen, William A. Irwin, *The Intellectual Adventure of Ancient Man*, Chicago, 1946, pp. 110-119.

64 *ANET*, 413.

mother gave birth to thee and all her bringing thee up as well. Do not let her blame thee, nor may she have to raise her hands to the god, nor may he have to hear her cries.[65]

The ideal of silence appears in Ani's counsel to his son: "Do not talk a lot. Be silent, and thou wilt be happy. Do not be garrulous. The dwelling of god, its abomination is clamor. Pray thou with a loving heart, all the words of which are hidden, and he will do what thou needest, he will hear what thou sayest, and he will accept thy offering. . . ."[66]

Egyptian instructions, like many of the Hebrew proverbs, taught the ideal of marital fidelity and warned against the dangers of indiscretions in the matter of a man's relations with women. The vizier Ptah-hotep had cautioned the visitor in a house about approaching the women and said: "A mere trifle, the likeness of a dream—and one attains death through knowing her. . . . Do not do it—it is really an abomination—and thou shalt be free from sickness of heart every day."[67]

A folk tale from a thirteenth-century papyrus tells how a young man was falsely accused by the wife of his older brother of proposing adultery to her. The circumstances are similar in plot to the biblical story of Joseph and Potiphar's wife in Genesis 39:1-20. The story is of interest not only because of this parallel, but because it documents with a specific story the proverbial sayings which warn Egyptian young men of the wiles of an evil woman.

The scrupulous young man, Bata, lived with his elder brother, Anubis, and his wife; he was accustomed to sleep, however, in the stable. One day as the two brothers were plowing in the field, they ran out of seed for the planting. Anubis sent his younger brother, Bata, to the house for more grain, saying:

[65] *ANET*, 420-421.   [66] *ANET*, 420.   [67] *ANET*, 413.

"Go and fetch us seed from the village." And his younger brother found the wife of his elder brother sitting and doing her hair. Then he said to her: "Get up and give me some seed, for my younger brother [*sic*, but read "elder"] is waiting for me. Don't delay!" Then she said to him: "Go and open the bin and take what you want! Don't make me leave my combing unfinished!" Then the lad went into his stable, and he took a big jar, for he wanted to carry off a lot of seed. So he loaded himself with barley and emmer and came out carrying them.

His brother's wife asked him about the size of the load of grain he was carrying and continued the conversation by flattering him:

"There is great strength in you! Now I see your energies every day!" And she wanted to know him as one knows a man.

Then she stood up and took hold of him and said to him: "Come, let's spend an hour sleeping together! This will do you good, because I shall make fine clothes for you!" Then the lad became like a leopard with great rage at the wicked suggestion which she had made to him, and she was very, very much frightened. Then he argued with her, saying: "See here—you are like a mother to me, and your husband is like a father to me! Because—being older than I—he was the one who brought me up. What is this great crime which you have said to me? Don't say it to me again! And I won't tell it to a single person, nor will I let it out of my mouth to any man!" And he lifted up his load, and he went to the fields. Then he reached his elder brother, and they were busy with activity at their work. . . .

In the meantime the wife of his elder brother became frightened because of the proposal she had made and set about to slander the younger brother.

Then she took fat and grease, and she became like one who has been criminally beaten, wanting to tell her husband: "It was your younger brother who did the beating!" And her husband left off in the evening, after his custom of every day, and he reached his house, and he found his wife lying down, terribly sick. She did not put water on his hands, after his custom, nor had she lit a light before him, and his house was in darkness, and she lay there vomiting. So her husband said to her: "Who has been talking with you?" Then she said to him: "Not one person has been talking with me except your younger brother. But when he came to take the seed to you he found me sitting alone, and he said to me: 'Come, let's spend an hour sleeping together! Put on your curls!' So he spoke to me. But I wouldn't listen to him: 'Aren't I your mother?—for your elder brother is like a father to you!' So I spoke to him. But he was afraid, and he beat me, so as not to let me tell you. Now, if you let him live, I'll kill myself! Look, when he comes, don't let him speak, for, if I accuse him of this wicked suggestion, he will be ready to do it tomorrow again."[68]

When eventually the husband learned the truth about his wife, he killed her and "threw her out to the dogs"[69]— a fate not unlike that which befell Jezebel, the wicked queen of Israel.[70]

BABYLON'S WISE MEN

According to the Bible, Babylon as well as Egypt had its wise men.[71] A small residue of their sayings, in the form of proverbs written on clay tablets, has made its appearance in the excavations of remains from Sumerian times down to the Assyrian period. The Sumerians made collections of proverbs on clay tablets, just as they prepared lists of

68 *ANET*, 24.   69 *ANET*, 25.
70 II Kings 9:33, 36.   71 Jer. 50:35.

words and names, and used them frequently as school tablets.[72] Moralistic sayings from the first third of the second
millennium B.C. have come from Nippur: "The ship bent
on honest pursuits sailed off with the wind; Utu finds
honest ports for it." "He who drinks much beer must drink
water." "By marrying a thriftless wife, by begetting a thriftless son, unhappiness is my store."[73]

Shrewd observations about life in the form of clever
sayings are also found in Akkadian literature. Some people
are accompanied by bad luck wherever they go: "You are
placed into a river and your water becomes at once stinking;
you are placed in an orchard and your date-fruit becomes
bitter."[74] "He consecrated the temple before he started it,"
reminds one of the biblical, "Let not him that girdeth on
his armour boast himself as he that putteth it off."[75] Industry is required for success: "As long as man does not exert
himself, he will gain nothing."[76]

Instructions of wisdom are also found on Assyrian tablets, as: "As a wise man, let your understanding shine
modestly, let your mouth be restrained, guarded your
speech."[77] "Unto your opponent do no evil; your evildoer
recompense with good."[78] "Give food to eat, give date wine
to drink; the one begging for alms honor, clothe: over this
his god rejoices, this is pleasing unto the god Shamash, he
rewards it with good. Be helpful, do good."[79]

A frequent theme of the biblical Book of Proverbs is the
warning against the harlot. This finds its analogue in the
Assyrian counsels:

> Do not marry a harlot whose husbands are six
> thousand.
> An Ishtar-woman vowed to a god,
> A sacred prostitute whose favors are unlimited,

[72] *Journal of the American Oriental Society*, vol. 74, 1954, p. 82.
[73] *ibid.*, p. 84.   [74] *ANET*, 425.   [75] I Kings 20:11.
[76] *ANET*, 425.   [77] *ANET*, 426.   [78] *ANET*, 426.
[79] *ANET*, 426.

Will not lift you out of your trouble:
In your quarrel she will slander you.
Reverence and submissiveness are not with her.
Truly, if she takes possession of the house, lead
    her out.
Toward the path of a stranger she turns her mind.
Or the house which she enters will be destroyed,
    her husband will not prosper.[80]

Religious observances and feelings are enjoined and
prosperity is promised as a reward for paying one's religious
obligations:

Pay homage daily to your god
With sacrifice, prayer and appropriate incense-offering.
Towards your god you should feel solicitude of heart:
That is what is appropriate to the deity.
Prayer, supplication, and prostration to the ground
Shall you offer in the morning: then your might will
    be great,
And in abundance, through god's help, you will
    prosper.[81]

On the level of speculative thought about life's values,
there has long been known a composition containing a
dialogue between a master and his obliging servant. It con-
sists of a dozen stanzas, in each of which the master makes
a proposal for a certain course of action. The obliging
servant replies with an appropriate proverb or cliché which
supports the course suggested by the master. Whereupon,
the master changes his mind and suggests the opposite
course. To this also the wise servant has ready at hand an
equally good supporting proverb. This clever composition
has long been seen as a dialogue of pessimism, in that it
seems to deny that there are any fixed values in life, since
an equally good reason can be given for doing and for not

80 *ANET*, 427.   81 *ANET*, 427.

doing a particular thing. However, recently two cuneiformists have independently come to the conclusion that
the composition is a caricature, and that it was intended as
a broad satire and not as ponderous philosophizing.[82]

Whatever the intention of the author, the work is rem-
iniscent of the attitude of the "gentle cynic" who wrote the
biblical Book of Ecclesiastes. Parts of the dialogue follow:

Dining:

"Servant, obey me."

Yes, my lord, yes.

"Bring me at once water for my hands, and give it
to me: I wish to dine."

Dine, my lord, dine. To dine regularly is the opening
of the heart [i.e. brings joy]. To a dinner eaten in
happiness and with washed hands the sun-god Shamash
comes.

"No, servant, I shall not dine."

Do not dine, my lord, do not dine. To be hungry and
eat, to be thirsty and drink, comes upon every man.

Rebellion:

"Servant, obey me."

Yes, my lord, yes.

"I intend to start a rebellion."

Do it, my lord, do it. If you do not start a rebellion
what becomes of your clay? Who will give you something
to fill your stomach?

"No, servant, I shall not do something violent."

Do it not, my lord, do it not. The man doing something violent is killed or ill-treated, or he is maimed,
or captured and cast into prison.

Love:

"Servant, obey me."

Yes, my lord, yes.

"A woman will I love."

[82] E. A. Speiser, *Journal of Cuneiform Studies*, vol. 8, 1954, pp. 98-105.

Yes, love, my lord, love. The man who loves a woman forgets pain and trouble.

"No, servant, a woman I shall not love."

Do not love, my lord, do not love. Woman is a well, woman is an iron dagger—a sharp one!—which cuts a man's neck.

Sacrifice to a god:

"Servant, obey me."

Yes, my lord, yes.

"Bring me at once water for my hands, and give it to me:

I will offer a sacrifice to my god."

Offer, my lord, offer. A man offering sacrifice to his god is happy, loan upon loan he makes.

"No, servant, a sacrifice to my god will I not offer."

Do not offer it, my lord, do not offer it. You may teach a god to trot after you like a dog when he requires of you, saying, "Celebrate my ritual" or "do not inquire by requesting an oracle" or anything else.

Public service:

"Servant, obey me."

Yes, my lord, yes.

"I will do something helpful for my country."

Do it, my lord, do it. The man who does something helpful for his country,—his helpful deed is placed in the bowl of Marduk.

"No, servant, I will not do something helpful for my country."

Do it not, my lord, do it not. Climb the mounds of ancient ruins and walk about: look at the skulls of late and early men; who among them is an evildoer, who a public benefactor?

Suicide and murder:

Servant, obey me."

Yes, my lord, yes.

"Now, what is good? To break my neck, your neck, throw both into the river—that is good."

Who is tall enough to ascend to heaven? Who is broad enough to embrace the earth?

"No, servant, I shall kill you and send you ahead of me."

Then would my lord wish to live even three days after me?[83]

Whether the author was essentially a cynic as to values in life, or merely a caricaturist, one cannot be certain. But that he was a shrewd observer of human nature, there can be no doubt. Truly he was one of the wise men of Babylon.

Along the banks of the Tigris and Euphrates rivers there developed, through the course of several millennia, a civilization built, as E. A. Speiser has recently phrased it, upon the "dynamics of Mesopotamian law."[84] In this area, where various ethnic groups with different languages have partaken of a civilized life under a system of law, the underlying continuity which appears most conspicuously is in the authority of law, which has been documented by the collections of cuneiform laws recently made available.

The debt that Hebrew culture, which has made its own significant contributions to three religions of the world, owes to Mesopotamian concepts of law and authority has only lately become apparent. Quite apart from substantive borrowings—some of which have been apparent in the examples we have cited above—the Hebrew concept of *torah*, "law," as a way of life regulated by principles of justice has its counterpart in the well-defined rules for each class of society in the Code of Hammurabi. In this respect the long-remembered tradition of the coming from Baby-

---

[83] *ANET*, 438.
[84] *The Canadian Bar Review*, October, 1953, pp. 863-877.

lonia of Abraham, the father of the people of Israel, is in a cultural sense strikingly authenticated by the recovery of Mesopotamian law.

In contrast to Mesopotamia, Egypt seems to have had no written laws, but to have relied upon the king, who was considered divine, for law and authority.[85] But social wisdom did accumulate and was preserved in the form of instructions and wise sayings which served for centuries as a medium for the instruction of youth. Hebrew "wisdom" writings seem to reflect, if not to copy—as in the case of Proverbs 22:17-24:11, which has many sayings in common with the Egyptian instruction of Amen-em-Opet—this well-documented practice of the Egyptian sages through many centuries. Some, at least, of "all the wisdom of Egypt," was known and appreciated in ancient Israel.

An author of a history of Israel's early wars with the Philistines for the land of Canaan wrote of a brisk trade which Israelite farmers carried on with their enemy: "All the Israelites went down to the Philistines, to sharpen every man his plowshare, and his coulter, and his axe, and his mattock."[86] In the light of recent archaeological discoveries, it is no discredit to ancient Israel to assert that the Israelites were indebted to Babylon for certain concepts of law and authority, and that her wise men may well have had their wits sharpened by frequent contact with both Egyptian and Babylonian wisdom.

[85] J. A. Wilson, in *Supplement to the Journal of the American Oriental Society*, no. 17, July-September, 1954, pp. 1-7.
[86] I Sam. 13:20.

POSTSCRIPT

LIKE SAUL, who had gone in search of his father's strayed asses and found a kingdom, the archaeologist who went out to the lands of the Bible found far more than he had expected. At most, the span of time covered by the Bible is two thousand years; the mounds and caves of the Near East have borne evidence to document human culture extending over a period several times the length of this biblical span. Jericho was a walled city some four thousand years or more before its walls fell before Joshua, and the cities of lower Mesopotamia had a written literature some fifteen hundred years before Abraham left Ur. The story of man in the ancient Near East is longer and more complex than the seventeenth-century biblical chronology of Archbishop James Ussher, still printed in the margin of many Bibles, allowed one to believe.

Modern research has not only extended the time span of antiquity; it has enlarged the area of the known ancient world. New peoples, with languages which have been deciphered and translated, have made their appearance on the scene. In the rich harvest of written materials which have come from what was once called narrowly "Bible lands," new claims for detailed research have been staked out; special disciplines have arisen, such as Egyptology, Hittitology, Sumerology, and Akkadian and Ugaritic studies—each with its own set of problems of language and history.

In the Bible there are a few scattered references to a people called Horites, but little more than the name appears. It is now known that these biblical Horites were none other than the Hurrians, a group of people who played a major role in the history of the Near East during the second millennium B.C. For these few barren references in the Bible there is full documentation: a language, legal concepts, and a wealth of cultural detail which the excavations at Nuzi have revealed.

Perhaps the most notable achievement of Near Eastern archaeology in the past century is the new perspective in time and space for viewing the ancient world. Peoples once known only from the Bible, for so many centuries the sole witness to the pre-Greek world, have now been recovered and documented from other sources. The map of the ancient world has been filled in, to provide a better view of both a history of human culture and the distinctive contribution of the people of Israel. It is fair to claim, I think, that the Bible has moved, in the relatively brief period of modern discovery, out of the isolation which it has for centuries enjoyed as "sacred" into the main stream of world history.

A century of exploration and excavation in Palestine has produced a reliable map. Archaeology has given a trustworthy profile of history for many of the important places on it. And the daily life of biblical times has been generously documented by illustrations of cultural details such as dress, housing, plans of cities, occupations and crafts, religious practice, writing, and many others.

Fig. 77. Silver model of a boat from about the twenty-fifth century B.C. This was found in the "King's Grave" at Ur.

The picture of the religion of Canaan which has emerged in the century since Renan first went to Syria in 1860 has served to reveal the true significance of the conflict between the intractable Elijah and the prophets of Baal on Mt. Carmel, when the prophet of the Lord challenged, "if the Lord be God, follow Him; but if Baal, follow him." The Canaanite polytheism and its aim to achieve fertility stand revealed as something utterly different from the monotheistic religion of Israel.

The recovery of the history of ancient Assyria has served to anchor the chronology of Israel's history firmly into the scheme of world events. The authority of the Book of Kings as a historical source needs no longer to rest on the theological dogma of inspiration; numerous details have been adequately confirmed by the discovery of Assyrian records which supply independent witness to the events described. Assyria, that wolflike enemy of Israel, which frequently proved to be a catalyst for Hebrew prophecy, has emerged as the terror which Isaiah had pictured.

Ancient Near Eastern mythology, as it has come to light from Assyria, Babylonia, and Anatolia, has, like Canaanite theology, served to emphasize the unique character of Hebrew monotheism. From such stories as those of the Flood and Creation found in Sumero-Akkadian writings, it is clear that certain cosmological notions were widely spread in the ancient world and that the Hebrews utilized some of the universally held views as a setting for their own distinctive monotheistic and ethical beliefs. Yet, one must say, I think, that the contrast is more apparent than the likeness. Again, the newly-discovered mythology of the ancient Near East supports the claim that Israel was in, but not of, the ancient world.

The cases in which there may have been direct borrowings on the part of the Hebrew writers of law and wisdom from their colleagues in Mesopotamia and Egypt are few; and even these few cases are open to question. Nevertheless, a variety of basic concepts and concerns turn out to be common property in the writings from Palestine, Egypt, Mesopotamia, and Anatolia. A respect for law and authority was shared by the Hebrews and by those whose life was regulated by the cuneiform codes. Themes of worldly wisdom propounded by the wise men of Egypt are not without their counterparts in the Book of Proverbs.

As one surveys the list of those who have contributed to the enlargement of biblical knowledge in the past century, he cannot ignore the fact that this period of study marks a new epoch. The Bible as sacred history was for many centuries the particular province of the priest, the scribe, the monk, and the theologian. In the most recent period, its history has been the concern of such a varied group as consular agents, adventurers, royal engineers, an apprenticed bank-note engraver, epigraphists, philologists, and professional archaeologists. Important discoveries have been made by Renan, the skeptic, by de Vaux, the Dominican Father, by Parker, the adventurer, and even by a shepherd boy of the Taamireh Bedouin. As the Bible has moved into the main stream of world history, its study has become the interest and concern of a larger and more varied group of scholars.

One may well ask, Have the rich mines of antiquity been exhausted? A moral which emerges from this review of modern discovery is that the unexpected has come to pass time and time again. The finding of Canaanite poetry at Ras Shamra in 1929, the discovery of the Dead Sea Scrolls and the buildings of the community at Qumran, the turning up of a fragment of the Gilgamesh tablet at Megiddo on a dump heap, the discovery of three codes of law older than Hammurabi in the span of less than a decade, the unearthing of jar-handles inscribed with "Gibeon" at el-Jib, Neolithic and New Testament Jericho—these are some of the surprises of archaeology in recent years. Near Eastern archaeology does not yet seem to have reached the point of diminishing returns.

GLOSSARY

ADAD: Babylonian god of rain and storm.

AKKADIAN: Semitic language which was spoken in Babylonia and Assyria, and written in cuneiform.

AMON: Egyptian god of the sky and chief among the gods.

AMON-RE: Egyptian sky-god, identified with the sun.

ANATH: Canaanite war-goddess, called "the Maiden Anath" at Ugarit.

ANU: Sumero-Akkadian sky-god and head of the pantheon. Also spelled An and Anum.

ANUNNAKI: A collective term for a group of Babylonian gods.

APIS: The bull sacred to the Egyptian god Ptah of Memphis.

APSU: Babylonian primordial god of the fresh waters.

ASHERAH: Canaanite goddess, consort of El and mother of the gods. At Ugarit, called "Lady Asherah of the Sea."

ASHTAR: Canaanite god, a son of Asherah, who was chosen to rule from Baal's vacated throne; called the "Tyrant."

ASHTAR-CHEMOSH: Moabite god, known from the Mesha stone.

ASHTART: Semitic goddess of love and fertility, appearing in the Bible as Ashtoreth; became the Greek Astarte.

ASHTORETH: Hebrew form of the name of the Semitic goddess Ashtart.

ASHUR: Chief god of the Assyrians and the name of the capital city of Assyria.

BAAL: Semitic god of rain and fertility, known at Ugarit as "the Rider of Clouds."

CHEMOSH: God of the people of Moab in Transjordan.

DAGON: Semitic god of grain: at Ugarit, the father of Baal; in Philistia, the god of Ashdod.

DEBEN: Egyptian unit of weight.

EA: Wise earth- and water-god of the Babylonian pantheon.

EL: Chief of the Canaanite pantheon, called "King Father Shunem" and "Bull El" at Ugarit.

ELATH: Another name for Asherah, mother of the gods.

ENLIL: Babylonian wind- and storm-god, responsible for the Flood.

ERRAGAL: Same as Nergal, god of the nether-world.

ESAGILA: Temple of Marduk in Babylon.

GIZZIDA: Babylonian nether-world deity.

HOR-DEDEF: A son of the pharaoh Khufu, legendary for his wisdom.

II-EM-HOTEP: A high official of the pharaoh Djoser, legendary for his wisdom.

ISHTAR: Babylonian goddess of love and fertility, and queen of heaven.

KHIRBET: A form of an Arabic word meaning "ruins."

KINGU: Leader of the forces of the goddess Tiamat, from whose blood mankind was fashioned.

LEVIATHAN: Mythological monster, equivalent to the Ugaritic Lothan.

MARDUK: God of Babylon, and head of the pantheon during the time of the Babylonian empire.

MASSORETIC: A system of vowels and critical apparatus in our present Hebrew text of the Bible; while written down in the seventh century A.D., the system follows a tradition of pronunciation established by Jewish scribes in the first century A.D.

MINA: Babylonian unit of weight, equivalent to 60 shekels.

MOT: Ugaritic god of rainless season, associated with the nether-world.

NEBO: Babylonian god of writing; also name of city and mountain in Jordan.

NINURTA: Sumero-Akkadian god of war.

NUDIMMUD: Another name for the god Ea.

OSTRACON: Piece of broken pottery bearing an inscription; plural: ostraca.

POTSHERD: Fragment of broken pottery. Most abundantly preserved evidence in archaeological remains.

RE: Egyptian cosmic god of Heliopolis, whose name signifies the sun.

SAPPER WORK: The undermining of the foundation of a besieged fortress.

252

SHAMASH: Babylonian sun-god.

SHAPSH: Canaanite sun-goddess, called "Torch Shapsh" at Ugarit.

SHEKEL: Babylonian unit of weight; 60 shekels make 1 mina.

SQUEEZE: A facsimile of an inscription or other carving, made by pressing it with a plastic substance.

STELA: An upright stone slab, usually with inscription or carving.

TAMMUZ: Babylonian god of vegetation, inhabiting the nether-world.

TELL: Arabic for an artificial mound built up by a series of human occupations. Same word appears in the Hebrew of Joshua 11:13, "cities that stood on their tells."

TIAMAT: Babylonian primordial goddess of marine water and mother of the gods.

UGARITIC: Canaanite language of ancient Ugarit in Syria.

URUK: City in Babylonia, the home of Gilgamesh; biblical Erech; modern Warka.

UTU: Sumerian sun-god.

WADI: Arabic for valley; Anglicized plural: wadies.

ZIUSUDRA: Sumerian hero of the Flood, corresponding to Utnapishtim and Noah.

SOURCES FOR ILLUSTRATIONS

Allegro, John M.: 17, 19. Archives Photographiques, Paris: 35, 38. British Museum: 7, 8, 9, 44, 50, 51, 52, 53, 54, 57, 58. Cameron, G. G.: 46. Department of Antiquities, Israel: 5. Dunand, M.: 36. Éditions "TEL," Paris: 59, 65, 75. Foto Marburg: 28. Gaddis, A., Luxor: 26. Giraudon, Paris: 61, 70. Hereford Cathedral: 21. Hessische Treuhandverwaltung des früheren preussischen Kunstgutes, Wiesbaden: 12, 29, 30, 74. Iraq Museum: 68. Metropolitan Museum of Art, New York: 67. Musées Royaux d'Art et d'Histoire, Brussels: 24. Museo di Antichità, Turin: 49. Oriental Institute, Chicago: 13, 14, 42, 43a, 43b, 48, 69. Palestine Archaeological Museum, Jerusalem: 6, 11, 15. Petrie, Ann: 2. Pierpont Morgan Library, New York: 60. Pritchard, J. B.: 27, 31, 32, 37, 41, 62, 76. Psichari-Renan, Henriette: 34. Schaeffer, C. F. A.: 40. Starcky, J.: 18. Trustees of the late Sir Henry S. Wellcome: 10. Union Theological Seminary and James Muilenburg, New York: 22. University Museum, University of Pennsylvania: 73, 77. Yale University News Bureau: 71.

ILLUSTRATIONS FROM BOOKS

4: F. J. Bliss, *A Mound of Many Cities*, London, 1898, pl. 2 (copy by D. M. Spence). 16: L. H. Vincent, *Jérusalem de l'Ancien Testament*, Paris, 1954, pl. 65 (copy by D. M. Spence). 39: *Orientalia*, vol. 19, 1950, p. 374. 47: V. Place, *Ninive et l'Assyrie*, vol. 3, plates, Paris, 1867, pl. 18bis. 55: A. H. Layard, *The Monuments of Nineveh*, London, 1849, pl. 62,2. 56: *Iraq*, vol. 1, 1934, fig. 1. 63: F. H. Weissbach, *Babylonische Miscellen*, WVDOG, 4, Leipzig, 1903, p. 16, fig. 1. 64: A. H. Layard, *A Second Series of the Monuments of Nineveh*, London, 1853, pl. 5. 66: L. Delaporte, *Malatya: Arslantepe, I*, Paris, 1940, pl. 22, 2.

INDEX

Abel, Père F. M., 62
Abel-beth-maacah, 149
Abner, 90
Achshaph, 68
Acre, 68, 70
Adad, 147, 167
Adad-'idri, 145
Adam, 200
Adapa, 193, 196-200
Addaya, 77
Adonis, 124
Ahab, 129, 145-147
Ahaz, 148, 152
Ahimiti, 138
Ahiram, 99, 100
Akh-en-Aton, 6, 75, 194, 195
Akko, 156
Akzib, 156
Alashiya, 81-82
Albright, William F., 9, 45, 83, 84, 90, 109
Allenby, General Edmund H. H., 29
Alt, Albrecht, 60, 84, 87
Amariah, 90
Amarna, see Tell el-Amarna
Amarna letters, 75-77
Amen-em-Opet, 245
Amen-hotep III, 75, 194
Amman Museum, 85
Amon-Re, 79
Amos, 35
Anata, 59
Anath, 102, 111, 113, 116-118
Anathoth, 59
Ani, instruction of, 236, 237
Anu (An, Anum), 167, 179, 191, 196-199, 204, 210, 217
Anubis, 237
Anunnaki, 167, 168
Aphek, 68
Aphrodite, 124, 125
'Apiru, 77
Apis, 125
Apsu, 165, 185, 186, 190, 192
Aqhat, 120

Ararat, Mt., 170
Armageddon, 25
Aruna, 25, 26
Aruru, 173
Arvad, 156
Asdudimmu, 138
Ashdod, 91, 136, 138, 139, 156, 157
Asherah, 91, 102, 109, 111, 112, 117
Ashkelon, 34, 68, 74, 151, 156
Ashtar, 117
Ashtar-Chemosh, 106
Ashtaroth, 68, 70, 150
Ashtart, 102, 126
'Ashtart-Shem-Baal, 97
Ashtoreth, 91, 95, 102, 124
Ashur (city), 164, 215
Ashur (god), 138, 156
Ashurbanipal, 153, 163, 164, 183, 196, 201
Ashurnasirpal II, 153
Astarte, 126
Astartu, 150
Athenaeum, 154, 161
Aton, 195
Avva, 137
Awad, 142
Azariah, 90
Azekah, 15, 16
Azuri, 138
Azuru, 156

Baal, 91, 95, 102, 109, 111-113, 115-120, 124
Baalath, 33
"Babel and Bible," 184, 206
Babylon, 186
Banai-Barqa, 156
Barthélemy, Abbé, 101
Bata, 237
Bauer, Hans, 109
Beder, 79, 80
Beeroth, 59, 70, 87
Behistun, 129, 130-132
Beisan, 85, 86; see also Beth-shan
Ben-Hadad, 103

Besant, Sir Walter, 1, 63
Beth-Ammon, 156
Beth-Dagon, 156
Bethel, 86
Beth-haraphid, 16
Beth-horon the nether, 33
Beth-shan, 68, 70, 85, 86, 91
Beth-shemesh, 68
el-Bireh, 59, 86
Biridiya, 75
Bit-Ammon, 151
Bit-Zitti, 156
Black Obelisk, 139-145
Bombay, 144
Botta, Paul Emile, 129, 134-136, 153
bread of life, 199
Breasted, James Henry, 29-31
Bridson, D. G., 171
British Broadcasting Corporation, 171
Brunton, Guy, 12
Budge, E.A.W., 193
Bull of Heaven, 179
Burrows, Millar, 44
Byblos, 79-81, 93, 97-100, 102, 124, 156, 194

Cadastral Survey, 54
Canning, Sir Stratford, 140
Carthage, 102
Cedar Forest, 175, 178
Chemosh, 91, 105, 106
Chephirah, 59
cherubim, 100
City of Salt, 49
Clermont-Ganneau, 86, 105
Colt, Mr. H. Dunscombe, 12
Conder, Claude Reignier, 8, 63-65, 82
Coniah son of Elnathan, 15
copy desk from Qumran, 50
Corpus Inscriptionum Semiticarum, 100, 101
Coutts, Miss Burdett, 36
Creation, 183-193, 204
Cuthah, 137
Cyprus, 79, 82

Dagon, 91, 95, 97, 117
Daily Telegraph, London, 162, 184
Dalman, Gustaf, 41

Damascus, 70, 145
Daniel, 120
Dante, 54
Darius, 129-132
David, 90, 179
Dead Sea Scrolls, 42-52, 249
decipherment of cuneiform, 129-134
Delitzsch, Friedrich, 184, 185, 206
Deluge, see Flood
de Morgan, Jacques, 206, 207, 210, 215
de Saulcy, F., 47
de Vaux, Père Roland, 47, 49, 249
Dhiban, 103
Dhorme, Père P., 109
Dibon, 70
Dilmun, 204
Djefti, 26
Dor, 79, 97
Dothan, 70
Drake, C. F. Tyrwhitt, 64
Dudu, 202
Dunand, Maurice, 100

Ea, 165, 170, 182, 186, 191, 196-200
Eden, 196
Edom, 152, 156
Eglon, 3, 4; see also Tell el-Hesi
Ekron, 156, 157
El, 109, 111, 112, 114, 116-121, 124
Elah, 149
Elath, 112, 117
elephants, hunt for, 70-71
Elijah, 248
Eltekeh, 156
Enkidu, 173-176, 179-181
Enlil, 169, 170, 191, 204, 210, 217
Eridu, 196
Erragal, 167
Esagila, 192
Esarhaddon, 127
Esharra, 190
Eshmunazar, 95-97, 99
Eshnunna, laws of, 218, 219, 221, 223-227
Essenes, 44
Ethba'al, 156
Ethiopia, 138, 139
Eusebius, 86
execration texts, 66-68

fall of man, the, 196
Fara, 165
fertility cult, 124-126
figurines, nude female, 122-123
filial piety, 120
Fisher, Clarence S., 29-31
Flood, 160-170, 201-204

Galilee, 149
Galling, Kurt, 109
Gates, F. T., 30
Gath, 138
Gaza, 152, 157
Gazru, 151
Geba, 70
Gezer, 33, 70, 75, 77, 82, 86, 194
Gibeon, 59, 86-90, 249
Gideon, 187
Gihon, 39, 41
Gilead, 149
Gilgamesh, 164, 165, 170, 171, 173, 175-183, 249
Gizeh, Great Pyramid of, 2-3
Gizzida, 197-199
Gladstone, Mr. W. E., 160
Glueck, Nelson, 84, 85, 90
Goetze, Albrecht, 218
Gomorrah, 47
Gozan, 136
Gunkel, Hermann, 189
Guy, P.L.O., 31

Habor, 136
Hadadezer, 145
Halah, 136
Hamath, 70, 137, 145
Hammurabi, Code of, 177, 206-215, 216-218, 221, 222, 225, 227, 244, 249
Hananiah, 90
Hanish, 167
Hanno, 152
Hanya, 77
Harding, G. Lankester, 47
Harper, song of the, 234-235
Hattusa, 164
Hazael, 103
Hazazu, 147
Hazor, 33, 68, 70, 149
Hebron, 60
Hereford Cathedral map, 54, 55

Hezekiah, 18, 22, 39-41, 129, 154, 156-159
Hincks, the Rev. Edward, 129, 132, 133, 148
Hittite laws, 215, 216, 221, 222, 224
Hodaviah son of Ahijah, 15
Hor-dedef, 235
Horites, 246
Hoshaiah, 13-15, 17
Hoshea, 129, 149-151
Humbaba, 175, 177-179
Hurrians, 246
Huwawa, 175, 176

Ibleam, 70
Ii-em-hotep, 235
Ijon, 149
Ilabrat, 197
Ipuwer, 232, 233
Irhuleni, 145
Isaiah, 127, 139, 154
Ishtar, 167, 178, 179, 240
Isin, 217

Jacotin, Pierre, 56, 62
Janoah, 149
Jehoahaz, 151, 152; see also Ahaz
Jehu, 129, 141, 143-145
Jensen, Peter, 170, 171
Jeremiah, 10, 17, 59, 68, 90
Jericho, 249
Jerome, 53, 201
Jerusalem, 17, 29, 35-42, 52, 68, 75, 121, 156-159, 194
Jezebel, 239
el-Jib, 59, 86-89, 249; see also Gibeon
Joab, 90
Jonah, 153
Joppa, 70-74, 97, 156
Joseph, 228, 237
Joshua, 75, 106
Josiah, 27, 28
Juvelius, Walter, 40

Kadesh, 27
Karkar (Karkara), 145-148
Karnak, 25, 26, 75, 77, 78
Kaushmalaku, 152
Kedesh, 149
Kefir, 59
Kenyon, Sir Frederic, 43

Keret, 120
Keveh, 33
Khirbet Qumran, 47-52
Khorsabad, 134-138, 159, 172
King, L. W., 185
Kingu, 191
Kish, 164
Kitchener, H. H., 65
Klein, the Rev. F. A., 103
Knudtzon, J. A., 194
Kramer, Samuel N., 219
Kurkh, 145
Kuyunjik, 134; *see also* Nineveh

Lab'ayu, 75, 76
Lachish, 4, 6, 9-25, 86, 158; *see also*
    Tell ed-Duweir
Lagash, 188
Laish, 68, 70
Layard, Austen Henry, 22-24, 129,
    139-143, 148-150, 152-154, 161, 183
Le Hir, 93
Leonard, William Ellery, 171
Lepsius, C. R., 7
Leviathan, 121, 122, 189
lex talionis, 221-224
Lightfoot, Dr. John, 193
Lipit-Ishtar law code, 217, 218, 221
Loftus, 184
Lothan, 122
Lucian of Samosata, 124

Mahalliba, 156
Malta, 101
Marduk, 138, 186-189, 191, 192
Marseilles tariff, 102-103
Megiddo, 24-35, 52, 70, 75, 76, 100,
    123, 164, 194, 249
Menahem, 129, 148-150
Meri-ka-Re, instruction of, 235, 236
Merom, 70
Mesha, 103-106
Mesha stone, *see* Moabite stone
Middle Assyrian laws, 215, 221
Milkilu, 77
Minet el-Beida, 107
Mitinti, 151, 157
Moab, 68, 151, 156
Moabite stone, 103-106
Molech, 91

Mond, Sir Robert, 12
Montet, Pierre, 99, 100
Mot, 111, 116, 118
Mt. Carmel, 25, 79, 248
Muhammad adh-Dhib, 44
Muhammad Pasha, 140
Mummu-Tiamat, 185
Musru, 138

Napoleon III, 92
Napoleon Bonaparte, 56
Naphtali, 149
Nassr ed-Din, 207
Nazareth, 29
Nebi Samwil, 86
Nebo (god), 138
Nebo (town), 106
Nebuchadnezzar, 10, 18
Nefert-iti, 195
Ni, 70, 71
Nimrud, 126, 140-142, 144, 148-150,
    152, 159, 187
Nineveh, 22, 24, 145, 150, 152-155,
    157, 159-164, 174, 196, 201; *see also*
    Kuyunjik
Ningirsu, 188
Ninsum, 176
Ninurta, 167
Nippur, 164, 203, 217, 240
Nisir, Mt., 160, 168-170
Noah, 170, 203
Nudimmud, 190, 192
Nuzi, 247

"obliging servant, the," 241-244
Omri, 105, 129, 144
Onomasticon, 86, 87
Oppert, Dr. Jules, 133
Orontes, 147
ox, the goring, 225-226

Padi, 156, 157
Palestine Exploration Fund, 1, 4,
    40, 62, 63, 65, 82
Parker, Captain Montague, 40, 41,
    249
Pekah, 129, 149, 151
Pella, 68, 70
Petrie, W. M. Flinders, 1-12, 43, 82,
    90
Pharaoh-necoh, 28

Philistines, 79, 85
Pococke, Richard, 86
Potiphar's wife, 237
pottery, importance of, 6-9
pottery, surface exploration for, 82-85
prophet, 15, 80, 232
Ptah-hotep, 228-230, 236, 237
Pul, 149; see also Tiglath-pileser III
Puzur-Amurri, 167

Quatremère, 93
Qumran, see Khirbet Qumran

Rabbah, 70
Rahab, 189, 190
rape, laws on, 224-225
Rassam, H., 183-184
Ras Shamra, texts from, 106-122, 190, 249; see also Ugarit
Rawlinson, Henry C., 129-133, 144, 150, 153, 154, 160, 161
Rehob, 68, 70
Remaliah, 149
Renan, Ernest, 92-101, 248, 249
Ritter, Carl, 57
Robinson, Edward, 37, 57-62, 82, 85, 86, 90
Rockefeller, John D. Jr., 24, 29
Röhricht, Reinhold, 53
Royal Asiatic Society, 132, 133, 144
Ruad, 93

Safed, 64
St. George and the Dragon, 190
Sakkarah, 66
Salamanu, 151
Samaria, 82, 136, 137
Samsimuruna, 156
Samuel, 80
Samuel, Metropolitan-Archbishop Athanasius Yeshue, 44
Sanders, Marshal Liman von, 29
Sanipu, 151
Sargon II, 127, 134-139, 172
Saul, 80, 85, 91
Sayce, Professor A. H., 39
Sayid Taha Baqir, 218
Schaeffer, Claude F. A., 107, 108
Scheil, Père Jean Vincent, 210
Schick, Herr Conrad, 36, 37

Sekhmet, 72
Selim el-Kari, 105
Semachiah, 16
Sennacherib, 18-22, 24, 39, 127, 153, 154, 156
Sepharvaim, 137
Seth, 73
Seti I, 77, 78, 85
Shalmaneser III, 127, 136, 141, 143-148, 153
Shallum son of Jaddua, 15
Shalyat, 122
Shamash, 176, 177, 180, 211, 240
Shapsh, Torch, 116
Sharon, 97
Shechem, 68
Shemaiah, 16
Shullat, 167
Shunem, Father, 111, 114, 116
Shuruppak, 165
Shushan, 209, see Susa
Shutruk-nahhunte, 209
Sidon, 79, 80, 93, 95-97, 99, 102, 103, 156
Sidqia, 156
Siduri, 180, 181
Sillibel, 157
Siloam tunnel, 10, 36-42
Sippar, 164, 209
Socho, 70
Solomon, 24, 32-34, 91, 100, 228
Smith, Eli, 57-59, 62
Smith, George, 150, 160-162, 164, 165, 183, 184, 189, 193, 205
Smithsonian Institution, 85
Smyth, Piazzi, 2
Speiser, E. A., 165, 171, 244
sphinx throne, 35, 100
Stanley, Dean and Lady Augusta, 160
Starkey, James Leslie, 10-13, 22-24
Steele, Francis R., 217
Stewart, Captain R. W., 63
Sukenik, Professor E. L., 44, 45
Sumerians, 201-205
Survey of Western Palestine, 62-65, 82
Susa, 206, 207, 209, 215

Taanach, 26, 33, 70
Tadmor, 33

Talbot, W. H. Fox, 132, 133
Tammuz, 197-199
Tanis, 79
Tartan, 139
Taylor, J. E., 145
Tell Abu Harmal, 218
Tell Asmar, 121
Tell Beit Mirsim, 84
Tell ed-Duweir, 10-18, 22, 86; *see also* Lachish
Tell el-Amarna, 193-195, 200-201
Tell el-Hesi, 4-9, 33, 43, 52, 82; *see also* Eglon
Tell en-Nasbeh, 87
Tell Jezer, 86
Tello, 188
tells, nature of, 82
Testevuide, M., 56
Thebes, 79, 194
theft, laws on, 226, 227
Thompson, R. Campbell, 159
Thoth, General, 71-73
Thut-mose III, 25-27, 68, 70-72, 75
Tiamat, 185, 186, 188-192
Tiglath-pileser I, 215
Tiglath-pileser III, 127, 148-152, 158
Timnah, 156
Tishpak, 226
Tjeker, 79, 80
Tobiah, 14, 15
Topheth, 68
torah, 244
Torczyner, Professor Harry, 10, 11
Trever, John C., 44, 45
Tuweileb, 60
Tyre, 68, 75, 79, 80, 93, 102, 103, 147, 194

Ubar-Tutu, 165
Ugarit, texts from, 106-122
Ur, 164, 219, 220, 247

Ur-Nammu, laws of, 219, 221, 223, 224
Ur-Nammu, stela of, 220
Urshanabi, 183
Uruk, 171, 175, 176, 179, 180, 183
Ushu, 156
Ussher, Archbishop James, 246
Utnapishtim, 165, 169, 170, 182, 183, 203
Utu, 204, 240

Van de Velde, 63
Vincent, Père H., 41, 42, 84, 90
Virolleaud, Charles, 107-109
von Troilo, Franz Ferdinand, 86
Vossische Zeitung, 109

Warren, Captain Charles, 36, 37
water of life, 199
Wellcome, Sir Henry, 12
Wen-Amon, 79-82
Weygand, General Maxime, 100
Wheeler, Sir Mortimer, 40
Wilson, Edmund, 42
Wilson, John A., 236
Wisdom, Babylonian, 239-245
Wisdom, Egyptian, 228-237
Wolff, the Rev. P., 184, 185

Yadi' Yalhan, 117
Yahamat Liimmim, 124
Yahweh, 14, 16, 17, 92, 106, 121, 189, 190
Yanoam, 78
Yaosh, 13-15, 17
York, Archbishop of, 63

Zaphon, 113, 116, 117
Zaribtu, 156
Zebulon, 68
Zimreda, 6
Ziusudra, 203, 204

INDEX OF
BIBLICAL REFERENCES

Gen. 2-3	174, 205	II Kings 15:29-30	149
Gen. 3:22	200	II Kings 16:7-8	152
Gen. 6-9	169-170	II Kings 17:6	136
Gen. 39:1-20	237	II Kings 17:24	138
Gen. 50:26	228	II Kings 20:20	39
Ex. 21:2	214	II Kings 23:29-30	29
Ex. 21:24-25	221	II Chr. 32:30	39
Ex. 21:29	226	Job 9:13	190
Ex. 22:6-7	227	Ps. 74:13-14	122
Lev. 7:32	102	Ps. 89:11	190
Lev. 24:19	221	Ps. 92:10 (Eng. 92:9)	119
Deut. 15:12-18	214	Ps. 145:13	119
Deut. 22:23-27	224	Prov. 22:17-24:11	245
Deut. 23:18-19	125	Eccles. 9:7-9	182
Josh. 15:62	49	Isa. 20	139
Judg. 6:36-40	187	Isa. 20:1	136
I Sam. 13:20	245	Isa. 27:1	122
I Sam. 15:22	236	Isa. 51:9	190
I Sam. 18:7	179	Isa. 51:18	121
I Sam. 19:24	80	Jer. 19:11-12	68
II Sam. 2:13	90	Jer. 28:1	90
II Sam. 9:8	14	Jer. 38:4	17
I Kings 9:15-19	33	Jer. 50:35	239
I Kings 10:26-29	33	Ezek. 5:5	53
I Kings 20:11	240	Ezek. 38:12	53
II Kings 9:33, 36	239	Hos. 4:13-14	125
II Kings 15:19-20	149		

MI